MASTER THE GED SCIENCE

2nd Edition

UPDATED FOR THE ALL-NEW GED!

THOMSON

ARCO

Australia • Canada • Mexico • Singapore • Spain • United Kingdom • United States

An ARCO Book
ARCO is a registered trademark of Thomson Learning, Inc., and is used herein under license by Peterson's.

About The Thomson Corporation and Peterson's
With revenues approaching US$7.2 billion, The Thomson Corporation (www.thomson.com) is a leading global provider of integrated information solutions for business, education, and professional customers. Its Learning businesses and brands (www.thomsonlearning.com) serve the needs of individuals, learning institutions, and corporations with products and services for both traditional and distributed learning.

Peterson's, part of The Thomson Corporation, is one of the nation's most respected providers of lifelong learning online resources, software, reference guides, and books. The Education Supersite℠ at www.petersons.com—the Internet's most heavily traveled education resource—has searchable databases and interactive tools for contacting U.S.-accredited institutions and programs. In addition, Peterson's serves more than 105 million education consumers annually.

For more information, contact Peterson's, 2000 Lenox Drive, Lawrenceville, NJ 08648; 800-338-3282; or find us on the World Wide Web at: www.petersons.com/about

ACKNOWLEDGEMENTS: An American BookWorks Corporation Project. We would like to thank the following individuals for their assistance: Aart Hoogenboom, James Liptack, James Lucey, Barbara Maynard, and Elaine Silverstein.

ISBN: 0-7689-1000-5

Printed in the United States of America

10 9 8 7 6 5 4 3 2 1   03 02 01

CONTENTS

INTRODUCTION

This is the first step to advancing your academic career. Whether you are taking the GED in preparation of attending college, or looking for the career opportunities that become available after completing the GED, you are not alone. Between 1949 and 1999, an estimated 14.2 million adults earned a GED credential. It is estimated that in the United States today, 1 out of every 7 high school students will complete their education with the GED Exam

GED tests were originally developed to help veterans returning from service in World War II regain academic skills or complete an education that had been interrupted by the war. Many returning veterans used the knowledge from the GED Testing Services to gain jobs. Over the years, the emphasis of these tests has changed from knowledge required for industrial jobs to knowledge needed for today's information-driven world.

This book was designed to assist you with successfully passing the Science portion of the GED test. Skills essential to passing all areas will be covered, key science concepts will be addressed, and plenty of practice with the types of questions you will encounter on the real exam will be provided.

WHAT IS THE GED?

The acronym GED stands for the tests of General Educational Development. The tests are a national examination created by the GED Testing Service of the American Council of Education. GED tests cover topics that are normally tested in high school: Language Arts, Reading; Language Arts, Writing; Social Studies; Mathematics; and Science. Each of these tests covers topics specific to that course. The ultimate goal in passing these exams is a certificate equivalent to a high school diploma.

WHAT IS COVERED ON THE GED TESTS?

The GED consists of tests in five content areas. The chart below tells you what will be on each test, how many questions there will be, and how much time you will have to complete each exam.

Test	Content Areas	Number of Questions	Time Limit (minutes)
Language Arts: Writing I	Correction - 45% Revision - 35% Construction Shift - 20%	50	75
Language Arts: Writing II	Essay	250 words	45
Social Studies	US History - 25% World History - 15% Geography - 15% Civics & Government - 25% Economics - 20%	50	75
Science	Life Science - 45% Earth Science - 20% Physical Science - 35% (Physics, Chemistry)	50	75
Language Arts: Reading	Poetry - 15% Drama - 15% Fiction - 45% Nonfiction Prose - 25%	40	65
Mathematics Booklet One: Calculator Booklet Two: No Calculator	Numbers, Number Sense, Operations - 25% Data, Statistics, Probability - 25% Geometry and Measurement - 25% Algebra, Functions, Patterns - 25%	50	90

To pass the **Language Arts, Writing Test,** you will need to know how to communicate with the written word in today's world. Business communications are a large part of the knowledge you will need: How to write letters and memos, how to write reports and complete applications. Since all of these require proper grammar and punctuation, this skill is part of the testing process. What is not tested is "every day" spelling, since so much writing and composition is done today on computers and other machines with spell checkers. The test on Writing also looks for composition skills—do the thoughts flow in a normal sequence? Is there a smooth or logical transition between paragraphs? All of these are part of writing. An essay is required and will be graded.

The **Language Arts, Reading Test** looks for comprehension and analysis of what has been read. Most of the focus will be on fiction, but there will also be some content on nonfiction, including reading a business document. The test will also see if you can apply what you've read.

The **Mathematics Test** covers algebra, geometry, number relations, and data analysis, including statistics. The candidate should be able to look at data and statistics and analyze the numbers in relation to questions posed. In addition, problem-solving skills will be tested. Calculators are allowed during the first part of the exam, but not the second part.

The **Science Test** requires knowledge of a wide range of subjects and is based on the National Science Education Content Standards. The topics include: earth and space science, physics, chemistry, environmental science, and health science. Tested will be an understanding of concepts and problem-solving skills. More about this later.

The **Social Studies Test** covers U.S. history, world history, economics, civics, and government.

WHAT IS NEEDED TO PASS THE GED TESTS?

To pass the GED tests, the candidate must obtain a minimum score of 225 points over the five exams, as well as a minimum score per test. The number of points received for correct answers varies from question to question, test to test. You will need to check with the GED Testing Service in your state to determine what minimum score is permitted for each test. It is essential that you keep in mind both the score on each individual test as well as the overall score of the combined tests. To illustrate this more clearly, look at the chart below.

	Sally	Anton	Maria
Test 1	56	44	42
Test 2	33	46	54
Test 3	44	45	39
Test 4	49	41	45
Test 5	44	48	47
Total	226	224	227

We will assume that these students took the test in Iowa. The minimum score for all five exams is 225 points. The minimum score on any one exam is 35 points. With these testing requirements, Maria would have been the only person to have successfully passed the GED requirements. Sally earned the minimum of 225 points, but she fell below 35 points on Test 2. Anton scored over 35 on all of his tests, but failed to earn a total of 225 points.

STUDY SKILLS AND TIPS

Everyone has a different way to study. Some people take notes based on what they are reading and then review the notes later to reinforce the reading material. Others highlight passages in their texts and skim those passages later to reinforce the reading. Others employ both methods to ensure that they absorb the most information from their reading.

Be sure to give yourself plenty of time to study before taking the exam. Many candidates find that taking a course with an instructor gives them the needed structure to accomplish their goals. Others have the self-discipline to study on a regular basis without a class.

Regardless of which method you use to study, be sure that your study area is away from distractions (such as children, television, etc.) and that you study on a regular basis. Above all, develop and practice the skills you will need to pass the exam. This means that you need to read as much as possible from as many different sources as possible.

Practice, practice, practice!

WHAT WILL I FIND ON THE SCIENCE TEST?

THE GED SCIENCE TEST

The GED Science Test is a measurement of your understanding of science concepts as well as your ability to solve science problems. Many of the items on the test will focus on application of science to daily living, such as environmental science, technology, research, and workplace skills.

CONTENT AREAS

Science is Test 3 of the GED Tests. It consists of the following three content areas. The percentage of questions in each area is given in parentheses:

Life science (45%): The study of life processes and patterns and the study of humans and the environment

Earth and space science (20%): The study of Earth's structure, atmosphere, weather, and resources, as well as space science

Physical science (35%): The study of matter (chemistry) and energy (physics)

TYPES OF QUESTIONS

When you take the GED Science Test, you will have 80 minutes to answer 50 multiple-choice questions. Approximately one half of these will be stand-alone questions that will test your understanding of basic scientific concepts, processes, and methods of inquiry. The other half will be questions based on graphs, charts, diagrams, or paragraphs of information. Each question will based on one of the six science standards developed by the National Science Education Council: fundamental understandings, unifying concepts and processes, science as inquiry, science and technology, science in personal and social perspectives, and history and nature of science. Of these, 60% will represent fundamental understandings, 17% will test science in personal and social perspectives, 8% will test science as inquiry, 8% will test history and nature of science, 3.5% will test science as technology, and 3.5% will test unifying concepts and processes.

Fundamental Understandings

This strand tests your knowledge of basic scientific concepts and principles—your science literacy. Questions may cover your understanding of basic laws of motion (physical science), the theory of evolution (life science), or the Earth's place in the solar system (earth and space science). In the following example, read the passage and answer the question that follows:

Black holes are regions of space with such dense gravity that not even light can escape. Therefore, black holes cannot be observed directly by astronomers. In order to study this mysterious phenomenon, scientists will use the next generation of particle accelerator, such as the Large Hadron Collider. This massive device, now under construction in Switzerland, may allow scientists to create miniature black holes and to detect their existence by tracking the energy they release when they disappear. This in turn may allow physicists to determine if black holes really exist.

1. Scientists cannot see black holes because
    (1) they are very far away.
    (2) they trap light.
    (3) they do not really exist.
    (4) larger telescopes are needed
    (5) they cannot track the energy the black holes release.

The correct answer is (2). To answer this question correctly, you must not only understand the passage, but also understand several fundamental facts about science, including the fact that objects must give off light in order to be seen through a telescope. The other choices are incorrect statements that are not based on a fundamental understanding of scientific knowledge.

Unifying Concepts and Principles

Unifying concepts and principles require you to understand how information is organized, how basic principles are interrelated, how scientists use measurement, and how form is related to function. The following question, also based on the passage above, is an example:

2. Which statement about the nature of light is suggested by this passage?
    (1) Light cannot travel through a vacuum.
    (2) Light is a form of electromagnetic radiation.
    (3) White light can be broken down into the colors of the spectrum.
    (4) Light is made of particles of matter.
    (5) Light waves and sound waves behave in similar ways.

The correct answer is (4). To answer this question correctly, you must understand not only that scientists think of light as a stream, but also that gravity acts on all matter. Choices (1) and (5) are incorrect, and choices (2) and (3) are correct, but not suggested by the passage.

Science as Inquiry

Questions on the GED that test this strand will require you to think like a scientist—to weigh evidence, think critically, and understand the scientific process. Here is an example:

3. A scientist suspects that the large-size particles of soot emitted by a steel mill are dangerous to people's lungs. How can she test this hypothesis?
    (1) Compare the lung function of people who live near the mill with that of people who live in a different place.
    (2) Remove and biopsy one lung from a sample of people who live near the mill.
    (3) Ask people to relocate closer to the mill and test their lung function before and after the move.
    (4) Compare the lung function of children and adults who live near the mill.
    (5) After people die, perform autopsies to determine the degree of lung damage caused by living near the mill.

The correct answer is (1). If the scientist conducted this experiment, she would be comparing two groups: an experimental group who is exposed to the condition of interest and a control group who is not. The results would be a valid test of her hypothesis. The other choices either present ethical problems, as in choices (2) and (3), or do not represent valid tests of the hypothesis, choices (4) and (5).

Science as Technology

4. The wings on a plane provide lift because air moves faster across the curved top of the wing than across the flat bottom, and faster-moving air has lower pressure. Based on this principle, an engineer might design a plane with greater lift by
   (1) increasing the size of the engine.
   (2) increasing the weight of the plane.
   (3) modifying the shape of the wing.
   (4) increasing the size of the wheels.
   (5) making the plane more aerodynamic.

The correct answer is (3). The principle stated in the item is Bernoulli's principle and leads to the shape of an airplane wing: curved on top and flat on the bottom. Therefore, modifying that shape might provide more lift. Choices (1) and (2) would be more likely to decrease lift than to increase it, and choices (4) and (5) are unrelated to lift.

Science in Personal and Social Perspective

This strand includes the knowledge you need to understand scientific information about health and the environment, as well as to develop decision-making skills. Read the following passage and answer example 5:

The great increases in the human lifespan that developed countries have enjoyed over the past 100 years result from two factors: improved living standards, which include both nutrition and sanitation, and medical advances, such as the discovery of antibiotics. Both advances result from fundamental research into human nutritional needs and the nature of health and illness. Scientists could not look for drugs that would kill microbes until they knew that microbes caused disease. They could not find ways to clean up water supplies until they knew that drinking water could harbor disease-causing organisms, and they could not develop vaccines until they understood the nature of the immune system. Similarly, current information about nutrition, exercise, and the risks of smoking and drinking is based on our current state of knowledge of basic biology and is subject to change as that knowledge evolves.

5. According to the passage, which of the following would be considered a medical advance that has improved human health?
   (1) Widespread use of the polio vaccine
   (2) Use of sunscreen to prevent skin cancer
   (3) Widespread testing of drinking water
   (4) Discoveries about the dangers of high-fat diets
   (5) Improved safety of food supplies

The correct answer is (1). According to the passage, the other answer choices merely relate to improved *knowledge* about human health.

History and Nature of Science

This strand will test your knowledge of scientific advances and the way in which scientific discoveries build on the work of earlier scientists. The following example is also based on the passage above:

6.   According to the passage, scientific information about human health is based on
     (1) knowledge of antibiotics and the nature of disease.
     (2) information about water supplies.
     (3) improved living standards.
     (4) knowledge of common health risks.
     (5) a history of scientific discoveries.

The correct answer is (5). The passage implies that the nature of scientific knowledge is subject to change as more discoveries are made. Choices (1), (2), (3), and (4) are all partially correct, but only choice (5) is universally correct.

Pretest

Chapter 1

PREVIEW

Pretest

Answer Sheet

1	①	②	③	④	⑤	6	①	②	③	④	⑤	11	①	②	③	④	⑤
2	①	②	③	④	⑤	7	①	②	③	④	⑤	12	①	②	③	④	⑤
3	①	②	③	④	⑤	8	①	②	③	④	⑤	13	①	②	③	④	⑤
4	①	②	③	④	⑤	9	①	②	③	④	⑤	14	①	②	③	④	⑤
5	①	②	③	④	⑤	10	①	②	③	④	⑤	15	①	②	③	④	⑤
16	①	②	③	④	⑤	21	①	②	③	④	⑤	26	①	②	③	④	⑤
17	①	②	③	④	⑤	22	①	②	③	④	⑤	27	①	②	③	④	⑤
18	①	②	③	④	⑤	23	①	②	③	④	⑤	28	①	②	③	④	⑤
19	①	②	③	④	⑤	24	①	②	③	④	⑤	29	①	②	③	④	⑤
20	①	②	③	④	⑤	25	①	②	③	④	⑤	30	①	②	③	④	⑤
31	①	②	③	④	⑤	36	①	②	③	④	⑤	41	①	②	③	④	⑤
32	①	②	③	④	⑤	37	①	②	③	④	⑤	42	①	②	③	④	⑤
33	①	②	③	④	⑤	38	①	②	③	④	⑤	43	①	②	③	④	⑤
34	①	②	③	④	⑤	39	①	②	③	④	⑤	44	①	②	③	④	⑤
35	①	②	③	④	⑤	40	①	②	③	④	⑤	45	①	②	③	④	⑤
46	①	②	③	④	⑤												
47	①	②	③	④	⑤												
48	①	②	③	④	⑤												
49	①	②	③	④	⑤												
50	①	②	③	④	⑤												

Pretest

ROAD MAP

Pretest

Answers and Explanations

Directions: Choose the <u>one best answer</u> for each item.

Items 1–3 refer to the following paragraph.

A virus is a small particle consisting of nucleic acid surrounded by a protein coat. Viruses are active only if they are in living cells because they reproduce more viruses by commandeering the host cell's machinery. If the nucleic acid is RNA, the virus is said to be a retrovirus. It is called a retrovirus because it must change its RNA to DNA before it can take over the host cell. When a retrovirus makes DNA from RNA, it uses an enzyme-reverse transcriptase. Viruses that contain DNA as their nucleic acid do not require this additional step and behave more like their hosts in that they follow the central dogma of modern biology: DNA makes RNA, which makes proteins.

1. In order for any virus to become pathogenic in a cell, it must
    (1) be alive.
    (2) contain RNA.
    (3) be a retrovirus.
    (4) have DNA.
    (5) have a protein coat.

2. Retroviruses are viruses that contain
    (1) only RNA and a protein coat.
    (2) RNA, DNA, and protein.
    (3) some of the host's machinery.
    (4) proteins that will convert RNA to DNA.
    (5) none of the above.

3. In order to harm a host, retroviruses must
    (1) be in the host's nucleus.
    (2) use the host's cellular machinery to make new virus particles.
    (3) use an enzyme that will convert their RNA to DNA.
    (4) commandeer the host's cell machinery.
    (5) all of the above.

Items 4 and 5 refer to the following diagram.

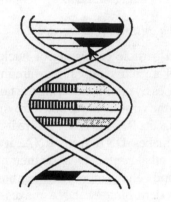

4. The diagram is an illustration of the structure of DNA, which was elucidated by
    (1) Wallace and Darwin.
    (2) Hershey and Chase.
    (3) Watson and Crick.
    (4) Venter and Collins.
    (5) Messelson and Stahl.

5. The arrow is pointing to a dark portion that represents a molecule joined with another that is not shaded. If the dark shading represents the molecule thymine, the nonshaded portion next to it represents a molecule of
    (1) guanine.
    (2) adenine.
    (3) cytosine.
    (4) a ribose sugar.
    (5) a pentose group.

Items 6–8 refer to the following table.

	Proton	Neutron	Electron
Mass	1	1	0.0005
Location	nucleus	nucleus	orbiting nucleus
Charge	+1	0	−1

6. Which particles are attracted to each other?
    (1) Protons and neutrons
    (2) Protons and electrons
    (3) Neutrons and electrons
    (4) Protons, neutrons, and electrons
    (5) None of the above

7. Which particles have mass?
    (1) Protons and neutrons only
    (2) Protons and electrons only
    (3) Neutrons and electrons only
    (4) Protons, neutrons, and electrons
    (5) Electrons only

8. Sodium has an atomic number of 11 and an atomic mass of 23. How many electrons are there in a neutral atom?
    (1) 11
    (2) 12
    (3) 34
    (4) 132
    (5) Not enough information is given to answer this question.

9. Carbon exists in at least two forms, carbon-12 and carbon-14. What is the difference between carbon-12 and carbon-14?
    (1) Carbon-12 has 12 protons and 14 neutrons.
    (2) Carbon-12 has 12 protons and 12 electrons, while carbon-14 has 12 protons and 14 electrons.
    (3) Carbon-12 has 12 protons, while carbon-14 has 14 protons.
    (4) Carbon-12 has 6 neutrons, while carbon-14 has 8 neutrons.
    (5) Carbon-12 has 6 protons, while carbon-14 has 8 protons.

Items 10–12 refer to the following information.

Many cities in the northeastern United States are faced with the yearly task of filling potholes after the snow melts each spring. Potholes are the direct result of ice wedging, a form of physical weathering. In the autumn, rainwater seeps into cracks in the pavement. During the winter, the water freezes and expands, causing the cracks to widen. Repeated freezing and thawing over the course of the winter expands the cracks in the pavement. By springtime, networks of cracks have formed and chunks of pavement may be dislodged. Continued driving on these roads over the winter only accelerates the process. Improved pavement materials with better expansion/contraction properties would decrease the number of potholes, but potholes, like flowers, are a mark of spring.

10. According to the passage, what process is responsible for the formation of potholes?
    (1) Biological weathering
    (2) Ice wedging
    (3) Heat expansion
    (4) Chemical weathering
    (5) Water erosion

11. Which of the following cities is least likely to experience the type of weathering discussed in the passage?
    (1) New York
    (2) Miami
    (3) Boston
    (4) Minneapolis
    (5) Seattle

12. Which of the following would be least likely to reduce the incidence of potholes on roads?
    (1) More elastic road surfaces
    (2) Application of road salts to prevent icing
    (3) Prompt repairs of cracked roadways
    (4) Sanding roads after a snow storm
    (5) Periodic repaving of busy roadways

13. Phase transitions, such as melting and boiling, occur at particular temperatures. What happens when ice melts in equilibrium with its surroundings?

    (1)   The temperature of the ice rises gradually as heat is added from the surroundings.

    (2)   The temperature of the ice remains constant as heat is added from the surroundings.

    (3)   The temperature of the ice falls as heat is given up to the surroundings.

    (4)   The temperature of the ice remains constant as heat is given up to the surroundings.

    (5)   No added heat is required from the surroundings.

Items 14–16 refer to the following information.

When atomic nuclei undergo radioactive decay, some of the nuclei are transformed into a different kind of nucleus, called the daughter nucleus in the decay chain. The same fraction of the remaining nuclei decay in each equal time interval. The figure below shows the fraction of nuclei left as a function of time.

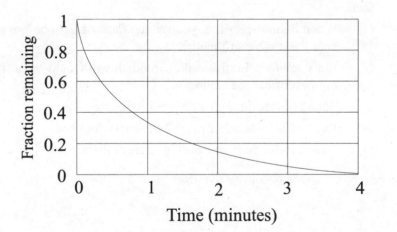

14. Radioactive decay involves changing

    (1)   one kind of atom into another.

    (2)   one kind of molecule into another.

    (3)   one kind of nucleus into another.

    (4)   the atomic number of a nucleus.

    (5)   the mass number of a nucleus.

15. According to the graph, what will happen after 3 minutes have elapsed?

    (1)   About one third of the initial sample will have decayed.

    (2)   About one half of the initial sample will have decayed.

    (3)   More than 90% of the initial sample will have decayed.

    (4)   All of the initial sample will have decayed.

    (5)   None of the initial sample will have decayed.

16. Which of the following statements is supported by the information given?

    (1)   The number of nuclei decaying each minute is the same.

    (2)   Fewer than half the nuclei decay in the first minute.

    (3)   More nuclei decay in the second minute than in the first.

    (4)   The daughter nuclei are also radioactive.

    (5)   The number of nuclei decaying per minute tends to zero after a long time.

17. Light and sound are both wave phenomena, but they are different in some ways. For example, light can travel in a vacuum, but sound cannot. Which of the following statements is a consequence of this fact?

    (1)   When lightning strikes, you see the flash of light before you hear the rumble of thunder.

    (2)   If a satellite in Earth's orbit exploded, you would see a flash but never hear the explosion.

    (3)   Sound passes through walls but light does not.

    (4)   Light reflects from surfaces but sound does not.

    (5)   Sound and light both travel in straight lines.

Item 18 refers to the following diagram.

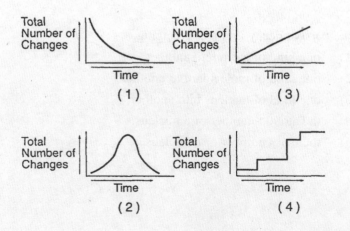

18. Niles Eldridge and Stephen Jay Gould are neo-Darwinists. While they believe that Darwin was essentially correct in his theory of natural selection and evolution, they feel there are points that should be refined as scientists learn more. Specifically, they feel that large and sudden changes in the environment will cause changes in the rate of speciation. Which of the following graphs best illustrates their position?

    (1)   1
    (2)   2
    (3)   3
    (4)   4
    (5)   1 and 3

Items 19 and 20 refer to the following diagram.

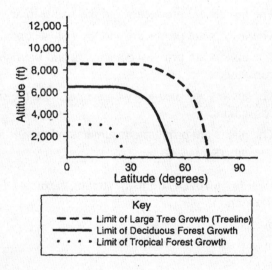

19. The diagram shows that most trees cannot live above
    (1)   3,000 feet.
    (2)   6,200 feet.
    (3)   8,200 feet.
    (4)   28 degrees latitude.
    (5)   52 degrees latitude.

20. One can surmise from the graph that
    (1)   going up 1,000 feet is like going north 1 degree.
    (2)   going up 1,000 feet is like going north 2 degrees.
    (3)   going up 1,000 feet is like going north 10 degrees.
    (4)   going up 1,000 feet is like going north 10 degrees.
    (5)   deciduous trees can exist in cold climates.

Items 21–23 refer to the following information.

Ecosystems are composed of communities of organisms in their habitats. An example would be a stream containing plants, insects, fish, and some birds. The ecosystem depends on continuous energy input, although materials can be recycled or new materials can be brought in.

21. The energy that is inputted in this ecosystem is
    (1) the heat energy of the stream.
    (2) solar energy.
    (3) kinetic energy.
    (4) chemical energy.
    (5) built up downstream in a lake.

22. Assume that the insects are herbivorous and the fish eat the insects. Which statement is then correct?
    (1) The insects are producers and the fish primary consumers.
    (2) The insects are producers and the fish secondary consumers.
    (3) The insects are primary consumers and the fish secondary consumers.
    (4) The insects are secondary consumers and the fish tertiary consumers.
    (5) The plants are primary consumers and the insects secondary consumers.

23. If there were a spill of DDT into the stream, the most DDT per kilogram would be found in
    (1) plants.
    (2) insects.
    (3) fish.
    (4) birds.
    (5) insects and fish.

24. Nerves can be classified as sensory, motor, or interneurons. Suppose that a person has his hand on a hot plate. He can feel the heat and knows that the plate is hot, but he cannot move his hand. This is indication of
    (1) sensory neuron damage.
    (2) motor neuron damage.
    (3) interneuron damage.
    (4) brain damage.
    (5) reflex reaction.

Item 25 refers to the following illustration.

The figure shows sunrise times for Fargo, North Dakota, plotted as a function of the number of days after December 1, 2000.

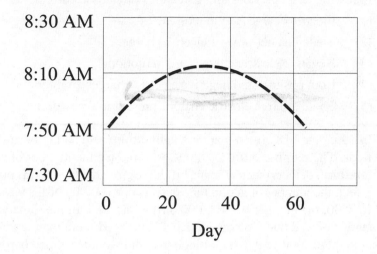

25. For approximately how many days does the sun rise after 8 a.m.?
    (1)   10
    (2)   20
    (3)   30
    (4)   40
    (5)   50

26. Galileo showed that the acceleration of falling objects does not depend on their mass. Yet light objects, such as feathers, fall much more slowly than heavy objects, such as bricks. What is the best explanation?
    (1)   Light objects experience a smaller gravitational force than heavy objects.
    (2)   Their accelerations are the same, but the speeds are different.
    (3)   Galileo's law does not apply to organic materials like feathers.
    (4)   Galileo's law assumes that air resistance can be neglected.
    (5)   Galileo was wrong.

27. Electric current in metals is carried by free electrons, while the positively charged nuclei remain at rest. In aqueous solutions, positive and negative ions moving in opposite directions carry current. Opposite charges moving in the same direction result in no current. Which of the following best describes all the features of electric current?

    (1)   Electric charges are in motion.

    (2)   There is a net flow of electric charge.

    (3)   Negative electric charges are in motion.

    (4)   Both positive and negative electric charges are in motion.

    (5)   There are free electric charges present in the material.

28. In 1998, the FDC ruled that the vitamin folic acid had to be added to flour. The purpose of this action was to reduce the number of neural tube birth defects (such as spina bifida). Before the policy was put into effect, the number of neural tube defects per 100,000 births was 37.8. In 2000, the number per 100,000 births was 30.5. In the same year, a study showed that women age 15–44 averaged more than double the amount of folic acid in their blood than did women studied before the mandatory fortification. Which of the following statements is correct?

    (1)   There was a 19% decrease in the number of neural tube defects between 1998 and 2000.

    (2)   There was a 7.3% decrease in the number of neural defects between 1998 and 2000.

    (3)   If women would double their intake of folic acid, they could reduce the number of birth defects by half.

    (4)   This study was faulty, because some women take vitamin supplements.

    (5)   The number of neural tube birth defects per million women in 2000 was 378.

29. Rust is the common name for iron oxide. A student wanted to prove that things in space wouldn't rust, so he got NASA to send a piece of iron on a space shuttle flight and have the astronauts place the iron outside the space station. A year later the iron was examined and was found to be without any rust. What is the best conclusion?

    (1)   The laws of nature do not apply to outer space.

    (2)   The space station was traveling too fast for any chemical reactions to occur.

    (3)   The temperature in outer space is too cold for rusting to occur.

    (4)   Rust cannot form in one year.

    (5)   There is insufficient oxygen in outer space for rusting to occur.

Items 30–32 refer to the following illustration.

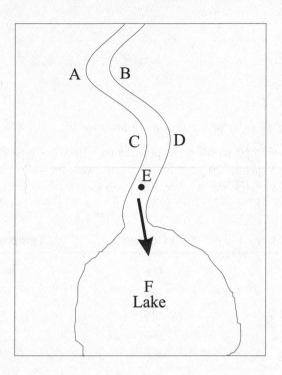

30. At which of the marked locations on the adjacent diagram would net erosion be greater than deposition?

    (1) C and D only

    (2) B and C only

    (3) A and D only

    (4) F and E only

    (5) All locations would erode equally.

31. At point F in the diagram, the river has the lowest velocity. This is because

    (1) the flow of the water, previously restricted by the riverbanks, can now spread.

    (2) natural currents in the lake are slower than river currents.

    (3) the sediment load of the water leaving the river slows the velocity.

    (4) natural formations on the lake bottom slow river velocity.

    (5) the lake at point F is much deeper than the river.

32. If the elevation is constant, at which point in the diagram would the river water be moving the fastest?
    (1)   A
    (2)   B
    (3)   C
    (4)   D
    (5)   E

Items 33 and 34 refer to the following information.

A student wanted to do an experiment to find the best conditions for growing brine shrimp. She set up 6 beakers with the following conditions and placed a half-teaspoon of eggs in each one:

Beaker Number	Salt Content	Temperature
1	0%	10° C
2	3%	10° C
3	5%	10° C
4	0%	20° C
5	3%	20° C
6	5%	20° C

She sampled them each day for five days, and she found that the greatest number of shrimp grew at 3% salt at either temperature.

33. In this experiment the dependent variable(s) is (are)
    (1)   percentage of salt.
    (2)   temperature.
    (3)   number of shrimp.
    (4)   number of days.
    (5)   percentage of salt and temperature.

34. The student was not satisfied with her results. She wanted results that could help her better distinguish the preferred growth conditions. To improve her experiment, she should
    (1)   use finer divisions for the percentage of salt.
    (2)   use finer divisions for the temperature.
    (3)   let the experiment run longer.
    (4)   be more careful about the volume of water the eggs were growing in.
    (5)   be more careful about adding a specific number of shrimp eggs.

Items 35 and 36 refer to the following information.

The four major blood groups in humans are A, B, AB, and O. People who are Type A have a certain protein on their red blood cells (RBCs) that is referred to as "A." People with Type B blood lack the "A" protein and have "B" instead. People with Type AB have both proteins, while those with Type O have neither protein on their RBCs.

People with type O blood are called universal donors because they can give blood to individuals of any other blood group, since the recipients will not form antibodies to the O blood, which carries neither protein. Every person receives half of his or her blood group type from the mother and half from the father, so that everyone has two alleles, or gene types, for the ABO blood groups.

35. Which of the following statements is incorrect, according to the information above and your knowledge of biology?
    (1)   People with blood Type AB cannot receive blood from a Type B donor.
    (2)   People with blood Type O cannot receive blood from a person with Type AB.
    (3)   People with blood Type A, whose mother is Type B, can donate blood to Type A individuals.
    (4)   Some people with blood Type AB had a parent whose Type was A.
    (5)   Antibodies are proteins formed by the recipient that attack the proteins on the donor's RBCs.

36. A man with Type B blood married a woman with Type O blood. Which of the following blood groups could their children inherit?
    (1)   Type AB
    (2)   Type B
    (3)   Type O
    (4)   Types AB and O
    (5)   Types B and O

37. Of the following technological advancements, the most recent was the
    (1)   sequencing of an archaebacterial genome.
    (2)   sequencing of the human genome.
    (3)   identification of the structure of the prb protein.
    (4)   invention of the scanning tunneling electron microscope.
    (5)   discovery of the deep sea vents by the submersible *Alvin*.

38. The most pressing problem for humans in their environment today is
    (1) global warming.
    (2) pollution.
    (3) overpopulation.
    (4) depletion of the ozone layer.
    (5) habitat destruction.

Items 39–41 refer to the following illustration.

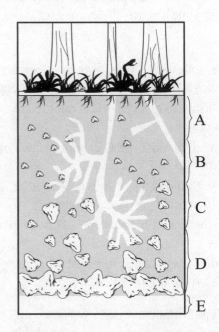

39. In which zone of the soil would you expect to find the most organic matter?
    (1) A
    (2) B
    (3) C
    (4) D
    (5) All layers will have equal amounts of organic matter.

40. Which letter in the diagram represents bedrock?
    (1) A
    (2) B
    (3) C
    (4) D
    (5) E

41. Soil profiles vary depending on the climate. Assume that the diagram represents a tundra soil profile instead of the temperate forest represented. How would the soil profile differ?

    (1)   The topsoil zone would be much thicker.

    (2)   The topsoil zone would be much thinner.

    (3)   The bedrock zone would be much deeper.

    (4)   All of the zones would be comparable.

    (5)   There would be greater variety of plants and animals.

42. The statement, "The core of the earth is metallic," is an example of a scientific

    (1)   fact.

    (2)   principle.

    (3)   hypothesis.

    (4)   observation.

    (5)   law

Items 43 and 44 refer to the following passage.

A student read reports of lead being removed from gasoline because it was harmful to humans. She hypothesized that it was harmful to other living things as well and developed a test for lead in water systems using small onions. She cut the end off the onions where the roots grew and placed each onion in a test tube containing lead nitrate solutions. The concentrations of lead are shown on the diagram. Here is a diagram of her experiment:

Onions

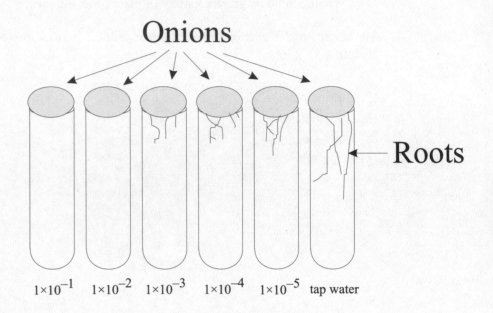

Roots

1×10^{-1} 1×10^{-2} 1×10^{-3} 1×10^{-4} 1×10^{-5} tap water

43. Which of the following statements is false?
    (1) The more lead in the solution, the less water.
    (2) Lead caused the onion roots to grow more slowly.
    (3) People should not eat onions that have been growing in lead.
    (4) From left to right, the concentration of lead increases.
    (5) Even small amounts of lead keep roots from growing.

44. Which of the following statements is true?
    (1) There is half as much lead in the first tube than the second tube (reading left to right).
    (2) The first tube has 100 times more lead than the third tube.
    (3) The amount of lead increases as you move left to right.
    (4) There is twice the amount of lead in the first tube than the second tube.
    (5) The fifth tube has five times the amount of lead as the first.

45. The idea that the atom was composed mostly of space came from experiments that
    (1) used the tunneling electron microscope.
    (2) measured the masses of magnesium and oxygen when they combined.
    (3) shot subatomic particles through gold foil.
    (4) measured the rate of radioactive decay in lead.
    (5) were done in the seventeenth century by Priestley.

Items 46–48 refer to the amino acid chart.

Messenger RNA (mRNA) Codes for Selected Amino Acids

Amino Acid	mRNA Code
Leucine	C–U–G
Arginine	C–G–A
Phenylalanine	U–U–U
Valine	G–U–U
Lysine	A–A–A

46. The mRNA sequence that would code for the polypeptide leucine-arginine-valine, or leucylargylvaline, is
    (1) CCA CGA UUU.
    (2) CUG CGA GUU.
    (3) CCG CGU AAU.
    (4) AAC AUC UGG.
    (5) GGT GCT CAA.

47. Which of the following DNA sequences codes for the dipeptide leucylarginine?
    (1) CCA CGA
    (2) CCC GAA
    (3) AAC AUC
    (4) TTG TAG
    (5) GAC GCT

48. Consider the following DNA sequence: AAA CAA. If C were replaced by A in DNA replication, the change would be considered a
    (1) silent point mutation.
    (2) missense point mutation.
    (3) nonsense point mutation.
    (4) chromosomal aberration.
    (5) translation error.

Items 49 and 50 refer to the following diagram of a flower.

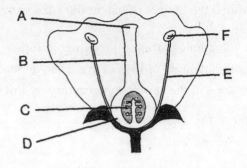

49. Pollen is produced in the structure labeled
    (1)   A.
    (2)   C.
    (3)   D.
    (4)   E.
    (5)   F.

50. The stamen is (are) part(s)
    (1)   A.
    (2)   A and B.
    (3)   F.
    (4)   E.
    (5)   F and E.

ANSWERS AND EXPLANATIONS

1. **The correct answer is (4). (Fundamental understandings)** A virus cannot commandeer the cell's machinery without using its own DNA.

2. **The correct answer is (4). (Fundamental understandings)** A retrovirus must contain reverse transcriptase, the enzyme (protein) that converts its RNA to DNA.

3. **The correct answer is (5). (Fundamental understandings)** DNA is found only in the nucleus. The rest of the answers are descriptive of a virus's interaction with its host.

4. **The correct answer is (3). (History and nature of science)** James Watson and Francis Crick shared the Nobel Prize in 1962 for their description of the structure of DNA.

5. **The correct answer is (2). (History and nature of science)** The helix has been described as a twisted ladder, with the sugar-phosphate backbone being the parts you would hold on to and the rungs being the nitrogen bases adenine, guanine, cytosine, and thymine. Adenine always bonds to thymine, and guanine always bonds to cytosine.

6. **The correct answer is (2). (Fundamental understandings)** The opposite charges attract one another.

7. **The correct answer is (4). (Fundamental understandings)** While the protons and the neutrons have approximately the same mass, even electrons have some mass.

8. **The correct answer is (1). (Fundamental understandings)** The number of electrons and the number of protons are always the same in an uncharged atom.

9. **The correct answer is (4). (Fundamental understandings)** Isotopes differ in the number of neutrons. Any element that has 6 protons will be a form of carbon. The atomic number is the number of protons, while the atomic mass is the number of protons and neutrons.

10. **The correct answer is (2). (Unifying concepts and processes)** The expansion of water when it freezes is responsible for the cracking caused by ice wedging. Repeated freezing and thawing causes the cracks to enlarge, and eventually portions of pavement dislodge.

11. **The correct answer is (2). (Science in personal and social perspective)** Miami has a tropical climate; therefore, the freezing temperatures needed for ice wedging are highly unlikely. All other cities listed suffer freezing temperatures regularly during winter months.

12. **The correct answer is (4). (Science and technology)** Sanding the roads after a storm improves traction but does little to the snow and ice. All other choices prevent or correct cracks in the roadway.

13. **The correct answer is (2). (Fundamental understandings)** Melting occurs at a constant temperature, the melting point. Heat added during melting does not increase the temperature of the ice, so choices (1) and (3) are incorrect. Heat is required to melt ice, however, so choices (4) and (5) are wrong.

14. **The correct answer is (3). (Fundamental understandings)** According to the passage, radioactive decay involves a change in the kind of nucleus.

15. **The correct answer is (3). (Unifying concepts and processes)** According to the graph, the fraction remaining after 3 minutes is less than 0.1, which means that more than 90% of the nuclei have decayed.

16. **The correct answer is (5). (Unifying concepts and processes)** As time goes on, the number of remaining nuclei tends to zero, as does the number that decay per minute. According to the graph, more nuclei decay in the first minute (more than half) than in any subsequent minute, so choices (1), (2), and (3) are incorrect. Choice (4) may or may not be true, but it is not supported by the passage or graph.

17. **The correct answer is (2). (Unifying concepts and processes)** Since sound requires a medium to propagate, it cannot travel from a satellite in orbit, which is in a vacuum. While choices (1) and (3) are true, they do not follow the facts stated in the problem. Choices (4) and (5) are not always true.

18. **The correct answer is (4). (Unifying concepts and processes)** The horizontal line parallel to the x-axis shows no change over time. The vertical lines parallel to the y-axis connote periods of numerous changes over very short time spans.

19. **The correct answer is (3). (Fundamental understandings)** The graph shows the limits of growth. For the tree line it is about 8200 feet and 72 degrees latitude.

20. **The correct answer is (3). (Fundamental understandings)** Trees grow from 0 latitude and 0 feet to around 72 degrees and 8300 feet. By division, that's 115 feet per 1 degree latitude, which is approximately 1000 feet per 10 degrees latitude.

21. **The correct answer is (2). (Fundamental understandings)** Streams, like most other systems, depend on the sun for energy. The sun's radiant energy is transformed by producers to chemical energy that other organisms can use.

22. **The correct answer is (3). (Fundamental understandings)** The food chain is plants —> insects —> fish —> birds, meaning that the insects eat the plants, the fish eat the insects, and the birds eat the fish. Plants are producers, in that they produce chemical energy from radiant energy. The organisms that eat plants are herbivores or primary consumers. The organisms that feed on primary consumers are secondary consumers.

23. **The correct answer is (4). (Fundamental understandings)** Biological magnification is the term used to describe this event. It means that nonbiodegradable substances taken in by organisms build up in the food chain. The rationale behind this is that many plants are eaten by the insect during the insect's lifetime before the insect is eaten by the fish. Of course, the fish eat many insects. Unfortunately, this is a true story, and even penguins in the South Pole region have DDT in their tissues although no spraying ever occurred there.

24. **The correct answer is (2). (Fundamental understandings)** Sensory neurons receive stimuli and pass the message to the interneurons in the central nervous system. The motor neurons take this information from the CNS to an effector: another nerve, a gland, or a muscle. In this case the information was processed as far as the CNS but somewhere in the motor neurons there was a fault.

25. **The correct answer is (4). (Science as inquiry)** The graph is above the 8 a.m. level from day 10 to day 50: about 40 days.

26. **The correct answer is (4). (Fundamental understandings)** Objects experience the same acceleration in a vacuum. While acceleration does not depend on mass, it is affected by other factors. While choice (1) is correct, it does not follow from this that the acceleration is different.

27. **The correct answer is (2). (Unifying concepts and processes)** Current requires the motion of charge, so choice (5) is incorrect. The charges can be of either sign, so choice (3) is incomplete and choice (4) is overly restrictive. Choice (1) is incorrect because there must be a net flow of charge.

28. **The correct answer is (1). (Fundamental understandings)** To figure the decrease, subtract the difference and divide by the current number: $(37.8–30.5)/37.8 = .19$ or 19%.

29. **The correct answer is (5). (Science as inquiry)** There is no available oxygen for rusting.

30. **The correct answer is (3). (Fundamental understandings)** The outer edges of a curve in a river or stream experience the greatest erosive effect, due to the angle at which the current meets the shore. All other points experience less force from the current on the shoreline.

31. **The correct answer is (1). (Fundamental understandings)** The banks of the river restrict the path of flow for a river. When the river empties into a lake or the ocean, the flow spreads and slows down.

32. **The correct answer is (5). (Fundamental understandings)** At point E, the river is flowing straight and the friction of the riverbank is minimized.

33. **The correct answer is (3). (Science as inquiry)** The **independent** variable is the **cause,** and the **dependent** variable is the **effect**. The independent variable is placed on the *x*-axis and the dependent on the *y*-axis when graphing results.

34. **The correct answer is (1). (Science as inquiry)** We know that temperature is not the variable to change since she tested at two different temperatures with the same result. The volume of water and the amount of eggs she put into each container are, or should be, controls. Controls are experimental conditions that should be the same so that the independent variable is the only thing that changes.

35. **The correct answer is (1). (Fundamental understandings)** Type AB is considered the universal recipient. Because people with AB have both proteins on their own RBCs, they won't produce antibodies to either A or B proteins on donated RBCs.

36. **The correct answer is (5). (Fundamental understandings)** A person with type B could have the alleles BB or BO.

37. **The correct answer is (2). (Science and technology)** The sequencing of the human genome was announced recently by both public and private groups.

38. **The correct answer is (3). (Science in personal and social perspective)** Overpopulation is causing most of the other problems.

39. **The correct answer is (1). (Fundamental understandings)** This level is closest to the surface and has plants and animals living within it. In deeper layers, there is less and less organic material.

40. **The correct answer is (5). (Fundamental understandings)** Bedrock is uneroded rock, represented in the diagram by E.

41. **The correct answer is (2). (Unifying concepts and processes)** Organic material decays slowly and less completely in colder climates. Since there would be less organic debris, the topsoil layer would tend to be thinner.

42. **The correct answer is (3). (History and nature of science)** Since it is impossible to actually see the core of the earth, the statement must be the most tentative of the listed choices (hypothesis).

43. **The correct answer is (4). (Science as inquiry)** As one moves from left to right, the concentration of lead goes down. 1×10^{-1} is the same as 0.1 M, while 1×10^{-5} is 0.00001M solution.

44. **The correct answer is (2). (Science as inquiry)** See number 43.

45. **The correct answer is (3). (History and nature of science)** Rutherford's experiment showed that only a few alpha particles bounced back, while most went through the foil.

46. **The correct answer is (2). (Fundamental understandings)** While there are several ways to code for most amino acids, only one is given for each in the table.

47. **The correct answer is (5). (Fundamental understandings)** Remember that each nitrogen base has its own "partner" with which it bonds in DNA, A to T and G to C. The rules apply also in transcription, the making of RNA from DNA, with one exception: in RNA there is no T (thymine), and U (uracil) takes its place. So, when you're going from DNA to RNA or vice versa, just take the complement base for each. Note that choice (3) must be an RNA sequence, not DNA, because it contains a U.

48. **The correct answer is (2). (Fundamental understandings)** The original strand (AAA CAA) is transcribed to UUU GUU, which would be translated as phenylalanine-valine. But the change would result in UUU UUU, which would be two phenylalanines together. When a nitrogen base changes with no resulting change in the amino acid, the change is called silent. When the amino acid sequence changes, it is a missense mutation. And when the change results in a "stop" message, it's called a nonsense mutation.

49. **The correct answer is (5). (Fundamental understandings)** Most flowers have both male and female structures. The male structure is the stamen, which is made of the filament (E) and the anther (F). The pollen is produced in the anther while the eggs are produced in the ovary (D).

50. **The correct answer is (5). (Fundamental understandings)** See number 49.

Review

PART 2

PREVIEW

LIFE SCIENCE

UNIT 1: THE NATURE OF SCIENCE

All of us need at least a basic knowledge of science, for several reasons. First, we need to use scientific information so we can understand news reports about scientific topics such as DNA, genetically modified food, AIDS, global warming, alternate energy sources, and the momentous scientific advance that occurred in the year 2000 with the identification of a human genome sequence. Second, we need to know how science works so we can use the scientific method in our daily lives. Not only is scientific literacy important for you as an individual, but it is also important for you as a citizen of this country and the biosphere. You need to understand what scientific break-throughs mean and how they may affect your future.

However, although you may accept the importance of science, you may find that studying science causes a certain amount of anxiety. If science anxiety is a problem for you, the most important strategy you can use is to allow enough time to study science. Most people cannot "cram" science into their heads just before a test. You need time to understand and assimilate scientific concepts. One of the best ways to assimilate the material is to be actively involved in your reading. Read to answer questions. If you take notes, take them in your own words. Do not use the words of the text, as you will only remember words and not concepts.

Just reading the material is deadly. It would put anyone to sleep even if the person knew the material. Be an active learner. Allow plenty of time for your study. Master one unit at a time. Then move on.

WHAT IS SCIENCE?

Science is the study of the natural world. It includes mathematics, physics, chemistry, biology, and the humanities. The term **science** is used to mean either a body of knowledge determined through scientific investigation or a special way of finding things out.

Science is an ongoing process. This is an important statement. Scientific results that are reported in scientific journals are tentative and subject to review and verification by other scientists.

Most scientific research arises from questions raised by previous research. A scientific question is stated in such a way that it can be answered by rigorous testing. A scientific study must be unbiased, which means that it must be free from all prejudice and favoritism, especially unintended prejudice, or **bias**. A scientific study must be fair.

A scientist must always report the method he or she used as well as the results of the study. For a scientific report to be accepted by the scientific community, other scientists must be able to reproduce the results. Reproducibility is a way to confirm, renounce, or use the study to further scientific knowledge. A scientific study is never accepted without replication of the method and results.

Nutrition information, as reported by the daily press, illustrates this point well. Every week yet another nutrition article seems to contradict previous nutrition information. For years we've been advised to take Vitamin C daily. Then a study is reported that finds that Vitamin C can harm DNA. The general public's response is that this proves that scientists don't know what they are talking about. In truth, this is science at work. Scientists do not accept results of only one study. Scientists must analyze, question, and try to duplicate the latest study before it can advance their understanding of the science of nutrition. Science is always a work in progress.

Scientists carry out that work by using the **scientific method**. Scientists first make observations that lead to a problem or a question. They then come up with a possible answer to the question, called the **hypothesis**. Next, scientists design **experiments** that yield mathematical measures (data) to test their possible answers. Experimental designs usually compare an experimental group or groups with a control group. The data obtained are then analyzed statistically, and a conclusion is drawn. Analysis either supports the hypothesis or does not support the hypothesis. Analysis usually leads to further questions to be studied.

We use the scientific method to solve everyday problems. Perhaps the *problem* is that the printer on your computer doesn't work. Your *hypothesis* might be that there must be something wrong with some of the connections. Your *procedure* would be to: (1) check out the electrical connection and (2) check out the cable connections between the printer and the computer. The *conclusion* is either that the printer prints or it doesn't. If it doesn't print, another hypothesis is needed. Maybe there is no ink in the cartridge or no paper in the tray.

A scientific question that was asked a couple of centuries ago was, "Does soil contribute to the mass of a tree that grows from a tiny acorn?" To investigate this question, scientists hypothesized that the amount of soil in a container in which an acorn was grown would lessen as the tree grew. Their procedure was to measure the soil placed in a container, plant an acorn, water the soil, and wait until the tree had grown. After a certain period of time, the scientists carefully removed the tree from the soil so as not to lose any soil. They remeasured the soil and weighed the tree. What they found was that the amount of soil was identical to the amount present when the tree was planted. The scientists concluded that soil did not contribute to the mass of the tree.

Many other questions were asked before scientists discovered the process of photosynthesis, which trees and other green plants use to obtain energy from sunlight, carbon dioxide, and water.

EXERCISE 1

Directions: Choose the <u>one best answer</u> for each item.

1. A hypothesis is
   - (1)   a statement that leads to further questions.
   - (2)   another name for an observation.
   - (3)   the statistical method used to collect and analyze data.
   - (4)   a measurable explanation of an observation.
   - (5)   another name for a conclusion.

2. A scientist hypothesized that certain kinds of foods would help travelers avoid jet lag. She fed Group A a high-protein diet and Group B a high-carbohydrate diet before a flight to Europe. She tested both groups 24 hours later for signs of jet lag. What is the most important element missing from this experimental design?
   - (1)   The scientist's observations are not included.
   - (2)   The scientist did not consider the age of the subjects.
   - (3)   The scientist did not include a control group.
   - (4)   There was no mention of the number of time zones involved.
   - (5)   The scientist did not include a high-fat diet.

3. A scientist has tied his research to preceding research, stated his hypothesis, described his methods, presented his data and statistical analyses, stated his conclusions, and published a paper in a prestigious scientific journal. It would be most correct to say that the scientist has
   - (1)   proven his scientific ideas.
   - (2)   advanced the frontier of scientific knowledge.
   - (3)   conducted a definitive research project that concluded all scientific research on the subject.
   - (4)   missed an important step in the scientific method.
   - (5)   presented his work to other scientists to see if they can reproduce his results.

4. Good scientists can be said to be
   - (1)   open-minded to criticism.
   - (2)   positive about their conclusions.
   - (3)   uninterested in possible bias in their research.
   - (4)   opposed to revising their hypothesis.
   - (5)   uninterested in publishing their work.

UNIT 2: THE CELL

The amazing thing about life is how basically simple and similar it is throughout the living world. All life is based on atoms and molecules. The basic life processes are chemical reactions. Therefore, all science is interrelated, and having knowledge of physical science, the subject of Chapter 3, helps in the study of life science.

CELL STRUCTURE

The basic unit of life in plants and animals is the **cell**. Cells are composed of a **cell membrane** that encloses the **cytoplasm** and a **nucleus** that contains genetic material. Several key types of molecules—those in the cell membranes, those that store energy within the cell, and those that comprise the genes—are essentially the same in plants and animals.

Two major classifications of cells are **prokaryotes** and **eukaryotes**. The word *Karyon* means "nucleus," so prokaryotes are an ancient group of cells that developed early in the history of life and lack a true nucleus. Prokaryotic cells are primitive cells whose ancestors have been on the Earth for at least 3.5 billion years. Prokaryotes are one-celled and mostly microscopic. Bacteria are prokaryotes, as are *Archaea*, which include microscopic, single-celled organisms that live in extreme environments.

Eukaryotes are cells that have a true nucleus and well-defined **organelles,** or subcellular chemical structures, within the cell. Eukaryotic cells appeared on the earth about 1.8 billion years ago. Eukaryotes may exist as single cells or as multicellular organisms and are the types of cells that make up plants and animals.

All eukaryotic cells have a cell membrane that separates the cell from the outside world. Membranes are composed of tightly packed fat, protein, and carbohydrate molecules and have some openings to the outside called pores. Contained in the membrane but outside the nucleus is a jellylike fluid called cytoplasm, which contains the highly specialized organelles that carry out cellular functions. Organelles may release energy from food, transport molecules such as amino acids, remove waste products, make new molecules such as hormones and antibodies, or store genetic material. Remember that most cell functions carried out by organelles involve chemical reactions.

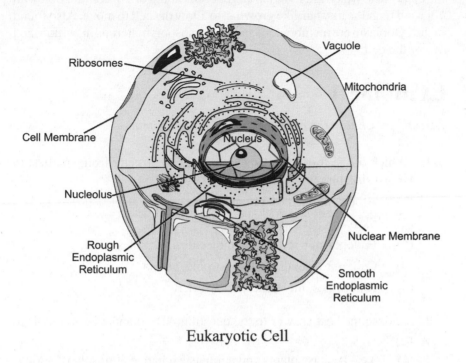

Eukaryotic Cell

It is important to look at the organelles and their functions in more detail. The nucleus is the organelle that contains the chromosomes. The nucleus controls the cell's growth and reproduction as well as the cell's metabolism. **Metabolism** refers to the total of all physical and chemical reactions that occur in a cell.

In the cytoplasm is the **endoplasmic reticulum**, an intricate, membranous canal system that assists in producing, manufacturing, or digesting large chemical molecules. The endoplasmic reticulum is a network of canals within the cytoplasm. It is abbreviated as ER. The ER may contain other organelles called ribosomes. If it does it is called a rough ER, or rER. If there are no ribosomes it is called a smooth ER, or sER. **Ribosomes** are structures that make proteins. **Proteins** are chemicals that are vital to life and exist in many forms in plants and animals.

Two other organelles found in the cytoplasm are the mitochondria (found in both plants and animals) and chloroplasts (found only in plants). Both of these organelles are concerned with energy transformation. **Chloroplasts** (in plant cells) convert light energy into chemical energy in a process called photosynthesis. Only plant cells contain chloroplasts, so only plant cells can perform this basic process on which all life depends. **Mitochondria** take the sugar molecules made in photosynthesis and transfer the chemical energy to a high-energy molecule called ATP that the cells can use readily. The process mitochondria use is called respiration.

An interesting structure in the cytoplasm is the cytoskeleton, which gives the cell its shape and along which the organelles move. It functions along with the centrioles, which are found in animal cells and work in conjunction with cilia and flagella, tiny hairlike growths, to allow the cell to move. Also found in the cytoplasm are membranous sacs that transport materials in, within, and out of the cell.

EXERCISE 1

Directions: Choose the <u>one best answer</u> for each item.

1. Which of the following lists is organized correctly from smallest to largest structure?
    (1)   Atoms, molecules, organelles, cells
    (2)   Skin, nucleus, nucleolus, cell
    (3)   Endoplasmic reticulum, molecules, vacuoles, atoms
    (4)   Cell, mitochondria, chromosome, atoms
    (5)   Ribosomes, molecules, atoms, rER

2. Choose the best answer to the question, "Do plants need animals to live?"
    (1)   Yes, because plants and animals exchange atmospheric gases.
    (2)   Yes, because plants do not have mitochondria.
    (3)   No, because plant cells have both chloroplasts and mitochondria and can store energy as well as release it.
    (4)   Yes, because animals help pollinate all plants.
    (5)   No, because animals eat the plants and kill them.

3. Which organelle is found only in plant cells?
    (1)   Endoplasmic reticulum
    (2)   Mitochondria
    (3)   Ribosomes
    (4)   Nucleoli
    (5)   Chloroplasts

4. The organelles that give the cell its shape and function in cell locomotion are the
    (1)   sERs.
    (2)   vacuoles.
    (3)   nucleoli.
    (4)   metabolic units.
    (5)   cytoskeletons.

THE CELL MEMBRANE

The cell membrane contains the material inside the cell and controls what enters and leaves the cell. It is composed of phosphate/lipid (fat/oil) molecules packed together in a sandwich-like structure. Studded throughout are large protein molecules and carbohydrate chains, which are used as markers or identifiers by the cell and external molecules. Some proteins act as pores in the membrane so that some materials may pass directly into the cell. Molecules may enter and leave the cells by chemical diffusion, osmosis, or active transport (which requires energy).

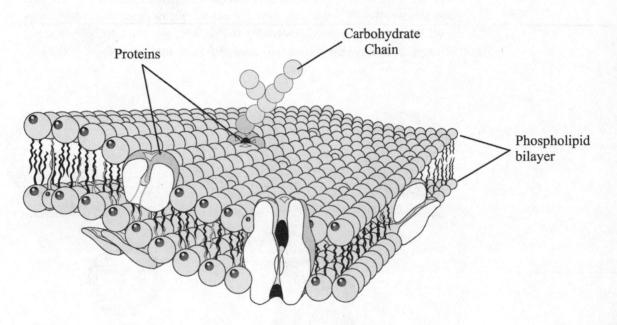

Proteins

Carbohydrate Chain

Phospholipid bilayer

Cross Section of Cell Membrane

CELL FUNCTIONS

Cell functions are chemical reactions that use the food we eat to provide energy and raw materials for the cell's use. Since food is composed of chemicals, cells break down the food and use the food molecules to make other molecules needed by the cell.

All metabolic activity (cellular metabolic reactions) is made possible by the action of protein catalysts (transformer molecules) called enzymes. **Enzymes** are protein molecules needed in very small amounts to bring about a chemical reaction. Once they finish with a chemical reaction they can be reused in another chemical reaction.

The cell stores information about how to make the proteins it is composed of in DNA (deoxyribose nucleic acid) housed in the cell nucleus. Segments of DNA, called **genes**, direct the making of numerous specific proteins needed by the cell. DNA also regulates which genes are active and which proteins are made. DNA regulation allows cells to relate to their environments. DNA also governs the growth of cells and their division.

CELL DIVISION IN EUKARYOTES

Plants and animals grow from one original cell that divides by a highly regulated process called **mitosis**. Mitosis is a type of cell division that is necessary for growth of an organism and for repair of damaged tissues and organs. The process of mitosis begins with one cell and produces two cells with the same number and kind of chromosomes as the original cell. The fact that almost all cells in the body have the exact same number of chromosomes is what makes the process of cloning possible. Mitosis is a continuous process, but scientists have divided it into four phases to make it easier to study.

Late Interphase

Prophase

Metaphase

Anaphase

Cytokinesis

Mitosis

1. *Prophase:* The nuclear membrane disappears; the chromosomes become distinct; a spindle appears.

2. *Metaphase:* The duplicated chromosomes are lined up on the equator of the cell.

3. *Anaphase:* The duplicated chromosomes split apart and travel to opposite poles of the cell.

4. *Telophase:* A nuclear membrane develops around the chromosomes at each pole; chromosomes become indistinct. During this phase the division of the cytoplasm, called cytokinesis, is completed. There are now two smaller cells in the space of the original cell.

CELL CYCLE

Mitosis is part of a cell cycle that includes interphase, the period of time between mitotic events. Interphase begins with the growth of the newly divided cell (G_1). It includes the S phase, which is the reproduction of DNA material, and the G_2 phase, in which the cell prepares for the next mitotic division.

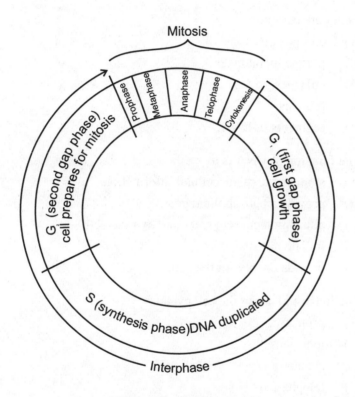

The Cell Cycle

The stained nuclear material that can be seen under a microscope during mitosis consists of **chromosomes.** Chromosomes are long, thin, coiled packages of a DNA molecule plus some proteins. Chromosomes carry the genes. A gene is the unit of heredity and is composed of a fragment of DNA (a sequence of DNA nucleotides). A gene carries the code for a single protein.

Through mitosis, a single cell divides into a multicellular organism. Each cell in an organism, except the reproductive cells, has the same number and kind of chromosomes as the **zygote**, or fertilized egg. In spite of having the same genetic composition, the developing cells, called **stem cells** in animals, multiply and differentiate to form specialized cells such as bone cells, blood, nerves, skin, muscle cells, and others in animals. Plant cells differentiate into sclerenchyma cells, vessels, sieve tube cells, and companion cells, for example. Specialized cells further develop into tissues and organs that comprise a multicellular organism, whether it is a plant or animal. Differentiation of cells is under the control of DNA, which regulates which genes express themselves and which genes are repressed. Therefore, DNA regulates the differentiation of stem cells.

EXERCISE 2

Directions: Choose the one best answer for each item.

1. Genes are composed of
   (1)   chromosomes.
   (2)   plasma membranes.
   (3)   enzymes.
   (4)   proteins.
   (5)   segments of DNA.

2. The function of DNA is to
   (1)   store and regulate cellular information.
   (2)   provide a phospholipid coat.
   (3)   allow molecules to enter and exit the cell.
   (4)   initiate mitosis.
   (5)   provide energy for the cell.

3. The longest phase of the cell cycle is
   (1)   prophase.
   (2)   metaphase.
   (3)   anaphase.
   (4)   telophase.
   (5)   interphase.

4. A cell membrane that lacked carbohydrate strands extending from it would
   (1)   not be able to keep organelles in the cell.
   (2)   lose energy.
   (3)   have trouble recognizing molecules on the outside of the cell.
   (4)   dehydrate.
   (5)   not be able to undergo mitosis.

UNIT 3: THE MOLECULAR BASIS OF HEREDITY

The instructions for growth and repair of the cells of all organisms—protists, fungi, plants, and animals—are carried in their DNA. DNA is the master code of life.

DNA is composed of four smaller units called **nucleotides**. Therefore, DNA is frequently called a polynucleotide. Each nucleotide is composed of a sugar molecule, a phosphate group, and one of four nitrogen bases: adenine (A), thymine (T), cytosine (C), and guanine (G). Thymine and cytosine molecules have a single ring structure and belong to a group called pyrimidines. Adenine and guanine have a double ring structure and are called purines.

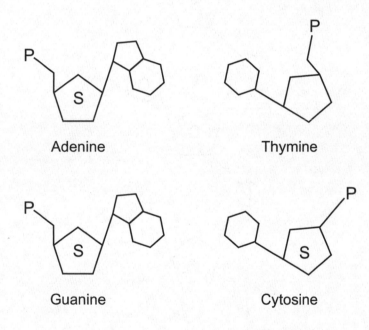

Adenine   Thymine

Guanine   Cytosine

DNA Nucleotides

Because DNA is a double-stranded molecule with a constant distance between the two strands, the nitrogen rings can only bind in certain ways. A pyrimidine can only bond with a purine (a single ring with a double ring molecule). So thymine can only bond with adenine, and cytosine can only bond with guanine. A-T and C-G are called complementary nitrogen bases. While that is the only pairing possible, the order of the nitrogen bases along a DNA strand can be varied. One strand of DNA is made up of alternating sugar and phosphate molecules with the nitrogen base attached to the side of the sugar molecule.

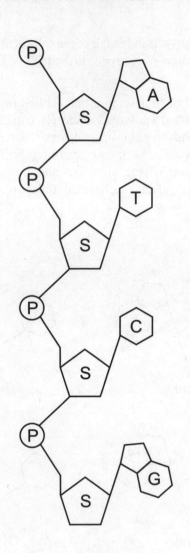

DNA Strand

The DNA molecule has two parallel strands of nucleotides united by hydrogen bonds at their complementary nitrogen bases. The molecule is coiled into a double helix shape. A single DNA molecule may contain more than 130 million base pairs, which may be arranged in any order. So the number of potential variations in nitrogen base sequences is enormous.

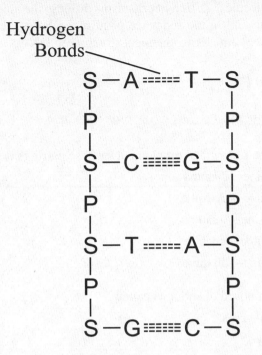

Uncoiled DNA Molecule

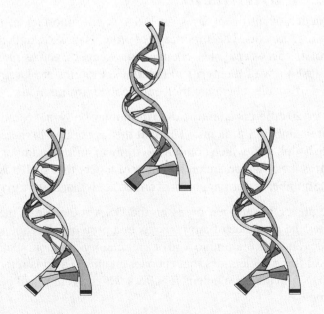

DNA Replication

The DNA in all organisms is composed of the same sugar, phosphate, and nitrogen base molecules. Different organisms differ in the amount of DNA their cells contain and in the sequence of nitrogen bases. But all living organisms have the same basic chemical structure in DNA.

EXERCISE 1

Directions: Choose the <u>one best answer</u> for each item.

1. Which of the following complementary base pairings is incorrect?
   (1)   Adenine—guanine
   (2)   Guanine—cytosine
   (3)   Cytosine—guanine
   (4)   Thymine—adenine
   (5)   Adenine—thymine

2. DNA is composed of subunits called
   (1)   amino acids.
   (2)   purines.
   (3)   pyrimidines.
   (4)   deoxyribose sugar.
   (5)   nucleotides.

PROTEIN SYNTHESIS

The sequence of nitrogen bases on DNA is all-important in making, or synthesizing, proteins. The importance of proteins to life cannot be exaggerated. Proteins act as enzymes, chemical messengers, and as muscle fibers, to name just a few of their critical functions. Proteins are large molecules composed of smaller chemical molecules called **amino acids**.

There are 20 different amino acids in the human body that combine to form an infinite number of proteins. Think of this as parallel to the 26 letters in the English alphabet, which combine to form an infinite number of English words. It is the arrangement and number of letters that spell a given word. So it is the number and arrangement of amino acids that make a given protein.

The sequence of nitrogen bases on the DNA molecule is the code that determines the sequence of amino acids in a protein. A sequence of three nucleotides encodes one amino acid or a regulatory function, such as "Stop." The unit of three nucleotides that encodes an amino acid is referred to as a **codon**. DNA in the cell nucleus regulates which protein will be made at a given time.

Actual protein synthesis, however, occurs on the ribosomes in the cytoplasm. Since DNA does not leave the nucleus, an intermediary molecule, RNA, is made from DNA. RNA (or ribonucleic acid) carries the code from the DNA to the cytoplasm. **Transcription** is the process of making RNA from DNA.

While RNA has the same nitrogen base sequence as DNA, it differs from DNA in three important ways: RNA is single-stranded, not double-stranded; RNA has a different sugar molecule from DNA; and RNA has a uracil (U) nitrogen base instead of the thymine (T) nitrogen base in DNA. Uracil is complementary to adenine, as is thymine in the DNA molecule.

There are three types of RNA with three different functions: rRNA makes up the ribosome, tRNA carries amino acids found in the cytoplasm to the ribosome, and mRNA carries the code from the nucleus to the ribosomes.

The entire process of protein synthesis consists of the following steps:

1. RNA molecules are made from DNA.

2. RNA molecules leave the nucleus and travel to the cytoplasm.

3. rRNA forms ribosomes, either on the endoplasmic reticulum or free in the cytoplasm.

4. mRNA carries the nitrogen base code signifying the amino acid sequence for a specific protein to the ribosome.

5. tRNA in the cytoplasm carries one amino acid to the mRNA-ribosome complex. tRNA carries a complementary codon to a codon on mRNA and can only bond at that point. This ensures that the "tag along" amino acid carried on tRNA will be joined in the proper sequence for that particular protein.

6. As different tRNAs reach the mRNA and bond with their complements, the various amino acids are positioned properly and bond together to form the designated protein.

7. The completed protein is released into the cytoplasm or packaged for secretion from the cell. Another similar protein may be made or the mRNA-ribosome complex may be recycled.

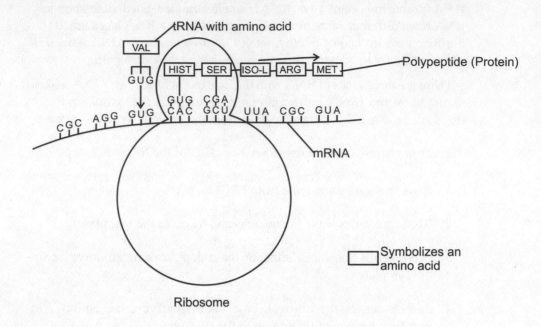

Protein Synthesis

MEIOSIS

The key to understanding the molecular basis of heredity is understanding how the DNA molecule is passed on to the next generation. This involves **meiosis**, a special type of cell division that occurs only in the formation of reproductive cells, such as the sperm and egg in humans. All human somatic cells (nonreproductive cells) contain 22 pairs of chromosomes plus a 23rd pair (XY) that determines sex. Reproductive cells called **gametes,** or sperm and egg, contain one half the number of chromosomes. In the case of humans, this is 22 individual chromosomes, plus one sex chromosome.

In order to produce sex cells with one half the normal number of chromosomes, several additional steps in cell division are necessary. Recall that in mitosis, during interphase, DNA replicates itself (makes an exact copy of itself). It does this by unzipping along the hydrogen bonds. Each half of the DNA molecule makes a new strand using free nucleotides in the nucleus. This provides enough DNA for the daughter cells after meiosis. Each chromosome remains attached to its exact copy until Metaphase II, as you will see below.

Meiosis consists of two divisions, one right after the other. As a result, one cell gives rise to four cells at the end of meiosis. Stages of meiosis are essentially the same as those of mitosis, with two major exceptions:

1. *Interphase:* DNA is replicated in preparation for cellular division. Just as in mitosis, DNA replication during interphase results in an exact copy of each of the chromosomes in a cell.

2. *Prophase I:* As in mitosis, the nuclear membrane disappears and chromosomes become distinct. However, in meiosis chromosome pairs come together in this stage and function as a unit.

3. *Metaphase I*: As in meiosis, the chromosomes line up on the mid-line of the cell.

4. *Anaphase I*: Unlike in mitosis, the chromosome pairs separate, with one half going to one pole (a developing daughter cell) and one half going to the other pole (a second developing daughter cell).

5. *Telophase I*: A nuclear membrane reforms around the chromosomes in each developing daughter cell.

6. *Prophase II*: Prophase now begins again without an interphase.

7. *Metaphase II*: The chromosomes line up in each of the two daughter cells.

8. *Anaphase II*: Each daughter cell now divides into two new cells, with exact copies of each of the chromosomes going to each daughter cell

9. *Telophase II*: There are four new daughter cells, each with one half the number of chromosomes the original cell had. They also have different assortments of these chromosomes.

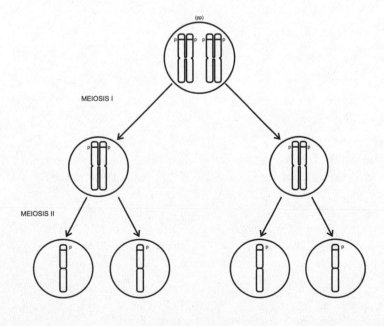

Meiosis

As the nuclear material is being divided exactly, the cytoplasm of the cell is also being divided in a process called **cytokinesis**, a splitting of the cytoplasm and organelles. However, it is not an exact division of cytoplasm and organelles between daughter cells.

Meiosis occurs in the formation of sperm cells and egg cells. When egg and sperm unite, a zygote with a new combination of chromosomes is formed as a result of sexual reproduction. This explains why offspring may have some characteristics of each parent. Sexual reproduction is the basis of evolution, because it provides the necessary variability of genes in the offspring of a species.

Mutations are sudden unpredictable changes in a gene that occur frequently but are usually corrected. Only mutations that occur in egg and sperm cells can be passed on to the next generation.

EXERCISE 2

Directions: Choose the <u>one best answer</u> for each item.

1. The nitrogen base uracil, found in RNA, is complementary to
   - (1)   thymine.
   - (2)   adenine.
   - (3)   cytosine.
   - (4)   guanine.
   - (5)   the phosphate group.

2. The unit of three nitrogen bases that carries the code for a specific amino acid is the
   - (1)   nucleotide.
   - (2)   chromosome.
   - (3)   codon.
   - (4)   tRNA.
   - (5)   DNA.

3. Where does meiosis occur?
   - (1)   In the nucleus of future egg or sperm cells
   - (2)   In the cytoplasm of future egg or sperm cells
   - (3)   In the nucleus of any dividing cell
   - (4)   In the cytoplasm of any dividing cell
   - (5)   In both the nucleus and cytoplasm of any dividing cell

4. Interphase is a period of the cell cycle in which
   - (1)   the cell is resting.
   - (2)   DNA is being replicated.
   - (3)   chromosomes migrate to the mid-line of the cell.
   - (4)   the cell wall or plate forms.
   - (5)   spindle fibers appear.

5. Which of the following is the significant event in Anaphase I during meiosis?
   - (1)   Like chromosomes pair.
   - (2)   New nuclei are formed.
   - (3)   The number of chromosomes is halved.
   - (4)   The nuclear membrane disappears from view.
   - (5)   The cytoplasm divides between the two daughter cells.

6. How many chromosomes does the nucleus of a zygote contain?
    (1)   4 complete set
    (2)   2 complete sets
    (3)   1 complete set
    (4)   1/2 set
    (5)   A random number

UNIT 4: BIOLOGICAL EVOLUTION

Evolution is defined as changes in gene frequencies in a population over time. Evolution is a basic concept in biology. It is important to understand that individuals do not evolve; species evolve. The basic principle underlying evolution is survival of the fittest: some individuals in a species have the right combination of genes to survive and reproduce in their environment. Their genes are, therefore, passed on to future generations, and those genes determine the future genetic composition of the species.

That evolution occurs is supported by three sets of observations. The first set of data is the great diversity of organisms that live on the earth today. All organisms are related in that they descended from a common ancestor, as evidenced by molecular similarities. The second set of data is found in the fossil record located in successive layers of rock and sediments that have formed over 3.5 billion years. The third set of data is seen in similarities in anatomy and molecular chemistry in diverse lifeforms.

Natural selection provides a scientific explanation for evolution. Natural selection is the general tendency for members of a species that are genetically better suited to their environment to survive and reproduce. This leads to changes in the genetic makeup of the species and eventually to the formation of new species over time. Natural selection involves three basic principles: First, a species can increase its population numbers greatly. Second, members of a species have great genetic variation due to sexual reproduction and mutations. Third, all members of a population compete for natural resources. Those individuals that are successful in obtaining natural resources live. Those that are not successful do not live.

The study of how organisms are related in an evolutionary sense is called **phylogeny**. A study of phylogeny shows that humans, gorillas, and chimpanzees are all very closely related. A related branch of biology, **taxonomy**, groups organisms into a classification scheme. Using taxonomy, biologists give each species a two-part name that designates its genus and its species. Under this system of **binomial nomenclature**, humans are classified as *Homo sapiens*, because we belong to the genus *Homo*, a group we share with several extinct but very closely related species, and the species *sapiens*, a name unique to our species.

Seven basic categories are used for naming organisms. Ranging from the smallest, most precise groupings to the largest, most inclusive, they are species, genus, family, order, class, phylum (or division), and kingdom.

Humans and chimpanzees belong to the same kingdom, phylum, class, and order. Our classification splits apart only at the family level.

Taxonomy tries to reflect evolutionary relationships in classification schemes. As new laboratory techniques become available, such as DNA testing, new relationships are found. This means that organisms are sometimes moved from one category to another. For example, it was discovered very recently that African elephants actually comprise two distinct species, not one, as biologists had long believed.

EXERCISE 1

Directions: Choose the <u>one best answer</u> for each item.

1. Which of the following conditions is necessary for evolution to occur?
   (1)   A stable environment
   (2)   A population with a stable genetic composition
   (3)   A lack of genetic mutations
   (4)   A population with genetic variability
   (5)   An unlimited amount of resources

2. The classification category below the level of phylum is the
   (1)   genus.
   (2)   family.
   (3)   order.
   (4)   class.
   (5)   kingdom.

3. A scientist would state that natural selection is
   (1)   a fact.
   (2)   a theory.
   (3)   a hypothesis.
   (4)   proven by the fossil record.
   (5)   proven by the classification of organisms.

4. What is the relationship between evolution and natural selection?
   (1)   Natural selection prevents evolution.
   (2)   Evolution causes natural selection.
   (3)   Natural selection is one cause of evolution.
   (4)   They are the same thing.
   (5)   They are unrelated.

UNIT 5: INTERDEPENDENCE OF ORGANISMS

The word "recycling" brings to mind the current practice of reusing paper, glass, and plastic products to protect the environment. However, nature has been recycling for millions of years. Atoms and molecules are continually recycled from the nonliving parts of the environment, such as soil minerals, air, and water, to living organisms. As living organisms die, decomposers return the atoms and molecules they are composed of to the nonliving environment so that they can be used again. There are numerous cycles that go on continuously, such as the water cycle, the nitrogen cycle, and the carbon cycle.

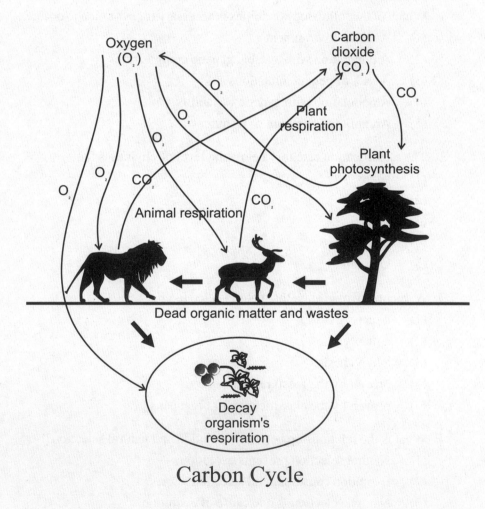

Carbon Cycle

Plants take up nonliving atoms and molecules such as water, minerals, and carbon dioxide from the soil, water, and air and convert them into biologically important compounds such as sugar. Plants use sugars for their growth and reproduction. Animals cannot convert nonliving atoms into food themselves, so they eat plants and use the plant sugars for their own growth and reproduction. Some animals, called **herbivores**, eat only plants. Others, called **omnivores**, eat both plants and animals. Even **carnivores**, animals that eat only other animals, depend on green plants for their food, because the animals that they eat themselves eat green plants.

An indication of the interdependence of organisms can be seen in a sketch of an ecosystem. An ecosystem consists of the nonliving parts (water, air, soil, rock), the **producers** (plants), the **consumers** (herbivores, omnivores, and carnivores), and the **decomposers** (bacteria and fungi) that live off dead plants and animals. Examples of ecosystems include a redwood forest, a desert, a rain forest, a prairie, or even a city park or backyard.

Just as life requires atoms and molecules, it also requires energy to survive. But there is a major difference between the two necessary groups. While atoms and molecules recycle, energy does not. This is an important concept. Energy flows from higher energy levels to lower energy levels in one direction only. In an ecosystem, the source of energy is the sunlight that is trapped by the plants. The plants use some of the energy to produce food and to carry out other activities, such as seed production. So a smaller amount remains to be passed on to the herbivores, who also use some energy. A still smaller amount remains to be passed on to the carnivores, and an even smaller amount to the decomposers. Energy is eventually lost from an ecosystem in the form of heat.

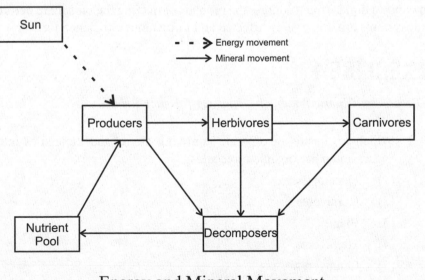

Energy and Mineral Movement
in Ecosystem

All the energy available to an ecosystem comes from the sun. Light energy, which animals cannot use for sustaining life, is converted by plants into chemical energy, which animals can use. Plants accomplish the transformation of energy by a chemical process called **photosynthesis**.

Organisms both cooperate and compete in ecosystems. An example of cooperation is insects that pollinate plants. Many of these insects have body shapes that complement flower shapes. By taking the nectar of flowers, insects pollinate the flowers, thus assisting in the sexual reproduction of plants for the next generation. An example of competition is birds that defend their territory against invasion by members of their own species. Such interactions are vital, stabilizing forces in an ecosystem.

Another major factor that brings about balance in an ecosystem is the interaction between population size and resources. Populations have the ability to increase continuously, but the environment and resource base cannot increase continuously. The resource base is finite, or limited. If population increases beyond the amount of food necessary to support it, members of the population die. This decrease in population continues until the population number is in equilibrium with the food supply. The search for resources, such as food, hiding places, nesting sites, or water, is a critical factor in the interaction of organisms.

Ecosystems can be small or they can be as large as the planetary biosphere, but they all have the same basic components. Humans live in the world's ecosystem as herbivores or carnivores. Humans have a far greater effect on the ecosystem than any other animal species. The human population is growing rapidly. Technology is increasing the standard of living, but it is also increasing pollution on the land, in the water, and in the air. Consumption of resources is increasing. Habitats and ecosystems are being destroyed throughout the world. It has been said that an ecosystem operates in a delicate balance. Humans must address the problems affecting the biosphere before ecosystems are irreversibly affected and thrown out of balance forever.

EXERCISE 1

Directions: Choose the one best answer for each item.

1. Which organisms incorporate nonliving atoms and molecules into sugars and other organic molecules?
    (1)   Decomposers
    (2)   Carnivores
    (3)   Plants
    (4)   Herbivores
    (5)   Omnivores

2. An ecosystem consists of producers, herbivores, carnivores, decomposers, and
    (1)   populations.
    (2)   the biosphere.
    (3)   communities.
    (4)   a social system.
    (5)   nonliving atoms and molecules.

3. The flow of energy in an ecosystem can best be described as a(n)
    (1)   cycle assisted by bacteria.
    (2)   atmospheric cycle.
    (3)   solar cycle.
    (4)   one-way downhill flow.
    (5)   back-and-forth flow through major components.

4. *Homo sapiens* (humans) function in the world ecosystem as
    (1)   producers.
    (2)   observers of ecosystem functions.
    (3)   herbivores and omnivores.
    (4)   decomposers.
    (5)   regulators.

UNIT 6: MATTER, ENERGY, AND ORGANIZATION IN LIVING SYSTEMS

Matter is anything that takes up space and has weight. Matter can be living or nonliving, but it is always composed of atoms and follows the laws of physical science (see Chapter 4). Of the 92 naturally occurring elements, six are found in all living things. These are carbon (C), hydrogen (H), oxygen (O), nitrogen (N), phosphorus (P), and sulfur (S). In order for these elements to function in living organisms, energy is required.

Energy is the most important factor for life. Without energy, animals cannot move or digest their food, and plants cannot grow and reproduce. Without energy, life cannot exist. Moreover, there must be a continuous supply of energy for living organisms to maintain their chemical and physical organization. When an organism dies, energy input stops and all of its living systems disintegrate.

Energy can exist in many forms, such as heat, electricity, light, and chemical energy. Plants use energy in the form of light to power the process of photosynthesis. Almost all energy for life comes from the sun in the form of light. Plants absorb light and transform light energy into chemical energy. This energy is stored in the chemical bonds that hold together the atoms in the organic molecules that plants produce. Plants and animals use the chemical energy in the organic molecules for life processes. Animals could not live without plants, because only plants transform light energy to chemical energy. Because plants can make their own food, they are called **autotrophs**. Animals are called **heterotrophs** because they must get their matter and energy from other living organisms.

Plants use the chemical process of photosynthesis to trap the sun's energy and build energy-containing organic molecules. In photosynthesis, plants absorb carbon dioxide (CO_2) from the air and water (H_2O) from the soil to form an energy-rich glucose molecule, $C_6H_{12}O_6$, a simple sugar, and give off oxygen to the atmosphere. Sunlight powers this reaction. The green pigment

chlorophyll, found in plant organelles called **chloroplasts**, captures the light energy.

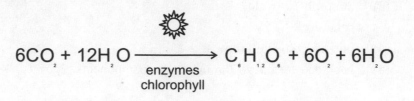

$$6CO_2 + 12H_2O \xrightarrow[\substack{\text{enzymes} \\ \text{chlorophyll}}]{} C_6H_{12}O_6 + 6O_2 + 6H_2O$$

Photosynthesis

The carbohydrate molecules that plants produce are then used to make the other molecules necessary for life. These are proteins, DNA, fats, and other sugars. Energy-storing chemical reactions that build molecules are called **anabolic** reactions.

Cellular respiration is the process that releases the chemical energy in molecules. The process is an energy-yielding, or **catabolic**, reaction that results in a breakdown of molecules. In aerobic respiration, oxygen is required to break down the glucose molecule into CO_2 and H_2O and a high-energy molecule called ATP. Cellular respiration occurs in organelles called mitochondria. **ATP** (adenosine triphosphate) is the molecule that supplies immediate energy for many cellular chemical reactions, such as the contraction of muscles, the transmission of nerve impulses, and the digestion of food.

$$C_6H_{12}O_6 + 6O_2 \xrightarrow[\substack{\text{enzymes} \\ \text{cytochromes}}]{} 6CO_2 + 6H_2O + ATP$$

Aerobic Respiration

All living organisms have evolved strategies to obtain the energy necessary to support life, to transport food internally, and to release it to the cell. Organisms evolved strategies to eliminate ingested matter also. Animals have various means of obtaining food and energy. Amoebae (one-celled animals) use pseudopods ("false feet") that engulf the food. Hydra have tentacles with nematocysts that sting the prey and bring the food to their mouth opening. A planarium has a mouth that extends from its body on a tube. Mollusks filter water and entrap food particles in mucous. A sea star inverts its stomach through its mouth and begins digesting food outside the body. Chordates (like humans) have complicated digestive systems with a mouth, esophagus, stomach, intestines, and anus.

Once the food is digested and absorbed, it is transported to the cells in the body. In chordates, the circulatory system carries the digested food in the blood to each cell in the body, where it undergoes cellular respiration. It is interesting to a biologist to compare the various systems throughout the living world to see how evolution enables organisms to obtain energy, transport it, and release it to the cells.

All living organisms are dependent on energy for life. Therefore, it is not surprising that matter and energy are key factors in an ecosystem that limit the distribution and size of populations. The flow of energy in an ecosystem must be consistent with the laws of physics. The First Law of Thermodynamics (also called the Law of Conservation of Energy) says that energy cannot be created or destroyed; it can only be transformed. As energy moves through an ecosystem, it is ultimately transformed into heat, which is a nonusable energy form. (As an example, think about how you get warm when you exercise.) The Second Law of Thermodynamics states that as energy is transformed to heat, there is a state of increased randomness and disorganization.

EXERCISE 1

Directions: Choose the <u>one best answer</u> for each item.

1. Which of the following statements about energy is correct?
    (1) High levels of energy result from the ability of ecosystems to recycle energy.
    (2) Plants create energy in the process of photosynthesis.
    (3) Animals do not derive energy from the sun.
    (4) Cellular respiration results in formation of the energy-rich molecule ATP.
    (5) Green plants use ATP to capture energy from the sun to produce sugar.

2. The raw materials used by plants in photosynthesis are
    (1) oxygen and water.
    (2) carbohydrates and carbon dioxide.
    (3) oxygen and carbon dioxide.
    (4) carbon dioxide and water.
    (5) carbohydrates and oxygen.

3. Photosynthesis occurs in special plant-cell organelles called
    (1) chloroplasts.
    (2) ribosomes.
    (3) nucleoli.
    (4) chlorophyll.
    (5) mitochondria.

4. Which of the following statements is correct?
   (1) The amount of usable energy is constantly being reduced as it passes through the ecosystem.
   (2) Energy is recycled in the same manner as carbon recycles in the ecosystem.
   (3) CO_2 and H_2O yield protein and oxygen.
   (4) O_2 and CO_2 in the presence of light and chlorophyll yield $C_6H_{12}O_6$ and H_2O.
   (5) Glucose is produced in mitochondria in animals and in chloroplasts in plants.

UNIT 7: BEHAVIOR OF ORGANISMS

Study of the behavior of complex, multicellular organisms reveals that behavior is under genetic, hormonal, and nervous system control. Some aspects of behavior interact with the environment and have evolved over time. The study of these behaviors, called **behavioral ecology**, includes both innate and learned behaviors.

INNATE BEHAVIORS

Many kinds of behavior, such as courtship rituals and nest building, are shared naturally by all members of a species. Such behaviors are said to be **innate** or genetically determined. Specific genes of the fruit fly have been linked to normal fly behaviors, such as sleeping, waking, mating, learning, and memory. Study of the fruit fly has also shown that genes control the embryonic development of the nervous system. The genetic basis of behavior is seen in many other animals: in tongue flicks of garter snakes, in some species-specific bird songs, and in the hunting or herding behaviors of certain breeds of dogs. Many biorhythms, such as when an organism falls asleep and how long it sleeps, are also genetically controlled.

Being able to identify genes responsible for behavior is very important in understanding some behaviors. In addition, identification of genes and enzymes that influence learning and memory may lead to treatments for Alzheimer's disease and other diseases of the brain.

HORMONAL CONTROL OF BEHAVIOR

The influence of **hormones** on behavior is well documented. It is known that hormones have powerful effects in even very low concentrations. Hormones travel through the body in the bloodstream and influence only certain specific cells, called target cells, which have specific receptor proteins on the cell membrane. Hormone secretion is influenced by the nervous system, by chemical changes in the blood, and by other hormones. Hormones control growth, sexual reproduction, and the well-known fight-or-flight response.

Pheromones are chemical signals exchanged between individuals of the same species that cause a specific behavioral response in the receiving animal. They are considered to be hormones, although they are secreted to the outside of the animal rather than into the bloodstream. Pheromones may cause a variety of actions in individuals and on populations. Dogs use pheromones to mark their territory. Ants use them to mark trails for other ants to follow. Pheromones are also important sexual attractants. In some species, a female's pheromone can attract males from a mile or two away.

THE NERVOUS SYSTEM AND THE SENSES

The nervous system is composed of the brain, spinal cord, nerve cells, and neuroglia cells, which protect and support nerve cells. The nervous system controls all systems of the body including the heartbeat, breathing, food digestion, and even the endocrine system, which produces hormones.

Nerve cells (or **neurons**) are the functional parts of the nervous system. Nerves communicate with one another or with other organs, such as muscles. Nerves conduct impulses rapidly along dendrites and long cell extensions called **axons**. Bundles of axons from many nerve cells make up the nerves. **Dendrites**, the tiny extensions of the nerve cell body, receive the impulses and transmit them to the cell body. The cell body sends impulses along the axon to an organ or to another neuron. Neurons communicate with one another indirectly, by sending impulses across a minute space called a **synapse**. Neurons communicate by means of chemicals called neurotransmitters, which are able to flow across the gap and excite or inhibit adjoining neurons or organs.

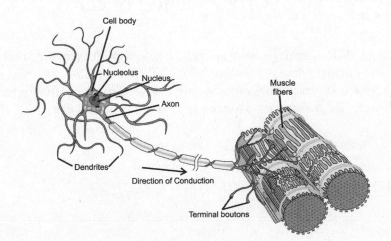

A neuron connecting to muscle fibers

The senses are an important part of the nervous system. The general senses include pain, touch, pressure, and temperature, which are sensed by neurons in the skin, organs, joints, and muscles. The special senses are taste, smell, hearing, balance, and vision. Taste and smell are the senses found in almost all animals. They are important for most basic animal activities, such as finding food and mates and avoiding predators. Many animals have additional senses. For example, some snakes can sense infrared radiation (heat) given off by animals. Fish may have mechanoreceptors that sense depth and force. Hearing (which is also mechanoreception) is much more sensitive in dogs and cats than in humans. Bats have a form of sensory perception called echolocation that allows them to detect echoes of sounds they transmit. Sharks and rays have electroreception, which detects the small electric currents that are produced by the heart or muscles of their prey.

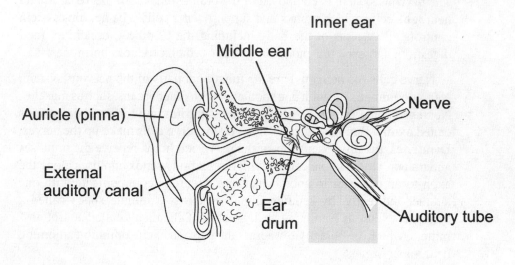

Cross section of ear

Vision differs greatly among animals. The octopus has an eye similar to that of humans, although it evolved along a different pathway. Insect eyes are compound eyes that detect the slightest movement even in dim light. The following illustration shows a cross section of the human eye.

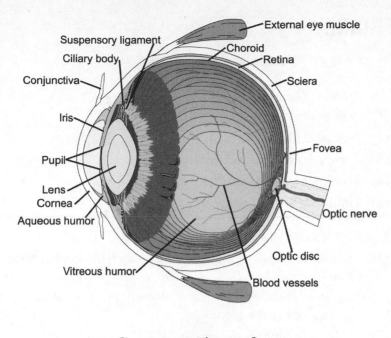

Cross section of eye

In summary, the nervous system enables animals to be aware of what is happening in their internal and external environment and to respond accordingly.

EVOLUTION OF BEHAVIOR

Behaviors used between members of the same species are called intraspecific behaviors. These include social dominance behaviors, mating behaviors, and territoriality behaviors used to establish a home range. Interspecific behavioral strategies, used between members of different species, include behaviors used to compete for resources and those used to divide environmental resources. Animals use different behaviors at different times of day or during different seasons to help apportion resources. All behaviors are the product of evolution: behaviors, like physical traits, evolve to ensure reproduction and survival of the species. The members of a species must be flexible enough to adapt and change in response to a changing environment. If members of the species cannot do that, they do not survive and reproduce.

Behavioral evolution occurs in plants also. Plants can change the color of their flowers over the growing season to attract seasonal pollinating insects. Plants have evolved chemical defenses against different predators. And, of course, the exquisite match of flower shape to the shape of specific pollinating insects and birds is well known.

EXERCISE 1

Directions: Choose the <u>one best answer</u> for each item.

1. An organism's behavior is governed by
   (1) environmental stresses.
   (2) interspecific competition.
   (3) genes, hormones, and the nervous system.
   (4) behavior learned from the mother.
   (5) intraspecific dominance.

2. Behavior has evolutionary significance in that
   (1) it is the only trait of organisms that undergoes natural selection.
   (2) organisms that behave successfully will produce future generations of the species.
   (3) behavior stabilizes the gene pool.
   (4) behavioral change can be demonstrated within one generation in an animal species.
   (5) behavioral change permits the dominant member of a group to continue to be a leader over time.

3. The particular pattern that a spider used to weave a web is an example of
   (1) behavior taught by parents.
   (2) intraspecific behavior.
   (3) innate behavior.
   (4) behavior learned by observation.
   (5) response to environmental change.

4. A synapse is a
   (1) place where neurons join together.
   (2) hormone.
   (3) neurotransmitter.
   (4) cell that supports neurons.
   (5) gap between neurons.

UNIT 8: SCIENCE AND TECHNOLOGY

It is important to understand the difference between science and technology. Science is the study of the natural world. Science includes mathematics, physics, chemistry, biology, astronomy, geology, and many overlapping disciplines, such as geophysics and biochemistry. Science tries to answer such questions as "How does the immune system work?", "How are continents formed?", and "Is the universe finite or infinite?" Scientific findings often challenge people's beliefs; many people today still question the validity of the theory of evolution on religious grounds.

To answer these fundamental questions about the natural world, scientists need creativity, imagination, and physical dexterity. Scientific research must be published and made public so that findings may be scrutinized by the scientific community for accuracy and reproducibility. The study of science involves tenacity in pursuing a question.

Technology is usually considered to be applied science. It involves taking scientific findings and applying them to solve human problems. However, technology can have an impact on scientific research as well. Consider the great technological push to miniaturize everything, including computer chips. As a result of miniaturization, scientists are able to put tracking collars on bears and turtles, which, with the help of orbital satellite positioning systems, enable them to trace the animal migrations. Because of technological advances, doctors can perform arthroscopic surgery on an athlete's damaged knee; psychiatrists can view the brain in action; and neurologists can begin to understand what happens in the brain when we learn something. Technological advances are often proprietary materials: they are patented or they are kept secret within a company to ensure the financial interests of the company. Technology, too, may create new problems, especially in the environment.

LOCAL, NATIONAL, AND GLOBAL CHALLENGES

Science and technology have tremendously changed most parts of the world over the past 250 years. Both disciplines are an essential part of the world society today. However, the challenges of deciding which scientific and technological advances should be embraced for the future should not and must not be left to the scientists. Society can and must affect the direction of scientific and technological progress. These decisions must be based on the study of alternatives, risks, costs, and benefits.

All people in a democratic society should understand basic concepts of science and technology before entering into the important economic, political, and ethical debates of current and yet-to-be-discovered science-and-technology-related challenges to the local, national, and global society.

EXERCISE 1

Directions: Choose the <u>one best answer</u> for each item.

1. Which of the following statements is NOT correct?
   - (1)   Science and technology are both parts of society.
   - (2)   Science can only indicate what can happen, not what should happen.
   - (3)   Individuals and society must decide on whether to use new technologies.
   - (4)   Active debate will not affect science or politics.
   - (5)   Decision on scientific and technological proposals should consider potential risks, costs, and benefits.

2. Scientific literacy involves
   - (1)   understanding the basic concepts and principles of science.
   - (2)   reading scientific journals.
   - (3)   writing for scientific journals.
   - (4)   conducting and carrying out scientific research.
   - (5)   a basic understanding of statistics.

UNIT 9: SCIENCE IN PERSONAL AND SOCIAL PERSPECTIVES

POPULATION GROWTH

Populations grow as a result of four major factors:

1. *Birth rate:* The birth rate, or **natality,** is the number of births per 1,000 individuals per year.

2. *Death rate:* The death rate, or **mortality**, is the number of deaths per 1,000 individuals per year.

3. *Emigration:* Emigration is movement out of a given area.

4. *Immigration:* Immigration is movement into a given area.

Population growth involves all organisms in any ecosystem, including plants, animals, fungi, and microorganisms. Of course, humans are part of the animal component.

An entomologist, L O. Howard, estimated that one female housefly lays 120 eggs at a time and that there are seven generations a year. Each generation is half male and half female. He calculated that one female would give rise to five trillion flies by the seventh generation. It is quite obvious that this does not occur or the world would be overrun by flies and other organisms that reproduce without restraint. Therefore, something must be restraining the growth of the housefly population.

All organisms have a biotic potential for growth at a given rate. Opposing this rate of growth is what is called environmental resistance. Environmental resistance involves factors such as food supply and other resources necessary for maintenance of a particular population size. A population initially grows at a slow rate, but then the rate increases. A population that has an explosive growth rate may grow beyond the capacity of the environment, in which case it will undergo a rapid population die-off. The **carrying capacity** is the maximum number of individuals that can be supported in a given environment. A natural ecosystem has a balance between the biotic potential of a population and environmental resistance.

Human populations have additional factors that influence population size. These are:

1. affluence and education, which lower the birth rate

2. importance of children in the labor force, which raises the birth rate

3. education and employment of women, which lowers the birth rate

4. infant mortality rates

5. costs of raising children

6. availability and reliability of birth control methods

7. religious beliefs and cultural norms concerning family size

Scientists who study human population are called **demographers**. Demographers use growth rates, fertility rates, and doubling times to explain the future of the human population. Demographers use population histograms to display the age and gender composition of a population.

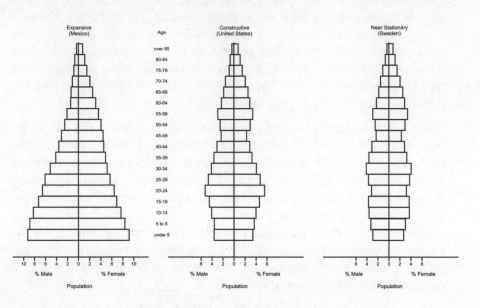

Population Histograms

From an ecological standpoint there are three main population subgroups: the prereproductive, reproductive, and postreproductive age groups. These groups give a very good idea of the future of the population. When the birth rate is high and the rate of population growth is exponential, then a population histogram is in the shape of a pyramid (shown on the left). A histogram with a tapering base shows a lower future growth due to the smaller prereproductive segment of the population (middle). A histogram that shows no constriction or expansion of the base shows a stationary population (right). These histograms are important to politicians, business leaders, and educators who have to plan for the future.

Science has shown that populations have limits to growth. Environmental resistance is seen in the availability of space, the number of people in relation to available resources, and the capacity of the natural systems (photosynthesis, biodiversity, nutrient cycles) to support human beings. Quality of life in the future must also be considered as a factor in human population growth.

Human population is increasing at an extremely rapid rate. Technology may be a big factor in enabling larger populations to live on the earth or, conversely, technology may lessen the carrying capacity of the earth.

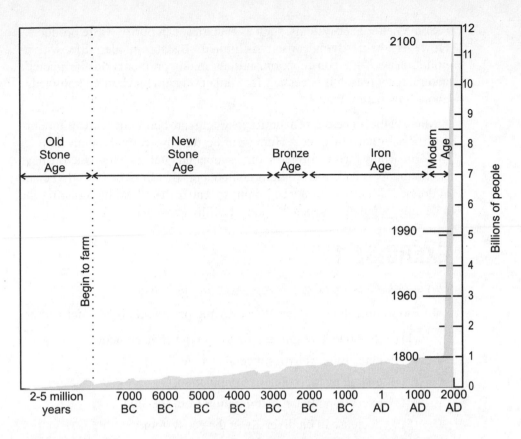

Human Population Growth

NATURAL RESOURCES

Human populations use natural resources to live in and to improve their standard of living. Natural resources include air, water, soil, forests, grasslands, wetlands, oceans, streams, lakes, wildlife, minerals, and element recycling systems. Nonrenewable mineral resources include copper, iron, and uranium. Energy resources include both nonrenewable resources, such as oil, coal, and natural gas, and the renewable resources, such as sun, wind, flowing water, geothermal heat, plant matter, biomass, and hydrogen. Included as a natural resource is biodiversity and the gene pool of all living things.

A **resource** is anything we obtain from the environment to meet our needs. Many natural resources, such as minerals and nonrenewable energy resources, are finite: when the supply is depleted, it will be gone forever. Overconsumption by humans places stress on some renewable natural resources such as air and water and the natural cycles that cleanse and recycle the components of the ecosystem. Too large a human population reduces habitats for other members of the planetary ecosystem.

Some natural ecosystems, such as estuaries, can purify waste products. However, the purifying capacity is limited. Because modern life, with its pollution and overconsumption, inflicts major problems on the planet's natural resources, it is necessary for humans to gain much more knowledge about how nature works.

Many of the processes of natural ecosystems are being changed by humans, with possibly harmful effects. Humans affect the physical and chemical cycles of Earth. Many factors influence environmental quality. These factors have economic, political, and religious components that must be considered and addressed. Many people are beginning to realize that a healthy economy and a healthy population depends upon a healthy ecosphere.

EXERCISE 1

Directions: Choose the <u>one best answer</u> for each item.

1. Environmental resistance to a growing population is best defined as
   - (1) the collective limiting factors in the environment.
   - (2) catastrophic environmental change.
   - (3) a large postreproductive population.
   - (4) exceptionally large emigration from the area.
   - (5) decrease in biodiversity in the ecosystem.

2. One of the least intrusive ways to reduce the birthrate in a country is to
   - (1) limit the number of children a family may have.
   - (2) use machinery in agriculture in place of children.
   - (3) educate and employ the women.
   - (4) ensure that women have many domestic duties.
   - 5) have male babies remain in the family but have female babies put up for adoption.

3. A population histogram plots
   - (1) wealthy countries against less-developed countries.
   - (2) the percent of the population in each age group by sex.
   - (3) population growth as well as limiting factors.
   - (4) the biotic potential against the environmental resistance.
   - (5) the rate of population growth for a given country.

4. Which statement about the population of the world is correct?

   (1) It has remained constant over the last two centuries.

   (2) It has reached the carrying capacity of the planet.

   (3) It has shown moderate growth over the last 300 years.

   (4) It has increased rapidly over the last 300 years.

   (5) It shows the effect of biotic potential and environmental resistance.

5. The difference between renewable resources and nonrenewable resources is that

   (1) renewable resources can be regenerated or repaired, while nonrenewable resources are consumed.

   2) renewable resources will be replenished in the near future, while nonrenewable resources will be replenished in the distant future.

   3) nonrenewable resources can be used up, because technology will find replacements for them in the future, while renewable resources will always be there.

   4) new deposits of nonrenewable resources will be located, while renewable resources go on indefinitely.

   5) there is no difference, as technology will compensate for any lack of resources.

NATURAL AND HUMAN-INDUCED HAZARDS

A hazard is a danger or a risk. In environmental terms, a hazard is anything that can cause injury, disease, or death to humans, to their personal or public property, or to parts of an ecosystem. Each different hazard carries a certain amount of risk, or likelihood that injury, disease, or death will result from exposure to the hazard. Risk analysis means evaluating the risks involved before exposure to the hazard. Another analysis that is used is **risk-benefit analysis**. This means evaluating whether the potential benefits of exposure to a hazard outweigh the risks. For example, radiation treatment carries potential risks, but cancer patients willingly subject themselves to those risks to avoid dying of cancer.

There are hazards that are present in our society on a daily basis. These include smoking, unsafe driving, overeating, drugs, and alcohol. Risks are involved in these activities, and we all do a personal risk-benefit analysis (or have a family member point out the risk-benefit) before exposing ourselves to the hazards.

Other hazards to humans and other organisms living on the earth occur and cannot be controlled. These include earthquakes, volcanoes, floods, tornadoes, and hurricanes. As we learn more about the natural processes that control these events, we can attempt to avoid them. For example, we can make informed decisions about how and where to build buildings to withstand local hazards, about placing pipelines and highways so they do not cross fault lines, about safe dam construction, and about coastline and flood plain ecosystems.

Biological hazards involve diseases such as AIDS and other sexually transmitted diseases, as well as malaria in developing countries. Diseases that once were restricted by geography to certain areas of the world are no longer so restricted. Due to ease of air travel, worldwide epidemics are a real possibility. Illegal import of animals such as bees and poisonous snakes are other sources of biological hazards.

Human-induced hazards are found in many places. One example is disposal of tons of waste produced in city and towns. In addition to biological wastes, these materials may include radioactive waste and poisonous metals. Other examples are sedimentation of rivers, lakes, and harbors; coastal erosion; degradation of soil; and loss of habitat.

It is necessary for humans to assess the potential dangers and risks before deciding what path society should use for future growth and development. An understanding of the natural world will allow humans to make decisions that benefit the country and the world.

EXERCISE 2

Directions: Choose the <u>one best answer</u> for each item.

1. Which of the following is NOT a daily hazard found in our society?
   (1) Excessive alcohol intake
   (2) Fast driving
   (3) Smoking
   (4) Groundwater pollution
   (5) Overeating

2. Which of the following is a human-induced hazard?
   (1) Earthquake
   (2) Malaria
   (3) Drought
   (4) Pollution
   (5) Smoking

ANSWERS AND EXPLANATIONS

UNIT 1: THE NATURE OF SCIENCE

Exercise 1

1. **The correct answer is (4). (Fundamental understandings)** A hypothesis is a possible answer to the problem or observation. Choice (1) is incorrect because the conclusion usually leads to further questions. Choice (2) is incorrect because a hypothesis is the result of observations (and the motivation for making future observations). Choice (3) is incorrect because the data are collected first and then a statistical analysis is done. Choice (5) is incorrect because a conclusion is drawn from the data collected.

2. **The correct answer is (3). (Science as inquiry)** A control group is always necessary in any experiment. The groups must be tested against a control, in this case a group of passengers who did not receive any special diet. Choice (1) is incorrect because the scientist's observations would have preceded the hypothesis. Choice (2) is incorrect because the age of the subjects in the experiment was not being tested (but the scientist should have considered age as a potential confounding variable). Choice (4) is incorrect because the time zones are not important as long as they remain constant between the groups. However, this would be important information to report, so that future work can investigate any interaction between diet and number of time zones. Choice (5) is incorrect because the scientist could have included a high-fat diet but it was not necessary and does not bias her results.

3. **The correct answer is (5). (Science as inquiry)** This scientist has presented his work to other scientists who now must duplicate his work and try to reproduce his results. Choice (1) is incorrect because it is up to the scientific community to support or refute the results. Because science is an ongoing process, conclusions are rarely, if ever, considered to be "proven." Choice (2) is incorrect because one scientific study does not advance the frontier of scientific knowledge until the results are confirmed by other scientists. However, one study with unexpected results can certainly change the course of science, as others explore the idea further. Choice (3) is incorrect because science is never final—it is always a work in progress. Choice (4) is incorrect because the scientist has gone through all the steps necessary for the scientific method.

4. **The correct answer is (1). (Unifying concepts and processes)** All scientists must be open to criticism and to the examination of their methods, data, statistical analysis, and conclusions. Only by looking at the problem from all angles can a scientist be sure that his or her research is "fair." Choice (2) is incorrect because conclusions must be

discussed and critically examined. As a result, new questions arise that require further research. Choice (3) is incorrect because scientists are always interested in bias. If bias is found in an experiment it negates all of the research. Choice (4) is incorrect because scientists should not be opposed to any revision that will make their research more accurate. Choice (5) is incorrect because a scientist must publish his or her work so the scientific community has a chance to support or reject it.

UNIT 2: THE CELL

Exercise 1

1. **The correct answer is (1). (Fundamental understandings)** Atoms make up molecules, which make up organelles, which make up cells. Choice (2) is incorrect because skin is a complex organ composed of cells. Choice (3) is incorrect because the ER is composed of atoms and molecules. Choice (4) is incorrect because cells are composed of atoms and molecules, mitochondria, and chromosomes. Choice (5) is incorrect because ribosomes are composed of atoms and molecules.

2. **The correct answer is (3). (Unifying concepts and processes)** Plants do not need animals to live. They have chloroplasts that transform energy from the sun into glucose as well as mitochondria that can release the energy for plant cell use. Choice (1) is incorrect because plants give off oxygen but also give off carbon dioxide. Choice (2) is incorrect, because plant cells have mitochondria, just as animal cells do. Choice (4) is incorrect because plants may be self-pollinated, wind-pollinated, or not pollinated, in the case of the seedless plants. Choice (5) is incorrect because animals eat some plants but so far have not eaten all plants.

3. **The correct answer is (5). (Fundamental understandings)** Chloroplasts are found only in plant cells and are responsible for photosynthesis. Choice (1) is incorrect because the ER is found in both plant and animal cells. Choice (2) is incorrect because mitochondria are found in both plant and animal cells. Choice (3) is incorrect because ribosomes are found in both plant and animal cells. Choice (4) is incorrect because nucleoli are found in both plant and animal cells.

4. **The correct answer is (5). (Fundamental understandings)** The cytoskeleton consists of microtubules and microfilaments that give the shape to the cell and function in locomotion. Choice (1) is incorrect because the sER is the membranous canal system in the cytoplasm. Choice (2) is incorrect because vacuoles are transport sacs in the cytoplasm. Choice (3) is incorrect because nucleoli are sacs in the nucleus that contain RNA. Choice (4) is incorrect because there is no such thing as metabolic units.

Exercise 2

1. **The correct answer is (5). (Fundamental understandings)** Genes are segments of the DNA molecule. Choice (1) is incorrect because genes are located on chromosomes. Choice (2) is incorrect because genes are located in the nucleus, which is part of the cell that the plasma membrane encloses. Choice (3) is incorrect because genes regulate production of enzymes. Choice (4) is incorrect because genes regulate production of proteins.

2. **The correct answer is (1). (Fundamental understandings)** DNA is the molecule that regulates the cell and stores cellular information. Choice (2) is incorrect because the phospholipid layer is found in the plasma membrane. Choice (3) is incorrect because DNA is a molecule, not a chemical process. Choice (4) is incorrect because DNA is a molecule that initiates protein synthesis. Choice (5) is incorrect because ATP is the energy molecule, not DNA.

3. **The correct answer is (5). (Fundamental understandings)** In interphase the cells grow to adult size, synthesize DNA, and store energy and materials for a new mitotic division. Choice (1) is incorrect because, while prophase may be a long phase, it is not the longest. Choices (2) and (3) are incorrect because metaphase and anaphase are both short. Choice (4) is incorrect because telophase, while longer than metaphase and anaphase, is not the longest.

4. **The correct answer is (3). (Fundamental understandings)** Carbohydrate strands recognize molecules outside the cell membrane. Choices (1), (2), and (4) are incorrect because carbohydrate strands do not function as a restraining part of the cell membrane, in the energy of the cell, or in water retention. Choice (5) is incorrect because DNA controls mitosis, not the carbohydrate strands.

UNIT 3: THE MOLECULAR BASIS OF HEREDITY

Exercise 1

1. **The correct answer is (1). (Fundamental understandings)** Complementary base pairs are adenine—thymine and cytosine—guanine. Adenine and guanine cannot form a pair bond.

2. **The correct answer is (5). (Fundamental understandings)** Nucleotides consist of a sugar, a phosphate, and a nitrogen base. Choice (1) is incorrect because amino acids are components of proteins. Choices (2) and (3) are incorrect because purines and pyrimidines are both groups of nitrogen bases. Choice (4) is incorrect because deoxyribose sugar is the sugar molecule in DNA.

Exercise 2

1. **The correct answer is (2). (Fundamental understandings)** Uracil replaces thymine and so is complementary with adenine. Choice (1) is incorrect because uracil replaces thymine in RNA. Choices (3) and (4) are incorrect because cytosine and guanine are complementary. Choice (5) is incorrect because the phosphate group is not a nitrogen base.

2. **The correct answer is (3). (Fundamental understandings)** A codon is a group of three bases that encode an amino acid. Choice (1) is incorrect because a nucleotide is a unit of DNA. Choice (2) is incorrect because a chromosome is a molecule of DNA. Choice (4) is incorrect because tRNA is found in the cytoplasm. Choice (5) is incorrect because DNA is a polynucleotide.

3. **The correct answer is (1). (Fundamental understandings)** Meiosis occurs in the nucleus of the future gamete. Choices (2) and (4) are incorrect because meiosis occurs only in the nucleus of sex cells. Choice (3) is incorrect because meiosis is a special division found only in sex cells. Choice (5) is incorrect because chromosome division only occurs in the nucleus.

4. **The correct answer is (2). (Fundamental understandings)** DNA is being replicated in interphase. Choice (1) is incorrect because interphase is a period of great cellular activity. Choice (3) is incorrect because chromosomes do not migrate during interphase. Choice (4) is incorrect because the cell plate forms during telophase. Choice (5) is incorrect because spindle fibers form during prophase.

5. **The correct answer is (3). (Fundamental understandings)** Like chromosomes separate in anaphase I of meiosis. Choice (1) is incorrect because like chromosomes pair during prophase. Choice (2) is incorrect because new nuclei form during telophase. Choice (4) is incorrect because the nuclear membrane disappears during prophase. Choice (5) is incorrect because the cytoplasm divides during telophase.

6. **The correct answer is (3). (Fundamental understandings)** A zygote, or fertilized egg, contains one complete set of chromosomes. In the case of a normal human zygote, there are 23 chromosomes from the sperm and 23 from the egg that fused to form the zygote. Together they make 23 pairs, or one complete set.

UNIT 4: BIOLOGICAL EVOLUTION

Exercise 1

1. **The correct answer is (4). (Unifying concepts and processes)** Gene frequencies cannot change if there is no genetic variability. Choices (1) and (2) are incorrect because evolution is more likely to occur in an

unstable environment and requires genetic variability. Choice (3) is incorrect because mutations can enhance evolution. Choice (5) is incorrect because, as population increases, resources become limited. At this point, natural selection can lead to evolutionary change.

2. **The correct answer is (4). (Fundamental understandings)** A phylum is a group of related classes of organisms. Choice (1) is incorrect because a genus is a group of related species. Choice (2) is incorrect because a family is a group of related genera. Choice (3) is incorrect because an order is a group of related families. Choice (5) is incorrect because a kingdom is the largest group of organisms, such as plants, animals, or fungi.

3. **The correct answer is (2). (Science as inquiry)** Natural selection has strong logical support for its conclusions. Choice (1) is incorrect because, although natural selection has strong evidence to support it, it is not considered a fact. Choice (3) is incorrect because a hypothesis must be testable. Choices (4) and (5) are incorrect, because, although the fossil record and taxonomy strongly suggest that natural selection has occurred, they do not constitute proof.

4. **The correct answer is (3). (Fundamental understandings)** Natural selection is one force that can lead to evolution. Choice (1) is incorrect because natural selection is a force that is responsible for evolution. Choice (2) is incorrect because the relationship works the other way. Choice (4) is incorrect because, although they are related, they are not the same thing. Choice (5) is incorrect; they are related.

UNIT 5: INTERDEPENDENCE OF ORGANISMS

Exercise 1

1. **The correct answer is (3). (Fundamental understandings)** Only green plants carry out photosynthesis, the process that uses energy and nonliving materials to create nutrients. Decomposers, choice (1), release nonliving atoms and molecules into the environment. Carnivores, choice (2), use plant-made organic molecules to live. Choices (4) and (5) are types of animals that eat plants to obtain their organic molecules.

2. **The correct answer is (5). (Fundamental understandings)** The nonliving elements are vital parts of an ecosystem. Choices (1) and (3) are incorrect because it is the individual organisms that make up populations and communities that are parts of an ecosystem. A biosphere, choice (2), is not part of an ecosystem. It is the largest ecosystem, the Earth. Choice (4) is incorrect because a social system refers to the interaction of animals in an ecosystem.

3. **The correct answer is (4). (Fundamental understandings)** Energy flows in only one direction through an ecosystem. Life depends on continual input of energy from the sun. Choices (1), (2), (3), and (5) are incorrect because energy does not cycle; it is used only once.

4. **The correct answer is (3). (Fundamental understandings)** Humans may function in an ecosystem as either herbivores or omnivores, but they are not producers nor can they regulate the ecosystem in any way.

UNIT 6: MATTER, ENERGY, AND ORGANIZATION IN LIVING SYSTEMS

Exercise 1

1. **The correct answer is (4). (Unifying concepts and processes)** ATP is a quick-energy molecule formed in the mitochondria of all cells. Choice (1) is incorrect because energy does not recycle, and choice (2) is incorrect because energy can neither be created nor destroyed. Choice (3) is incorrect because animals do not receive energy directly from the sun but indirectly from plants. Choice (5) is incorrect because energy is required for all levels of organization.

2. **The correct answer is (4). (Fundamental understandings)** The products of photosynthesis are glucose (a carbohydrate), oxygen, and water. The raw materials of photosynthesis are carbon dioxide and water.

3. **The correct answer is (1). (Fundamental understandings)** The plant organelle in which photosynthesis occurs is the chloroplast. Choice (2) is incorrect because ribosomes are organelles in which protein synthesis occurs. Choice (3) is incorrect because nucleoli are organelles found within the nucleus of the cell and contain RNA. Choice (4) is incorrect because chlorophyll is not an organelle but the green pigment of plants, found within chloroplasts. Choice (5) is incorrect because mitochondria are organelles in which cellular respiration occurs in both plants and animals.

4. **The correct answer is (1). (Unifying concepts and processes)** Choice (1) is correct because energy is constantly being degraded as it flows from one level to the other in an ecosystem. Conversely, choice (2) is incorrect because energy does not cycle. Choice (3) is incorrect because carbon and water yield carbohydrate and oxygen, and proteins are made later from carbohydrates. Choice (4) is incorrect because water and carbon dioxide are the raw materials for photosynthesis. Choice (5) is incorrect because glucose is produced only in the chloroplasts of plant cells.

UNIT 7: BEHAVIOR OF ORGANISMS

Exercise 1

1. **The correct answer is (3). (Unifying concepts and processes)** Behavior is controlled by the interaction of genes, hormones, and the nervous system. Choices (1), (2), (4), and (5) are incorrect because, although an organism does respond to the environment and to competition, its behavior is governed internally.

2. **The correct answer is (2). (Unifying concepts and processes)** Organisms that survive to reproduce will pass on their genes and their behaviors. Choice (1) is incorrect because natural selection works on all traits. Choices (3), (4), and (5) are incorrect because natural selection does not work within a single generation.

3. **The correct answer is (3). (Fundamental understandings)** Web weaving in spiders is innate and genetically transmitted. All members of a species weave the same types of webs. Choices (1) and (4) are incorrect because spiders are not cared for by their parents, and thus have no opportunity for social learning. Choices (2) and (5) are incorrect because web building is neither intraspecific nor interspecific, but rather genetically controlled.

4. **The correct answer is (5). (Fundamental understandings)** A synapse is a gap between neurons, not a chemical messenger or a cell, so choices (2), (3), and (4) are incorrect. Neurons do not join together, so choice (1) is incorrect.

UNIT 8: SCIENCE AND TECHNOLOGY

Exercise 1

1. **The correct answer is (4). (Science in personal and social perspectives)** In a democratic society, lively and open debate can make a difference in which technological advances are used and which discarded. The other choices given are correct statements.

2. **The correct answer is (1). (Science in personal and social perspective)** Scientific and technological literacy involves understanding basic concepts. The other choices are incorrect because reading and writing for scientific journals, conducting research, and understanding statistics are not necessary for scientific literacy.

UNIT 9: SCIENCE IN PERSONAL AND SOCIAL PERSPECTIVE

Exercise 1

1. **The correct answer is (1). (Science in personal and social perspectives)** Environmental resistance refers to the factors in the environment that limit populations. Choice (2) is incorrect, because catastrophic environmental changes may play a part in environmental resistance but are not the entire factor. Choices (3), (4), and (5) are incorrect because they do not refer to environmental resistance.

2. **The correct answer is (3). (Science in personal and social perspectives)** Education and employment of women reduce the birthrate and are less invasive than the other measures listed. Choices (1), (2), and (5) are very invasive, whereas choice (4) would not reduce the birth rate.

3. **The correct answer is (2). (Science in personal and social perspectives)** A histogram shows the percent of the population, by sex, in each age group. It does not show limiting factors, carrying capacity, or a break down of results by country. It also does not show rate of population growth; a line graph would be needed to do that.

4. **The correct answer is (4). (Science in personal and social perspectives)** Human population has shown extremely rapid growth over the past 300 years.

5. **The correct answer is (1). (Science in personal and social perspectives)** Choice (2) is incorrect because nonrenewable resources can never be replenished. Choice (3) is incorrect because technology may or may not be able to find replacements for nonrenewable resources. Choice (4) is incorrect because finding new deposits will just prolong the period of time before the resources become depleted. Choice (5) is incorrect because the two are not the same.

Exercise 2

1. **The correct answer is (4). (Science in personal and social perspective)** Groundwater pollution is a human-induced hazard, but it is not usually present in our daily lives. The remaining choices are hazards that are present every day in modern society.

2. **The correct answer is (4). (Science in personal and social perspective)** Pollution is a human-induced hazard. Choices (1) and (3) are physical hazards, choice (2) is a biological hazard, and choice (5) is a personal hazard.

GLOSSARY TERMS

science: a body of knowledge obtained through research, or a way of finding things out through research

bias: unintended prejudice that may affect the results of research

scientific method: method of testing hypotheses

hypothesis: possible answer to a question posed by a scientist

experiment: method used to test a hypothesis by controlling all factors except the one under study

cell: basic unit of which all living things are composed

cell membrane: a cell's outer covering, made of protein, fat, and carbohydrate molecules

cytoplasm: material inside the cell membrane that contains the organelles

nucleus: part of a cell that contains the genetic material

prokaryotes: ancient group of living things, composed of single cells and lacking a true nucleus

eukaryotes: cells that have a true nucleus and organelles

organelles: highly specialized chemical structures within the cell

metabolism: the total of all physical and chemical reactions that occur in a cell

endoplasmic reticulum: canal system within the cell that helps produce, manufacture, and digest large chemical molecules

ribosomes: structures within the cell that make proteins

proteins: chemicals that are vital to life and exist in many forms in plants and animals

chloroplasts: organelles in plant cells that convert light energy into chemical energy in a process called photosynthesis

mitochondria: organelles in plant and animal cells that carry out cellular respiration

enzyme: protein molecule needed in very small amounts to bring about a chemical reaction

gene: segment of a DNA molecule that directs the cell to produce a specific protein

mitosis: cell division that produces two cells identical to the original cell

chromosome: long, thin, coiled packages of a DNA molecule plus some proteins

zygote: a fertilized egg

stem cell: cells in an embryo that have not yet become differentiated

nucleotide: one of four phosphate-sugar bases (adenine, thymine, cytosine, and guanine) that make up the "rungs" of the DNA ladder.

amino acid: one of twenty different chemicals that proteins are made of

codon: the unit of three nucleotides that encodes an amino acid

transcription: the process of copying the nitrogen base sequence in a strand of DNA to produce a strand of RNA

gametes: reproductive cells, also called sperm and egg, each containing one-half the number of chromosomes of nonreproductive cells

cytokinesis: splitting of cytoplasm and organelles

mutation: a sudden, unpredictable change in a gene

evolution: the gradual change in gene frequencies in a population over time

natural selection: the tendency for members of a species that are genetically best suited to their environment to survive and reproduce

phylogeny: branch of biology that studies how species are related

taxonomy: branch of biology that groups species into a classification scheme

binomial nomenclature: a system of two-part taxonomic names that designate genus and species

herbivore: an animal that eats only plants

omnivore: an animal that eats both plants and animals

carnivore: an animal that eats only other animals

producer: the parts of an ecosystem that produce food (green plants)

consumer: the parts of an ecosystem that consume food produced by green plants

decomposer: living things, such as bacteria, fungi, and some insects, that break down and recycle dead organisms

photosynthesis: the process by which green plants convert energy from the sun into sugar, water, and oxygen

autotrophs: organisms that can make their own food

heterotrophs: organisms that must get their matter and energy from other living organisms

chlorophyll: the green pigment in plants that captures light energy

anabolic: a type of chemical reaction that builds molecules

catabolic: a type of chemical reaction that breaks down molecules

ATP: adenosine triphosphate, the molecule that supplies immediate energy for many cellular chemical reactions

behavioral ecology: study of the interaction between behavior and environment

innate: inborn, or genetically determined

hormones: chemicals produced by the body that act as messengers

pheromones: chemical signals exchanged between members of the same species

neurons: nerve cells; cells in the nervous system that send and receive signals throughout the body

axon: long extension of neuron that transmits nerve impulses

dendrite: short extension of nerve cell body that receives impulses

synapse: space between neurons across which impulses are conducted

natality: birth rate, or the number of births per 1,000 individuals per year

mortality: death rate, or the number of deaths per 1,000 individuals per year

carrying capacity: maximum number of individuals of a species that a given environment can support

demographer: a scientist who studies human population growth patterns

resource: anything humans obtain from the environment to meet our needs

risk-benefit analysis: an evaluation as to whether potential benefits outweigh potential hazards

Chapter

Earth and Space Science

Earth and space science encompasses all of the scientific disciplines that seek to understand the earth and the surrounding space. Earth science is usually broken down into geology, oceanography, meteorology, hydrology, and astronomy. **Geology** is the study of the solid earth and the dynamic processes that occur on and under the surface. **Oceanography** is the integrated use of scientific inquiry in the study of the oceans. Oceanography applies physics, chemistry, geology, and biology to ocean processes. **Meteorology** is the study of atmospheric processes, weather, and climate. **Hydrology** is the study of water on the earth's surface and underground. **Astronomy** is the study of the universe and Earth's relationship to it.

UNIT 1: GEOLOGY

Most scientists today believe that the earth, like all bodies in the solar system, originally formed from a **nebula**—a cloud of space gas and dust. Over a period of more than a billion years, gravity caused the earth's materials to contract and settle. In a process called differentiation, the materials that made up the forming planet sorted themselves out by density. Heavier (denser) materials sank to the center, and lighter materials rose to or near the surface of the proto-planet. The outer layer then cooled, creating the crust.

ROAD MAP

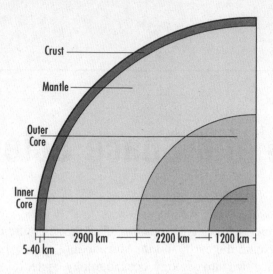

THE EARTH

The earth is a rocky planet with an overall diameter of approximately 12,750 km (7,900 miles) and an average density about 5.5 times that of water. The outermost layer, the crust, is the thinnest layer, with a thickness of 5 to 45 km (3 to 25 miles). It is composed of rocks made predominantly of silicate (silicon and oxygen) minerals. The crust is also the least dense layer, with a density of 2.5 to 3.0 g/cm^3. There are two types of crust, continental and oceanic. Continental crust is less dense (about 2.7 g/cm^3) than oceanic crust (3.0 g/cm^3).

Below the crust is the mantle, which extends about halfway to the center of the earth (approximately 2,850 km, or 1,800 miles). It is also composed of silicate minerals rich in magnesium and iron. The mantle is denser than the crust, with a density of 3.3 to 5.5 g/cm^3. Due to high temperatures and pressure, this layer of rock tends to flow like thick plastic.

The third layer is the outer core, which is molten, and is composed mostly of iron and nickel. This layer of the earth is denser yet. The outer core is approximately 2,270 km thick (1,400 miles). The inner core is also mostly iron, but unlike the outer core it is solid, with a density of 12.6 to 13.0 g/cm^3 and a radius of approximately 1,216 km (750 miles).

EXERCISE 1

Directions: Choose the <u>one best answer</u> for each item.

1. Which of the following supports the conclusion that the temperature of the earth's crust rises as you get deeper?
   A.   Oil pumped from deep wells is often very warm.
   B.   Air is hot at the bottom of deep mines.
   C.   Wells draw water from rock layers in the crust.
   - (1) A only
   - (2) B only
   - (3) C only
   - (4) A and B
   - (5) B and C

2. Which layer of the earth contains material of the lowest density?
   - (1)   Inner core
   - (2)   Outer core
   - (3)   Crust
   - (4)   Mantle
   - (5)   Asthenosphere

MINERALS

Minerals are the building blocks of the earth. A **mineral** is a naturally-occurring inorganic solid with a definite chemical structure. Minerals originally formed through natural processes in the earth's crust. Minerals are classified based on their chemical composition. Groups commonly used to classify minerals include oxides, sulfides, sulfates, native elements, halides, and carbonates. **Oxides** contain oxygen, the most common element in the crust. Sulfides and sulfites are minerals with sulfur complexes. **Halides** are salt compounds of various types, and **carbonates** contain carbon. Native elements are pure samples of inorganic elements, usually metals.

More than 4,000 unique minerals have been identified. Useful characteristics for identifying minerals include crystal structure, hardness, luster or shine, color, streak, cleavage/fracture, and specific gravity. Using these characteristics collectively, geologists can differentiate between mineral samples. All characteristics need to be considered, because many minerals share several of the basic characteristics. An example of different minerals with similar characteristics is gold and pyrite, or fool's gold. Both are dense, soft, and gold in color. Gold, however, will leave a gold streak when rubbed on a ceramic streak plate, while pyrite leaves a dirty brown residue.

ROCKS

Rocks are aggregates of different minerals. Rocks can be classified into three basic types: igneous, sedimentary, and metamorphic. All rocks form from the basic minerals of the earth. Except for the occasional meteor landing on Earth, all the building blocks for rocks have been here since the earth formed. The rock cycle describes how one rock can be transformed into other rock types and how physical processes of the earth, including erosion, weathering, heat, and pressure, interact to form and reform rocks.

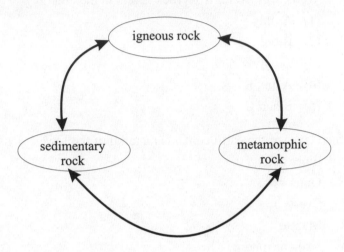

Igneous rock forms as a result of the cooling and crystallization of lava or magma. **Magma** is made of molten minerals located under the earth's surface, while **lava** is the same material once it is on the earth's surface. Igneous rocks formed from magma typically cool slowly within the earth, producing intrusive igneous rock, which has a coarser texture and larger crystal size than volcanic rocks. Granite is the most common type of intrusive rock. Volcanic rock, which cools much more quickly on the earth's surface, has a fine-grained texture. Basalt is an example of volcanic rock.

Sedimentary rock forms when rocks exposed at the surface undergo weathering and erosion, producing small rock fragments called sediments. Rain and wind carry these sediments away to a nearby body of water, where they fall to the bottom and are deposited in layers. The processes of compaction and cementation fuse the sediments into rocks. *Clastic* sedimentary rocks are formed from the sediments carried by water that settle on the bottom. These rocks are further classified by sediment size. An example of clastic sedimentary rock is sandstone. *Chemical* sedimentary rocks are formed from dissolved minerals when water evaporates. Limestone and chalk are common examples of this type of rock.

Metamorphic rock forms from existing rock. When rocks undergo heating and pressurization, the crystalline structure of the original or parent rock changes, and metamorphic rock results. Metamorphic rocks can form from igneous, sedimentary, or other metamorphic rocks. For example, shale, a sedimentary rock, becomes slate, and sandstone becomes quartzite.

A characteristic unique to metamorphic rocks is crystalline banding, or *foliation*. This occurs when minerals within a rock, in response to heat and pressure, realign within the rock and form stripes. The metamorphic rock gneiss, formed from granite, shows foliation.

EXERCISE 2

Directions: Choose the <u>one best answer</u> for each item.

1. You find a rock that is later identified as petrified wood. You are told that the fossil you have is NOT mineral-based. What is the justification for this claim?
   - (1)   The exact chemical composition is unknown.
   - (2)   Fossils are composed of matter that was once living.
   - (3)   The fossil crystal structure is cubic.
   - (4)   The fossil is not old enough to be a mineral.
   - (5)   All minerals come from the ocean.

2. You find a rock layer that is identified as sandstone in a hillside. Based on this finding, which of the following statements can be made about the hillside?
   - (1)   A volcano must be nearby.
   - (2)   The region must have been underwater at some point in time.
   - (3)   Heat and pressure from within the earth helped to form the rock layer.
   - (4)   A chemical test is required to identify the rock positively as sandstone.
   - (5)   There is a fault nearby.

WEATHERING, SOIL FORMATION, AND EROSION

Weathering is the process whereby rock breaks down into smaller and smaller pieces. This process occurs as a result of mechanical action, such as water freezing and thawing in the cracks of rocks; heat causing rocks to expand and crack; or by chemical changes, such as the dissolving of minerals in water or naturally occurring acids.

An important product of weathered rock is **soil**. Soil is a mixture of weathering residues (primarily sand, silt, and clay), decaying organic matter, living creatures (bacteria, fungi, worms, and insects), air, and moisture. The thickness of soils can vary from a few centimeters to several meters. Factors that affect the type of soil are the rock material from which it forms, the climate (temperature and moisture), and the terrain. Soil is very susceptible to degradation through poor management and use by human activity. Once severely damaged, soil is virtually lost to any productive use.

Erosion is the movement of rock or soil by forces of the earth. Water, wind, gravity, and glaciers are major forces that change the face of the earth. Erosion is a primary force reshaping the landscape of the earth.

Gravity is a constant force on Earth. Just as it pulls on all of us, gravity also pulls on all landforms. Rock slides are the result of gravitational erosion. Running water is a second significant cause of erosion. Moving water picks up sediments and carries them far from their place of origin. Fast-moving water can carry tons of sediments. The effects of water erosion are especially dramatic in areas where rain falls on hillsides barren of vegetation.

Wind is also a significant agent of erosion. Wind carries sediments long distances, and the abrasive effects of those sediments on other surfaces can create new sediments. A less common, but no less dramatic, agent of erosion is the movement of glaciers. The sheer size of glaciers, methodically moving across the landscape on a layer of melting ice and mud, results in significant abrasion. Yosemite Valley in California is a dramatic example of the force of glaciers in shaping the landscape.

EXERCISE 3

Directions: Choose the <u>one best answer</u> for each item.

1. A hillside is barren of vegetation. Which of the following agents of erosion would have a dramatic effect on the contour of the hillside?

    A. Water

    B. Wind

    C. Gravity

    (1) A only

    (2) B only

    (3) C only

    (4) A and B

    (5) A, B, and C

2. A tree grows on a cliff side. Over a number of years, the roots of the tree cause sections of the cliff to break away. This is an example of which type of weathering at work?

    (1) Ice wedging

    (2) Thermal expansion

    (3) Biological agents

    (4) Chemical agents

    (5) Wind

PLATE TECTONICS

Plate tectonics, the theory currently used to explain the interrelationship of the processes that shape the earth, is a unifying theory of geology. According to the theory, the surface of the earth is composed of large slabs of crust and upper mantle that are constantly shifting against one another. The theory explains earthquakes and volcanic action, the formation and location of mountain ranges, and the locations of the present continents. The plate tectonic theory attempts to explain evidence of continental movement and observed pressures at known plate boundaries.

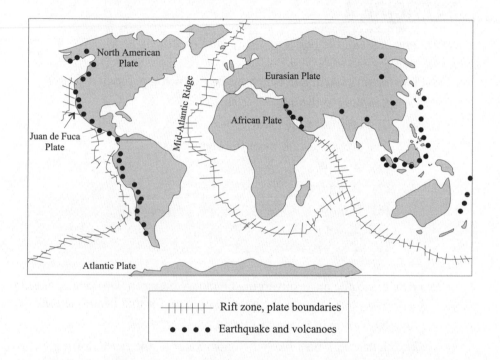

The earth's outer shell, or **lithosphere**, comprised of the crust and upper mantle, is relatively brittle and cold. The lithosphere moves in response to pressures exerted from beneath the **asthenosphere**, a plastic region of the upper mantle on which the lithosphere glides. The heat and pressure in the asthenosphere create convection currents that exert compression and tension forces on the lithosphere.

The theory of plate tectonics seeks to explain the earth's internal processes by arguing that the crust is comprised of distinct geologic plates that are in motion. Plate tectonic theory holds that the earth's lithosphere is divided into several major plates and many smaller ones. North America, South America, Africa, and Antarctica all reside on separate, identified tectonic plates. Eurasia, the Pacific Ocean, and the combined India-Australia landmass are all located on other major plates. Each plate is made up of continental crust, oceanic crust, or both. These plates are constantly moving over the underlying partially molten asthenosphere at speeds ranging from 1 to 12 cm (½ inch to 5 inches) per year. Evidence of this movement has recently been verified by satellite photographs that show the Atlantic Ocean is widening by several centimeters a year and that Mt. Everest is growing taller.

Processes within the earth cause these plates to move against each other. Most geologic activity, including earthquakes, volcanoes, and mountain building, occurs along plate boundaries. At the boundaries, plates spread apart, collide, or slide past each other. The Pacific Ring of Fire, a volcanically and seismically active region, corresponds to the boundary of the Pacific tectonic plate.

EXERCISE 4

Directions: Choose the <u>one best answer</u> for each item.

1. Plate tectonics explains which of the following geologic events?
   A.   Sea floor spreading
   B.   The origins of the earth
   C.   The present locations of the continents
      (1) A only
      (2) B only
      (3) C only
      (4) A and B
      (5) A and C

2. Japan is located on a converging boundary between two ocean plates. In 10,000 years, what is the most likely fate for that island nation?
   (1)   Nothing will happen to Japan.
   (2)   Japan will most likely be underwater as the crusts form a trench.
   (3)   Japan will be located 500 miles south of its present location.
   (4)   Japan will most likely be on a large mountain as crust rises from the sea.
   (5)   The fate of Japan cannot be predicted from the tectonic evidence.

LAND FORMS

The topography of the surface of the earth is the result of forces within the earth and forces acting upon the earth. The internal high temperatures and pressures, as well as the forces of erosion and weathering, combine to give us the earth we see today. Most often, compression and tension forces from within the earth cause folding and buckling of the crust, while the forces of erosion are primarily responsible for smoothing the surface back down.

Mountain Building. Mountains are as big below the surface as they are above. A foundation must exist within the crust for any landforms of significant elevation. The relative balance between the thickness of the crust above and below the surface is called **isostasy**. Think of this concept as similar to what happens when an iceberg floats. To balance the amount of ice floating above the surface of the water, there is a substantial counter-mass below the surface. Mountains are similar, in that only a fraction of their total mass rises above sea level with a large portion anchoring the visible mountains below ground level. The average thickness of continental crust is approximately 45 km (18 miles), but crust segments under mountain ranges can exceed 75 km (30 miles).

Mountain building is a slow process taking tens of millions of years to accomplish. Mountain building results when forces within the earth move segments of crust so that a previously flat surface is reshaped. Mountain types fall into several major categories.

Folded mountains develop in regions where sedimentary and/or volcanic rock layers are slowly but steadily compressed. The result is a wavelike undulation in the surface, looking much like a rumpled carpet. Over time, these folds increase in size and complexity, often yielding some of the most spectacular mountains in the world. The Appalachians, Himalayas, Alps, and the northern Rockies are all folded mountains.

Fault block mountains form where over time tensile forces are exerted along a crack in the crust. Fault block mountains are always bounded on at least one side by a normal fault of high-to-moderate angle. Gradual tensile forces stretch segments of crust, causing cracking and uplifting along the fault border. Two well-known mountain ranges in the United States that are comprised primarily of fault block mountains are the Tetons of Wyoming and the Sierra Nevada of California.

Volcanoes. Erupting volcanoes are some of the most dramatic events in geology. The forces at work causing volcanic eruptions are the same as with all igneous activity: the material under the lithosphere is under a great deal of pressure at very high temperatures. Periodically, materials work to the surface and partially decrease pressure through eruptions. Volcanism is most evident in areas where the tectonic plates are weakest, such as under oceanic hot spots and along plate boundaries.

Magma, which is hot and therefore less dense than the solid lithosphere, rises and encounters areas of low resistance. The magma either follows the boundary line or melts a hole in the crust. When the magma reaches the surface and spills out onto the outer surface, an eruption occurs. Some eruptions are violent and spectacular, while others look like quiet seepage.

There are three basic types of volcanoes. Cinder cones contain thick, granitic magma, rich in both the mineral silica and water vapor. Eruptions from this type of volcano are almost always violent, throwing tons of ash, dust, and debris into the atmosphere. Shield cones contain much thinner magma with considerably less water vapor and silica. Magma during shield cone eruptions is often classified as basaltic and usually flows like a quiet river. Usually, very little material is thrown into the atmosphere by shield cones. Composite cones can experience both explosive and quiet eruptions.

This happens due to moving currents within the magma below the volcano that changes the silica and water vapor content of the magma under the volcano. A general rule of thumb for violence of eruption is that the higher the water vapor and silica content of the magma, the more violent the eruption will be.

Earthquakes. Just as vulcanism is the result of pressures deep within the earth, so are earthquakes. Earthquakes are the vibrations caused by the shifting plates of earth's crust. Movement of tectonic plates at their boundaries, or along smaller cracks called faults, can temporarily reduce the tension and compression forces created by the convection currents within the asthenosphere. Quakes usually occur along tectonic boundaries or existing faults but sometime create new faults.

Faults are extensive cracks in rocks where crust segments slip or slide past each other. This motion is not steady but occurs in sudden jolts. The result of one of these slips causes large vibrations and tremors at the surface of the earth, producing an earthquake. Faults may or may not correspond to tectonic plate boundaries. The San Andreas Fault is an example of a fault that follows a plate boundary. **Normal faults** are cracks due to forces pulling a particular crustal plate away from another crust plate. **Reverse faults** are cracks due to forces pushing together two crust plates. **Strike-slip faults** are cracks where the particular crust plates are moving laterally against one another.

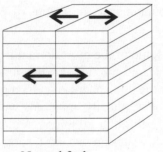
Normal fault

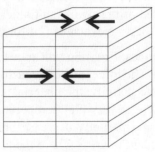
Reverse fault

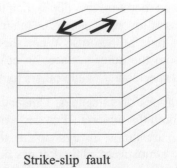
Strike-slip fault

When quakes occur, three different types of seismic waves are produced. Primary waves (P waves) are compressive in nature and travel very fast. Damage from P waves tends to be moderate. Secondary waves (S waves) are transverse (side to side) and travel at an intermediate speed. Damage from S waves is slightly more extensive. Both P and S waves are body waves, meaning that they travel within the earth's crust. Surface waves travel along the surface and shake both up and down and side to side. Surface waves are the slowest, but they cause the greatest damage.

EXERCISE 5

Directions: Choose the <u>one best answer</u> for each item.

1. What type of mountains result from prolonged compressive forces on a section of lithosphere?
   (1) Volcanoes
   (2) Island chains
   (3) Fault block
   (4) Folded
   (5) Craters

2. An extinct volcano has a gradual slope and layers of fine-grained rock all around. You readily identify the fine-grained rock as basalt. The evidence you see suggests that this volcano was a(n)
   (1) cinder cone.
   (2) shield cone.
   (3) composite cone.
   (4) island volcano.
   (5) fault-block mountain.

3. Reports arrive at your seismic station that an earthquake just occurred. Incoming data show a 3-minute differential between the arrival of primary and secondary seismic waves. Another seismic station is reporting 6.5 minutes between the arrival of primary and secondary waves. Given that primary waves travel faster than secondary waves, what is the cause of the differences in arrival time of the primary and secondary waves at the two seismic stations?
   (1) The calibration of the instruments at the other quake station must be off.
   (2) Your seismic station is closer to the epicenter than the other station.
   (3) Seismic waves can travel only short distances, so the scenario above is unlikely.
   (4) Your seismic station is further away from the epicenter than the other station.
   (5) Nothing can be determined with only two readings.

EARTH'S PAST

The most reliable evidence places the age of the earth at approximately 4.5 billion years. This age has been established using radioactive dating methods. This type of dating, which determines the specific age of a geologic strata or sample, is called **absolute dating** and is relatively new. Absolute dating takes advantage of the fact that each radioactive element decays at a specific rate, called the half-life. The half-life is the time required for 50% of a pure sample of a radioactive isotope to decay into other elements. By measuring the amount of a particular radioactive isotope in a sample, very accurate estimates of the age of the sample can be made.

Relative dating techniques, used prior to the widespread use of radioactive dating, are still used to sequence geologic events. Understanding the geologic history of a region requires an accurate means of sequencing events. Some very basic rules are used to establish the sequence of geologic events. The most important of these rules is the **Law of Superposition**. This most basic of rules states that all other factors being equal, geologic strata closer to the surface of the earth are younger than those beneath them. A second fundamental rule of relative dating is the **principle of original horizontality**. This rule states that sediments are deposited in flat horizontal sheets, all other factors being equal.

Another important concept in relative dating is the relative youth of **intrusions**. It is logical that when an igneous rock layer intrudes through another strata, it must be the younger. A fourth fundamental concept is the significance of **unconformities.** Unconformities, or breaks in the geologic record, result from a period during which erosion, rather than deposition, is the primary force molding the land. Unconformities appear in the geologic record as irregular boundaries. Using the principles outlined, a geologist can assemble the sequence of events that led to the geologic strata as seen today.

FOSSILS

Fossils are geologic evidence of past life forms. Fossils are found in geologic strata and can often provide clues as to the plants and animals living at the time that strata were formed. There are several types of fossils. Fossils can take the form of petrified remains, such as petrified wood, where the original organic material was replaced by minerals. They can also be the thin carbonaceous film left by the compressed body of the plant or animal. Mold and cast fossils form when sediments harden around an object, such as a shell, and later break open, leaving a mold of the original organism. Occasionally, the plant or animal dies and the entire body is preserved. An insect preserved in amber (petrified tree sap) is an example of this type of fossil. Trace fossils are the evidence of an organism's impact on the environment. These may be tracks, tooth marks, scratch marks, or evidence of nests.

EXERCISE 6

Directions: Use the diagram to answer questions 1–3.

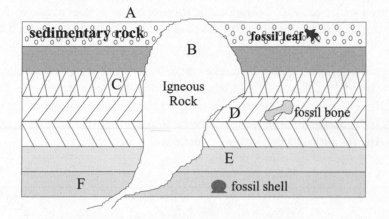

1. Which letter represents the oldest rock?
   (1)   B
   (2)   C
   (3)   D
   (4)   E
   (5)   F

2. Which letter represents an intrusion?
   (1)   A
   (2)   B
   (3)   C
   (4)   D
   (5)   E

3. Which statement about the area represented by the diagram is incorrect?
   (1)   Many different types of fossils may be found there.
   (2)   The sedimentary layers are older than the igneous rock.
   (3)   The sedimentary layers have been tilted at an angle from their original position.
   (4)   Layer F was underwater at one time.
   (5)   Weathering is most likely taking place at the point indicated by letter A.

UNIT 2: OCEANOGRAPHY

Earth is often called the blue planet, and for good reason. The oceans cover approximately 71% of the surface of the earth. Over 80% of the Southern Hemisphere is ocean. Approximately 360,000,000 km^2 of the earth is covered with oceans. Worldwide, the salinity of the oceans averages 3.5%. The primary salt in ocean water is sodium chloride (NaCl), common table salt.

Clearly defined currents circulate ocean water worldwide. These currents are primarily caused by global wind patterns and water temperature differentials. The currents help regulate temperature extremes in the oceans and within the atmosphere as well. Study the illustration to familiarize yourself with the locations of the world's oceans and continents.

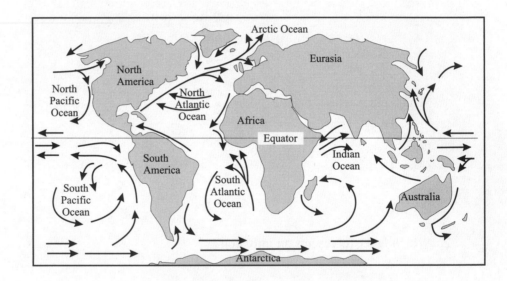

The continental margins are regions where the continents meet the oceans. The continental margins are, in turn, made up of a gently dipping continental shelf, a more steeply inclined continental slope, and (in some locations) a more gently dipping continental rise. The **continental shelf** extends outward from the coast to a depth of about 100 meters (325 feet). The continental shelf may have been dry land in the past during periods when the oceans were smaller. The continental shelf gives way to the continental slope, the true edge of the continent. The **continental slope** plunges steeply toward the ocean bottom, the **abyssal plain**, a region with a relatively constant depth of about 4 to 5 km (3 miles). The abyssal plain is analogous to a desert on land, as it is a bleak and barren place. Most sea life and vegetation is clustered in the shallow water along the shores.

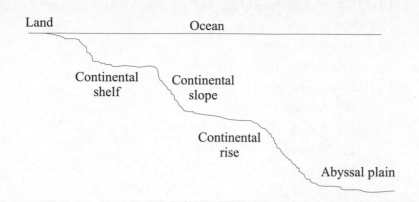

Common features of the sea floor include seamounts, ridges, and trenches. **Seamounts** are usually submarine volcanic peaks. When they reach above sea level, they form islands (the Hawaiian Islands are seamounts). **Mid-ocean ridges** form the longest linear feature on the planet's surface. Typically, mid-ocean ridges rise about 2.5 km (1.5 miles) above the surrounding ocean floor and are 2 km (1.2 miles) wide. The best known mid-ocean ridge, in the mid-Atlantic, defines the boundary between the North American/Caribbean and South American plates and the Eurasian and African plates. They are areas of intense seismic and volcanic activity. It is here that new ocean crust is created as the sea floor spreads apart.

Ocean **trenches** are features where the depth can reach 11,000 m, or 36,000 feet, although the average depth is 8,000 m (26,000 feet). Trenches are long and relatively narrow (about 100 km, or 60 miles). They may be found along a continental margin—the Peru-Chile Trench extends along western South America—or they may be found away from the margins as, for example, the Marianas Trench in the western Pacific Ocean. At trenches, two plates of the earth's crust are coming together, and one (always the denser oceanic crust) is descending back into the mantle, in a process called subduction.

EXERCISE 1

Directions: Choose the <u>one best answer</u> for each item.

1. The deepest part of the seafloor is called
   (1) a plain.
   (2) the continental slope.
   (3) the continental shelf.
   (4) a mid-ocean ridge.
   (5) a trench.

2. Of the following features of the sea floor, which are most directly caused by plate tectonics?

A. Mid-ocean ridge

B. Trench

C. Abyssal plain

(1) A only

(2) B only

(3) A and B

(4) A and C

(5) B and C

3. The most likely reason that most ocean life is found in shallow water is

(1) lack of predators.

(2) presence of warm currents.

(3) absence of human activity.

(4) presence of sunlight.

(5) pollution in deep waters.

UNIT 3: METEOROLOGY

All life on Earth is dependent on the atmosphere. The atmosphere is composed primarily of three gases. Nitrogen gas (N_2) comprises about 78%, oxygen (O_2) makes up about 21%, and argon (Ar) makes up about 0.93% of the atmosphere. Various other gases, including water vapor, comprise the rest.

One gas that forms a very small component in terms of abundance (only 0.035 percent) but has a big impact on weather and climate is carbon dioxide (CO_2). Carbon dioxide absorbs infrared radiation that leaves the earth's surface, resulting in the trapping of heat in the atmosphere. This process is known as the **greenhouse effect**. This is a natural process and is an important aspect of our atmosphere. Without it, our atmosphere would not be warm enough to sustain life as we know it, and our planet would probably be too cold for liquid water to exist.

However, human activity over the past century has increased and is continuing to increase the amount of carbon dioxide in the atmosphere. Extensive use of fossil fuels in cars, factories, and homes, and the burning of rain forests have increased the level of carbon dioxide in the atmosphere. Many scientists now believe that this increase will cause the atmosphere to become warmer, perhaps too warm. This effect is termed **global warming**. If global warming is occurring, the changes could have significant consequences to human culture. Currently, it appears that the temperature of the atmosphere is rising. Increasing carbon dioxide levels are not exclusively responsible for this rise in temperature. Industrialization is thought to play a role in the amount of solar energy reflected back into the atmosphere as well. Industrialization results in less forest areas and in more carbon dioxide in exhausts. Forests are important because the trees and other plants absorb CO_2 during photosynthesis and produce oxygen. Some scientists predict that if left unchecked, global warming could lead to changes in climate, crop failures, and the melting of the polar ice.

Another way human activities have an impact on the atmosphere concerns the ozone (O_3) layer. Ozone is a gas found in the upper atmosphere, where it filters harmful ultraviolet radiation from the sun. Without ozone, life could not exist on the surface of our planet. Human use of several chemicals has had a detrimental effect on the ozone layer. The best-known group of chemicals affecting the ozone layer are chlorofluorocarbons (CFCs), which are used as refrigerants and as propellants for aerosol sprays. CFCs cause the breakdown of ozone, thereby reducing its concentration. There have already been international treaties signed limiting the use of CFCs to reduce the threat to the ozone layer.

LAYERS OF THE ATMOSPHERE

The earth's atmosphere is divided into four layers based on temperature gradient. The bottom layer, the **troposphere**, extends to an altitude of approximately 8 to 18 km (5 to 12 miles) and is characterized by an average decrease in temperature of 6.5° C per kilometer increase in altitude (3.5° F per 1,000 feet). It contains approximately 80% of the mass of the atmosphere. Virtually all clouds and precipitation form in and are restricted to this layer. Vertical mixing in this layer is extensive.

Above the troposphere and extending to about 50 km (30 miles) is the **stratosphere**. Here, the temperature remains constant to about 20 km, then begins to increase with altitude. The stratosphere is important because it contains ozone (O_3), the gas that absorbs most ultraviolet light, keeping it from reaching the earth's surface and damaging life on the surface. The **mesosphere** lies above the stratosphere, and, here, as in the troposphere, temperatures decrease with increasing altitude. At about 80 km (50 miles), the temperature is approximately –90 °C (–130° F).

The layer above, with no well-defined upper limit, is the **thermosphere**. Here, temperatures rise again, due to the absorption of short-wave radiation by air molecules. Temperatures rise to 1,000 °C (1,800° F). Even though temperatures are very high, you would not feel hot if you were exposed to this air. Temperature is defined as the average kinetic energy of the atoms present in the material being measured. In the thermosphere, molecules of air are moving very fast and have a high kinetic energy and, therefore, high temperature, but the air is so thin that anything exposed has very few molecules striking it, resulting in little transfer of energy.

Energy from the sun is the most important control over the weather and climate of the earth. Solar radiation accounts for virtually all the energy that heats the surface of the earth, drives the ocean currents, and creates winds. Several factors affect the total amount of solar radiation captured by the atmosphere. Clouds reflect a significant portion of solar radiation, as do the oceans and paved or developed regions. The majority of this radiation travels back out into space. Of the solar energy captured by the earth, much of it is absorbed into the soil, to be radiated into the atmosphere after dark. The atmosphere works somewhat like a greenhouse: it keeps a portion of the solar radiation that reaches the earth from traveling back into space. Because of the atmosphere, there is a relatively small temperature variation between day and night and between seasons on Earth.

EXERCISE 1

Directions: Choose the <u>one best answer</u> for each item.

1. Which of the following gases is most common in Earth's atmosphere?
   (1) Nitrogen
   (2) Oxygen
   (3) Argon
   (4) Carbon dioxide
   (5) Methane

2. Scientists believe that the greenhouse effect is responsible for a gradual increase in the average temperature of the atmosphere. The clearing of the rainforests worldwide is greatly contributing to this problem because
   A. burning of the forest increases carbon dioxide levels in the air.
   B. trees are primary consumers of carbon dioxide and producers of oxygen.
   C. animals in the rainforest are primary users of carbon dioxide.
   (1) A only
   (2) B only
   (3) C only
   (4) A and B
   (5) A and C

WEATHER

Weather results from the unequal heating of the earth's surface. The equator receives the strongest radiation from the sun, and the poles receive the least. Areas with more solar energy tend to be warmer than the areas with less, and therefore the air at the equator is hottest and air at the poles is the coldest. Temperature differences also arise because the oceans and continents do not heat up equally. The movement of air, locally and worldwide, in an effort to equalize temperature, is the primary trigger for weather. The atmosphere is continually acting to redistribute solar energy from the equator toward the poles, and when air masses move, and air masses of different temperatures and water vapor content collide, weather happens.

An **air mass** is a large body of air with relatively uniform temperature and humidity. Air masses develop because of local conditions in their place of origin. The movement of air masses accounts for regional weather patterns. When two air masses of different characteristics collide, unstable weather conditions result as the two air masses mix. Rain, thunder, or violent winds can result when air masses mix. The boundary between the two air masses, where they interact, is called a **front**. When air masses collide, the warmer, less dense air mass always rises above the cooler, denser air mass, regardless of which of the masses was moving.

The cooling of air is accomplished mainly along fronts, where warm air is pushed upward over cooler air, and cool air is pushed down under warmer air. As air rises, it expands due to the decrease in pressure. As air expands, it also cools. If there is enough moisture, or if the temperature drops enough, condensation will occur and clouds will form. Clouds are formed of tiny ice crystals or of water droplets suspended in the air. If the ice crystals or water droplets become large and heavy enough to fall through the air, precipitation may occur. Since most clouds form high in the atmosphere, most precipitation begins as snow, even in the summer.

Cooling of air can also occur along mountain ranges where the air is forced upward to get over the mountain. **Orographic lifting** occurs when elevated terrain (e.g. mountains) forms a barrier to the flow of air currents, causing vertical air movement. As a result, the windward side of the mountains receive more precipitation than the leeward side. The leeward, or desert side, is referred to as being in a rain shadow. The moisture-rich air on the windward side cannot reach the leeward side with all of the moisture intact. Aside from the physical barrier of the mountains, the **adiabatic cooling** (cooling due to decreasing air pressure) occurs at higher elevations, decreasing the air's ability to retain moisture. Finally, the barrier of the mountains means that any storm system on the windward side will remain there longer, discharging more moisture before crossing over to the leeward side.

All air contains at least some water vapor. **Humidity** is a measure of the amount of water vapor in the air. The higher the air temperature, the more water vapor the air can hold. **Relative humidity** is a measure of the amount of water in the air in comparison with the amount it can hold. Relative humidity is expressed as the ratio of the current water vapor volume compared to the total water vapor capacity at a specific temperature. Water vapor condenses at the **dew point**, the temperature at which a given volume of water vapor causes saturation. Warm air can hold more water vapor than cold air can.

When air becomes saturated, clouds may form. Clouds are classified based on form and elevation. **Cirrus clouds** are high, thin, and usually made of ice crystals. **Cumulus clouds** are fluffy, often with a flat base. **Stratus clouds** appear as sheets that cover most of the sky. In addition, any storm cloud will carry the suffix "nimbus" in its name: thunderclouds are cumulonimbus clouds. Fog is generally classified as a cloud very near or at ground level.

Precipitation occurs when the atmosphere reaches saturation level for water vapor and attempts to reach equilibrium. Whenever the relative humidity exceeds 100%, precipitation is likely. While rain and snow are the most common forms of precipitation, there are others, such as hail and sleet.

Winds result from the unequal heating of the surface, moving from areas of higher atmospheric pressure (and lower temperature) to areas of lower atmospheric pressure (and higher temperature). Both localized winds and global winds follow this basic pattern. High-pressure centers occur when cool air sinks toward the surface and spreads laterally outward. In low-pressure centers, air is warmer and rises upward in the troposphere. Fronts form at the boundaries of air masses that have different temperature and moisture characteristics; fronts are generally sites of active weather, such as storms and precipitation.

EXERCISE 2

Directions: Choose the one best answer for each item.

1. The weather forecast calls for a cold front to move into your area overnight. If it is summer, what is the likely result?
   - (1) Humid weather for the next several days
   - (2) Rain as the front arrives
   - (3) Warmer weather as the front arrives
   - (4) Weather will be unchanged
   - (5) Hurricanes are likely

2. Thunderstorms occur on hot, humid days as a result of hot air rapidly rising and cooling. Thunderstorms often deposit heavy rains because
   - (1) storm clouds have high capacity for water vapor.
   - (2) rapidly cooling air loses much of its ability to retain water vapor.
   - (3) lightning is always accompanied by heavy rain.
   - (4) hail is much more common than rain with thunderstorms.
   - (5) thunderstorms are always short-lived.

UNIT 4: HYDROLOGY

Hydrology is the study of water on the surface of the earth and in the ground. The amount of water on Earth is finite, although it takes many forms. Water may be in the ocean; the polar ice caps; or rivers, streams, and lakes on the surface of the continents. Water may also exist as vapor in the atmosphere or in the clouds.

The **hydrologic cycle** describes the movement of water on and within the earth. Ninety-eight percent of the water on Earth is found in the oceans. Most water that falls as precipitation comes originally from oceans. Water is taken into the atmosphere through evaporation in the form of water vapor. Some water vapor also reaches the atmosphere through transpiration, which occurs when green plants produce water vapor during photosynthesis. Condensation occurs when the air is saturated, causing the vapor to condense into water droplets or freeze into ice crystals. Precipitation occurs when the droplets or ice crystals become too heavy to stay suspended in the atmosphere and fall toward the surface.

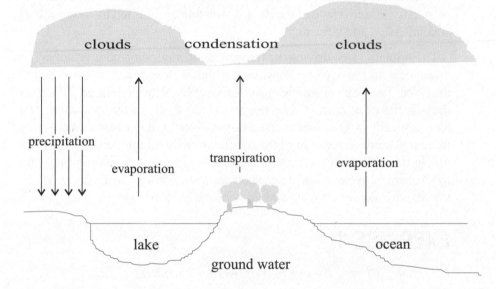

When precipitation falls on land, some water will stay above ground, where it forms runoff. Runoff water follows gravitational forces to feed river systems or collect in low areas. Standing water most often evaporates into the atmosphere. Other runoff collects to form streams, and these in turn feed rivers. Some runoff may go into lakes.

Water can also soak into the ground by infiltration and become groundwater. The level below which water in the ground is saturated is termed the **water table**. The depth of the water table depends on the climate of the area, as well as the terrain and the nature of the rocks. In general, groundwater flows from areas of higher topography to areas of lower topography and flows toward the oceans, just as rivers do. The movement of groundwater is much slower than that of surface water.

Aquifers are layers of rock and sediment that contain water. Water can be pumped out of aquifers and used by people. A common aquifer material is poorly cemented sandstone. An **aquiclude** is a rock through which water is unable to flow. Examples of aquicludes are shale and granite. Aquicludes form the bottom of a water table. In many regions of the United States, aquifers are the source of community drinking water. Because the movement of groundwater is so slow, aquifers are susceptible to contamination from pollutants and take time to replenish. Contamination of groundwater makes it unusable and very difficult to clean up.

WATERSHEDS

Rivers and streams are one of the means by which ground water and precipitation eventually return to the sea. The network of streams and rivers that drains a particular portion of land is called a **watershed**. Some watersheds cover small areas, while others cover hundreds or thousands of square miles. A tree is often used as a model to describe a watershed. The small streams are like branches, each leading to a larger stream (or branch), and eventually leading to a main river (trunk). The Mississippi River watershed stretches from the western side of the Appalachians all the way west to the eastern slope of the Rocky Mountains and is fed by thousands of smaller rivers and streams.

The primary force driving the movement of water on land is gravity. The origin of a stream or river is always at a higher elevation than the mouth of the river. The slope of the elevation a river moves through largely controls the velocity of its current. The steeper the slope, the faster the current of a river typically is. Over the course of time, rivers widen as erosion removes more and more material from the riverbank and geologic forces reduce the topographic slope. Young rivers tend to be narrow and fast-running with large changes in elevation over a short distance, while older rivers are much wider, with slower currents and less change in slope.

EXERCISE 1

Directions: Choose the <u>one best answer</u> for each item.

1. Water returns from the earth's surface to the atmosphere through
    A.   transpiration.
    B.   evaporation.
    C.   precipitation.
    (1)   A only
    (2)   B only
    (3)   C only
    (4)   A and B
    (5)   B and C

2. The force that drives the movement of water across and within the land is
    (1)   inertia.
    (2)   friction.
    (3)   kinetic energy.
    (4)   magnetism.
    (5)   gravity.

3. A tree is like a watershed because it

(1)   has many branches.

(2)   is made of roots, trunk, and leaves.

(3)   carries out photosynthesis.

(4)   goes dormant in the fall.

(5)   may cover hundreds of square miles.

UNIT 5: ASTRONOMY

For thousands of years, people have gazed at the sky and wondered about the vastness of the universe. In the past, people believed that the positions of the sun, moon, and planets in relation to the stars influenced events on Earth. Astronomy, the scientific study of space and the objects in it, has given today's scientists a much better understanding of the universe. We have even explored some of our near neighbors in the universe—the sun, planets, and moons—that, together with the earth, comprise the solar system.

More has been learned about the solar system in the last 30 years than in all of our previous history. The ancient Greeks called Mercury, Venus, Mars, Jupiter, and Saturn "planets" or wanderers, because these heavenly bodies appeared to move across the sky in relation to the stars, which appeared fixed in their positions. The Greeks believed that the earth was at the center of the universe, and that the sun, the stars, and the other planets moved around it.

Over time, however, the Greeks' model was proved faulty. In 1543, the Polish astronomer Nicolaus Copernicus argued that all the planets, Earth included, traveled in regular circular paths, called **orbits**, around the sun. Copernicus argued that planetary motions were best explained with a sun-centered, or heliocentric, model. Copernicus endured much criticism for his ideas, especially from the Catholic Church, because it went against the theological belief that man was at the center of the universe. In the early 1600s, the German astronomer Johannes Kepler modified the Copernican heliocentric model to place the planets in oval-shaped, or elliptical, orbits.

At about the same time, the Italian inventor and astronomer Galileo Galilei discovered the existence of moons around Jupiter and rings around Saturn using a new invention called the telescope. This was the first direct proof that not all heavenly bodies directly orbit the earth. Galileo also discovered that Venus has phases and therefore must orbit a source of light (the sun), and that the planets, moon, and sun have surfaces that are imperfect and blemished. Galileo strongly supported the Copernican helio-centric model, so much so that in 1616, the Church condemned his works. He was later convicted for promoting ideas against Church doctrine.

THE EARTH IN SPACE

The earth has two principal motions: rotation and revolution. **Rotation** is the spinning of the earth about its axis, the imaginary line running through the poles. The earth rotates once every 24 hours, producing the daily cycle of daylight and darkness. At any given time, half the earth is experiencing daylight while the other half is experiencing darkness.

Revolution is the motion of the earth around the sun. The distance between the earth and sun averages about 150 million km (93 million miles). The earth's orbit is not circular but slightly elliptical. Each year on about January 3, the earth is 147 km (91 million miles) from the sun, closer than any other time of the year (perihelion). On about July 4, the earth is 152 km (94.5 million miles) from the sun, farther away than any other time of the year (aphelion). Even though the distance from the sun varies during the course of the year, this accounts for only slight variation in the amount of energy the earth receives from the sun and has little consequence on seasonal temperature variations.

Term	Definition	Diagram
rotation	the spinning of a body on its axis, like a top	axis
revolution	the movement of a body around another body	earth sun

SEASONS

Probably the most noticeable aspect of seasonal variation is the difference in the length of daylight. Days are longest during the summer and shortest during the winter. However, this fact does not account fully for the seasons. Another factor that may not be as noticeable is the height of the sun above the horizon at noon. On the summer solstice, the longest day of the year, the sun is highest overhead at noon. It gradually retreats lower and lower in the sky from this day through the fall, until, on the winter solstice, it is at its lowest noon position in the sky. It then begins daily to get higher and higher in the sky again, repeating the cycle.

The altitude of the sun affects the angle at which the sun's rays strike the surface of the earth, resulting in a difference in the intensity of solar radiation received from the sun. The more direct rays of summer result in more energy reaching the earth's surface. In winter, when the rays are less direct, less energy is received, because the sun's energy is spread over a greater area. Also, the oblique rays must travel through more atmosphere before reaching the earth's surface, which means that they have more chance of being filtered, scattered, or reflected before reaching the earth's surface.

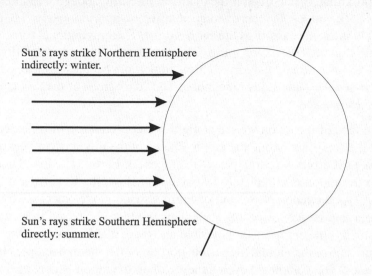

Sun's rays strike Northern Hemisphere
indirectly: winter.

Sun's rays strike Southern Hemisphere
directly: summer.

The revolution of Earth in its orbit around the sun causes this yearly fluctuation in the angle of the sun. The earth's axis is not perpendicular to the ecliptic (the plane of orbit around the sun) but is inclined at an angle of about 23° from the perpendicular. As the earth orbits around the sun, its axis remains pointed in the same direction (toward the North Star). As a result, the angle at which the sun's rays strike a given location on the earth changes continually. The change in angle varies as much as 47° over the course of the year. On one day during the year (the summer solstice), the Northern Hemisphere is tipped 23° toward the sun, and vertical rays of the noon sun strike the Tropic of Cancer at 23° north latitude. Six months later (the winter solstice), the Northern Hemisphere is tipped 23° away from the sun, and vertical rays of the noon sun strike the earth at the Tropic of Capricorn, 23° south latitude. At the vernal and autumnal equinoxes (first day of spring and autumn, respectively), the vertical rays of the noon sun strike at the equator. In short, the more direct the solar rays, the warmer the weather.

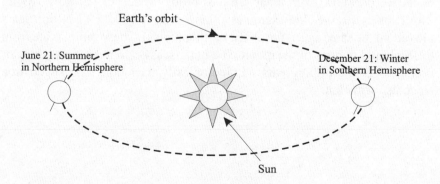

Earth's orbit

June 21: Summer
in Northern Hemisphere

December 21: Winter
in Southern Hemisphere

Sun

MOON

The earth has one natural satellite, the moon. Located about 384,400 km (238,300 miles) from Earth, the moon orbits once every 28 days. The moon is approximately one-quarter the diameter of Earth, about 3,475 km (2,150 miles). The moon has an average density of approximately 3.3 g/cm³, roughly the same density as the earth's crust. The gravitational force on the moon is about 1/6 that of Earth. The moon completes one rotation as it revolves once around the earth. This is important, because it means that we always see the same side of the moon. The "dark side" of the moon always faces deep space.

The face of the moon we see at night is a consequence of reflected light from the sun illuminating the moon. Phases of the moon occur because the moon, as it orbits the earth, passes in and out of Earth's shadow. On nights when the moon is completely in Earth's shadow, the moon is said to be "new." As the moon passes out of Earth's shadow over successive nights, a larger and larger crescent is seen. This process is referred to as waxing. Eventually, the entire moon is visible and there is a full moon. During the second half of the month, the visible portion of the moon decreases in size, or wanes. The completed cycle renews when the moon is new again.

Galileo observed the moon with his telescope in the early 1600s and noted that there seemed to be two distinct types of landforms. Galileo saw dark lowlands and bright, cratered highlands. Most of the lunar surface consists of densely cratered highlands. Because the moon has no atmosphere, and therefore no wind erosion, thousands of craters decorate the lunar surface. The smooth-appearing lowlands are much rarer and were later named *maria* ("seas" in Latin). The seas on the moon are actually large flats of basaltic lava that resulted from asteroid strikes millions of years ago.

The origin of the moon is unclear, although two theories are prevalent among scientists. The first theory states that the earth and moon formed at the same time, when the whole solar system was forming. A portion of material, a so-called proto-planet, was caught in Earth's gravity and began to orbit the earth instead of the sun. An alternative theory states that the moon actually formed from the earth when a very large asteroid struck the Earth's surface, perhaps several million years after the initial formation of the solar system. What we do know from lunar samples brought back to Earth by Apollo astronauts is that the oldest samples of lunar crust are about 4.5 billion years old (about the same age as the oldest Earth samples). These samples are from the highland regions of the moon. The lunar seas seem to be a bit younger, perhaps 3.2 to 3.8 billion years old. Geologically, the moon has changed little since its formation.

EXERCISE 1

Directions: Choose the <u>one best answer</u> for each item.

1. Which of the following is a result of the rotation of the earth?
   (1) Day and night
   (2) Winter and summer
   (3) Spring and fall
   (4) The movement of continents
   (5) Different stars are visible in the Northern and Southern Hemispheres

2. What evidence did Galileo present against the geocentric model of the solar system?
   (1) Rings around Saturn
   (2) Phases of Venus
   (3) Moons of Jupiter
   (4) Irregular surfaces of the sun and moon
   (5) All of the above

3. During July, North America is further from the sun than at any other time during the year, yet the average temperature is high throughout the continent. The best explanation is that
   (1) solar energy travels with the same concentration regardless of distance.
   (2) North America is receiving more direct sunlight due to Earth's axial tilt.
   (3) July is the Antarctic winter.
   (4) Northern Hemisphere oceans are better able to absorb energy in July.
   (5) all of the above are correct.

4. Why do we see only one side of the moon from the earth?
   (1) The moon's rotation is faster than its revolution.
   (2) The moon's revolution is faster than its rotation.
   (3) The moon orbits on an inclined orbital plane.
   (4) The moon's rotation and revolution rates are equal.
   (5) The moon does not rotate as it revolves around the earth.

SUN

At the center of our solar system is the sun. Like all stars, the sun is made of glowing, burning hot gases. Although on the small side of average for a star, the sun appears large in our sky due to its relative proximity, only about 93 million miles. The sun is the largest body of the solar system. Its diameter is 109 Earth diameters, or 1,390,000 km (864,000 miles). Yet, because of the gaseous nature of the sun, its density is less than the solid Earth's, very closely approximating the density of water. The sun's composition is 90% hydrogen, almost 10% helium, and minor amounts of other heavier elements. The sun has a surface temperature of 6,000° C and an interior temperature estimated at 1,500,000° C. The source of the sun's energy is nuclear fusion. In the interior of the sun, a nuclear reaction occurs, converting four hydrogen nuclei (protons) into a single nucleus of helium. In this nuclear reaction, some of the mass of the hydrogen nuclei is converted into energy. This results in the release of a tremendous amount of energy.

SOLAR SYSTEM

The solar system was formed approximately five billion years ago. The accepted theory of the origin of the sun and planets is the **nebular hypothesis**. This hypothesis holds that a nebula, or cloud, of gas existed consisting of approximately 80% hydrogen, 15% helium, and a small percentage of heavier elements. This cloud began to collapse or condense together under the influence of its own gravity. At the same time, the cloud had a rotational component to it, and, as its collapse continued, the rotational velocity increased. This rotation caused the nebula to form a disklike structure, and, within the disk, small nuclei developed from which the planets would eventually form. Most of the matter, however, became concentrated in the center, where the sun eventually formed.

As more and more matter collapsed inward, the temperature of this central mass began to rise due to compression. As the collapse continued, gravitational attraction increased, resulting in the increased compression and heating of the hydrogen gas. Eventually, the temperature became hot enough to begin nuclear fusion. The sun contains 99.85% of the mass of the solar system. The rest is found within the planets, moons, asteroids, and comets.

There are nine planets in the solar system. They are, in order of increasing distance from the sun, Mercury, Venus, Earth, Mars, Jupiter, Saturn, Uranus, Neptune, and Pluto (remember the mnemonic, "My Very Excellent Mother Just Served Us Nine Pies"). Based upon their gross physical characteristics, the planets fall within two groups: the terrestrial planets (Mercury, Venus, Earth, and Mars) and the Jovian (Jupiterlike) planets (Jupiter, Saturn, Uranus, and Neptune). Pluto is not included in either category, because its position at the far edge of the solar system and its small size make its true nature a mystery. The terrestrial planets are so called because of their Earthlike characteristics; all four are composed primarily of solid, rocky material. Size is the most obvious difference between the two groups.

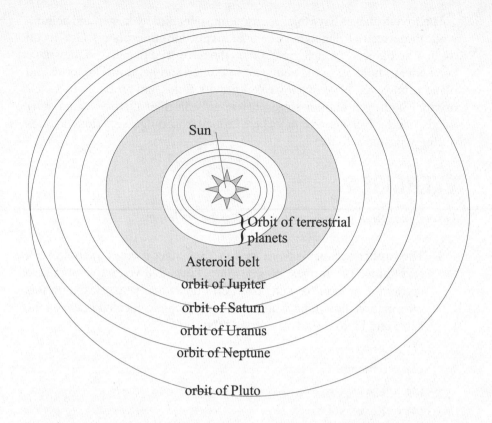

Mercury is the least massive planet, at about 0.06 the mass of Earth. Jupiter, with a diameter of 143,000 km, or 89,200 miles, is the most massive planet at 318 times the mass of Earth. Earth is the most massive terrestrial planet. Venus is about 80% as massive. Uranus is the least massive Jovian planet at 14.6 times the mass of Earth. The densities of the terrestrial planets average about 5 g/cm^3, or five times the density of water. The Jovian planets, despite their large masses, have an average density of about 1.5 g/cm^3. Compositional variations are responsible for the differences in densities.

The materials of which both groups are composed can be divided into three groups: gases, rocks, and ices. Gases are those materials with melting points close to absolute zero, or –273 °C (absolute zero is the lowest theoretical temperature). Hydrogen and helium are the gases. The rocky materials are made primarily of silicate minerals and iron and have melting points greater than 700° C. The ices have intermediate melting points and include ammonia (NH_4), carbon dioxide (CO_2), methane (CH_4), and water (H_2O).

The terrestrial planets consist mainly of rocky and metallic material with minor amounts of gases and ices. The Jovian planets consist of a large percentage of hydrogen and helium with varying amounts of ices. This composition accounts for their low densities. All the Jovian planets are thought to contain a core of rocky metallic material similar in composition to the terrestrial planets.

The Jovian planets have thick, dense atmospheres of hydrogen and helium, while the terrestrial planets have comparatively thin atmospheres. Gravity on the Jovian planets is much greater than the terrestrial planets, so they have been able to hold on to the abundant hydrogen and helium. The terrestrial planets, however, have much weaker gravity fields and probably lost their original hydrogen-helium atmospheres early in their history to the solar winds. On Earth, a second atmosphere formed from outgassing (loss of gases during volcanic activity).

EXERCISE 2

Directions: Choose the one best answer for each item.

1. The further a planet is from the sun, the longer it takes to complete a revolution. The farthest planet, Pluto, takes 248 years to complete a revolution around the sun. The Earth takes one year. Based on this information, how long would it take for Jupiter, located between the earth and Pluto, to revolve around the sun?

    (1)   1 day
    (2)   6 months
    (3)   1 year
    (4)   12 years
    (5)   250 years

2. The Jovian planets are much more massive than the terrestrial planets. Given this fact, what would be the effect on your weight upon landing on Saturn?

    (1)   You would weigh the same on Saturn as on Earth.
    (2)   You would weigh more on Saturn than on Earth.
    (3)   You would weigh less on Saturn than on Earth.
    (4)   You would become more massive, since Saturn is more massive.
    (5)   Because Saturn is gaseous, you cannot land there.

STARS

Our sun is the closest star to Earth. The next closest star is Proxima Centauri, approximately 4.3 light years away (about 25 trillion miles). The universe is very large, and stars, even close ones, are incredibly distant. Scientists believe that all stars have similar properties to our sun. They use a variety of criteria to classify and differentiate one star type from another. These criteria include stellar brightness (magnitude), color, mass, temperature, and size.

The magnitude of a star refers to its brightness. There are several reasons to explain a star's apparent dimness. Some stars appear dim due to their distance from Earth, while others are just not as bright. To distinguish between these two situations, magnitude is classified in two ways. **Apparent magnitude** is the observed brightness of a star as seen from Earth. **Absolute magnitude** is the true brightness of a star. With both scales, the lower the number (including negative numbers), the brighter the star. The sun is slightly dimmer than the average star but appears very bright to us because of its proximity. It is assigned an apparent magnitude of –26.7 (very bright) and an absolute magnitude of 5.0 (fairly dim). In general, a magnitude difference of 1 refers to a difference in brightness of 2.5. In other words, a star with a magnitude of 3 is 2.5 times brighter than a star with a magnitude of 4.

Temperature differences in stars are reflected in their colors. Very hot stars, with average surface temperatures of about 30,000 K, primarily emit short-wave radiation, which appears blue to the observer. Cooler stars, especially those with surface temperatures below 3,000 K, emit longer wave radiation that is observed as red light.

The relationship of temperature, color, and magnitude is summarized in the Hertzsprung-Russell (H-R) diagram. Stars are plotted by luminosity and temperature. Generally speaking, the brightest stars are also the hottest, while the least luminous are the coolest. About 90% of all stars follow this relationship and fall into the so-called main sequence. In the H-R diagram below, the main sequence stars appear from the upper left to the lower right. Our sun is a yellow main sequence star, and its approximate location on the diagram is marked with the X. The stars in the upper left corner are blue giants, and those in the lower right are red dwarves.

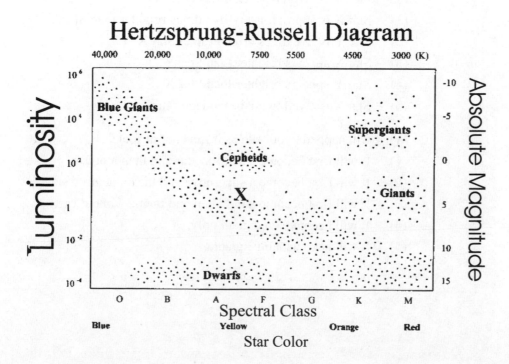

Astronomers theorize that stars spend the majority of their life span as main sequence stars. As its hydrogen fuel becomes used up, late in its life cycle, a star can leave the main sequence on one of three different paths, depending on its original stellar mass.

Low-mass red main sequence stars continue to burn until they run out of fuel, at which point they collapse into dense, hot white dwarves. Medium-mass yellow stars (those with a mass between one-half and three times that of the sun) gradually expand into red giants as gravitational energy is converted to heat. Once the red giant has exhausted its remaining fuel, it too collapses into a white dwarf. Sometimes as the red giant collapses, it releases its outer gas atmosphere, creating a glowing sphere of gas called a planetary nebula.

Stars larger than three times the mass of the sun, referred to as blue giants, have relatively short life spans and expire spectacularly as novas or supernovas. It is theorized that the core of a star that is transformed into a supernova collapses into either a very dense object called a **neutron star** or into an even denser black hole. A black hole is so dense that not even light can escape it. Neutron stars that send out radio signals at regular intervals are called **pulsars**.

EXERCISE 3

Directions: Choose the <u>one best answer</u> for each item.

1. Star X has an absolute magnitude of 2. Star Y has an absolute magnitude of 4. Which statement is correct?
   (1) Star X is approximately five times brighter than Star Y.
   (2) Star Y is five times brighter than Star X.
   (3) Star X appears brighter than Star Y.
   (4) Star Y appears brighter than Star X.
   (5) Star X is a yellow main sequence star.

2. What will happen to our sun as it runs out of fuel?
   (1) It will first become a neutron star and then a pulsar.
   (2) It will first become a supernova and then a neutron star.
   (3) It will first become a red giant and then a white dwarf.
   (4) It will become a red giant only.
   (5) It will become a blue giant.

3. Arrange the three types of main-sequence stars in order, from highest to lowest mass.

   A. Yellow main-sequence stars

   B. Blue main-sequence stars

   C. Red main-sequence stars

   (1) A, B, C

   (2) B, C, A

   (3) C, B, A

   (4) B, A, C

   (5) A, C, B

ANSWERS AND EXPLANATIONS

UNIT 1: GEOLOGY

Exercise 1

1. **The correct answer is (4). (Unifying concepts and processes)** Of the reasons supplied, only A and B involve heat. Warm oil and hot air are both evidence of heating.

2. **The correct answer is (3). (Fundamental understandings)** According-ing to the text, the lightest layer of materials formed on the outside and the denser minerals sank into the earth. The outer layer of the earth is the crust.

Exercise 2

1. **The correct answer is (2). (Fundamental understandings)** The definition of a mineral states that the substances forming a mineral must have a nonliving source. Petrified wood certainly has a living origin, choice (2). Crystal structure, choice (3), and chemical compo-sition, choice (1), are useful to identify types of minerals. Choices (4) and (5) are also incorrect.

2. **The correct answer is (2). (Fundamental understandings)** Sedi-mentary rocks form under water or when water evaporates; therefore for sandstone to be present, water must have been present in the past. Volcanism, choice (1), is related to igneous rocks and heat and pressure. Choice (3) is associated with metamorphic rocks. Choice (4) ignores that sandstone was identified in the question. Choice (5) is the result of crustal movements.

Exercise 3

1. **The correct answer is (5). (Fundamental understandings)** Wind, water, and gravity are all significant agents of erosion. On a barren slope with no vegetation to assist in stabilizing the soil, all three would have dramatic effects.

2. **The correct answer is (3). (Fundamental understandings)** By definition, weathering caused by tree growth would be classified as biological in origin.

Exercise 4

1. **The correct answer is (5). (Science as inquiry)** The theory of plate tectonics was developed to explain the reasons for evidence suggesting the surface of the earth was constantly moving. Geologic evidence shows continental shift over millions of years and changing dimensions for the sea floor, statements A and C. Plate tectonics does not address the origin of the earth, statement B.

2. **The correct answer is (2). (Science in personal and social perspective)** Converging plates either cause mountains or trenches. Mountain building, choice (4), typically occurs when continental crusts are involved. Japan is on oceanic crust, and compression at oceanic plates usually results in trenches. Japan does actually sit on a plate boundary where trenching is taking place. Choice (2) is the result of trenching over some years. No evidence suggests lateral movement, choice (3), is expected, and choices (1) and (5) are incorrect.

Exercise 5

1. **The correct answer is (4). (Fundamental understandings)** Folded mountains are the result of compressive forces. Fault block mountains, choice (3), are the result of pulling forces; volcanoes, choice (1), are the result of the earth's internal heat.

2. **The correct answer is (2). (Fundamental understandings)** Shield cones are characterized by large-diameter cones with gradual slopes that produce basaltic lava. Cinder cones, choice (1), typically produce granitic lava and have a much steeper slope profile. Composite cones, choice (3), can have basaltic lava for periods but will often have evidence of granitic lava as well.

3. **The correct answer is (2). (Science as inquiry)** Since secondary waves (S waves) are much slower than primary waves (P waves), as distance from the epicenter increases, time lag between arrival of the two wave forms also increases. Given this information, when comparing different seismic records, the one with the larger differential between P and S waves is the farther from the epicenter. Since the other station in the passage had the larger time lag, it had to be further away. This makes choice (2) correct.

Exercise 6

1. **The correct answer is (5). (Fundamental understandings)** The principle of superposition states that the lowest strata were laid down first. Therefore, letter F, the bottom layer, represents the oldest rock.

2. **The correct answer is (2). (Fundamental understandings)** Letter B represents an igneous intrusion. Intrusions that break through rock layers, as shown, are younger than the rock in which they are found.

3. **The correct answer is (3). (Science as inquiry)** This question brings together all of the information on Earth history and fossils in the text. Choice (1) is correct because the diagram shows at least three different types of fossils. Choice (2) is correct because we know that intrusions are younger than the surrounding sedimentary layers. Choice (3) is incorrect because the sedimentary layers are horizontal, as they were when they were laid down. Choice (4) is correct because the fossil shell suggests that the area was once underwater. Choice (5) is correct because weathering has revealed the top of the igneous intrusion at the surface.

UNIT 2: OCEANOGRAPHY

Exercise 1

1. **The correct answer is (5). (Fundamental understandings)** The text states that trenches are the deepest feature on the ocean floor. The abyssal plain, choice (1), is also deep, though not as deep as the average depth of a trench.

2. **The correct answer is (3). (Fundamental understandings)** Trenches are areas where one plate is moving under another, and mid-ocean ridges are areas where plates are moving apart. Therefore, both are examples of tectonic features.

3. **The correct answer is (4). (Unifying concepts and processes)** Life is abundant in shallow seas because the penetration of sunlight allows plants to grow, and all animal life is dependent on plant life. Choice (1) is incorrect because the absence of predators is the result, not the cause of lack of living things. Choice (2) is incorrect because both warm and cold currents can support life. Choice (3) is incorrect because most human activity actually takes place in shallower coastal waters. Choice (5) is incorrect because both deep and shallow ocean waters are now polluted.

UNIT 3: METEOROLOGY

Exercise 1

1. **The correct answer is (1). (Fundamental understandings)** Choice (1), nitrogen, is approximately 78% of the atmosphere. Choice (2), oxygen, is about 21% of the atmosphere. Argon, choice (3), comprises about 0.93 % of the atmosphere. All other gases make up the remaining 0.7%.

2. **The correct answer is (4). (Fundamental understandings)** Trees are important because photosynthesis uses carbon dioxide and produces oxygen, statement A. In addition, burning of trees releases carbon dioxide into the atmosphere, statement B. Animals are producers of carbon dioxide, not consumers, statement C. Statements A and B are true, so the correct choice is (4).

Exercise 2

1. **The correct answer is (2). (Fundamental understandings)** Fronts are most commonly accompanied by rain, due to the instability caused by mixing of air masses of different temperatures and water vapor contents. Choice (3) might be an option except during the summer air temperature is fairly high, with associated high water vapor content in the air. When that warm air meets the colder air at the front, the temperature drop releases large amounts of water into the air.

2. **The correct answer is (2). (Fundamental understandings)** Rapidly cooling air has a suddenly-decreased capacity to retain water vapor. The resulting condensation within the clouds releases large quantities of rain.

UNIT 4: HYDROLOGY

Exercise 1

1. **The correct answer is (4). (Fundamental understandings)** According to the text, water reaches the atmosphere from the earth's surface through evaporation and transpiration. Therefore, choice (4), A and B, is correct. Precipitation is the term for water that reaches the surface of the earth from the atmosphere.

2. **The correct answer is (5). (Unifying concepts and processes)** Gravity, which makes objects move toward the center of the earth, causes water to move downward. This is ultimately responsible for the flow of rivers and for the movement of water toward the oceans.

3. **The correct answer is (1). (Fundamental understandings)** The text states that the tree analogy applies to the watershed's structure, as it is composed of many branches. Choices (2), (3), and (4) are incorrect because they are true of trees but not of watersheds. Choice (5) is incorrect because it is true of watersheds but not of trees.

UNIT 5: ASTRONOMY

Exercise 1

1. **The correct answer is (1). (Fundamental understandings)** As the earth rotates, it is day on the side that faces the sun. Choices (2) and (3) are incorrect because the seasons do not depend on daily rotation of the earth. Choice (4) is unrelated to rotation. Choice (5) is a function of what part of the galaxy the hemisphere is facing.

2. **The correct answer is (5). (History and nature of science)** Each of the four listed statements is a piece of evidence that Galileo presented in support of heliocentrism and against the older theory of geocentrism.

3. **The correct answer is (2). (Unifying concepts and processes)** The angle of sunlight is the most significant factor in the warming of the atmosphere. Higher concentrations of solar energy are obtained when the light is most direct and the least amount of atmosphere is penetrated. During July in North America, the sun is most direct. Choice (1) is correct in that the energy is unchanged by space travel, but it does not account for the important fact that it must disperse over a wider region with longer distance. In addition, the more atmosphere that is penetrated, the more energy that is reflected prior to reaching the ground. Choice (3) is correct but irrelevant to the question, and choice (4) is inaccurate.

4. **The correct answer is (4). (Fundamental understandings)** The moon's rotation and revolution take the same amount of time—approximately 28 days. Therefore, the same side of the moon always faces the earth. The other statements are incorrect.

Exercise 2

1. **The correct answer is (4). (Fundamental understandings)** According to the information supplied, the time it takes for Jupiter to revolve around the sun should be between that of Earth (1 year) and that of Pluto (248 years). Only choice (4) fits this information.

2. **The correct answer is (2). (Unifying concepts and properties)** Weight is a measure of the force of gravity. More massive objects exert more gravitational force. Given that Saturn is much more massive than Earth, a person would weigh much more on Saturn than on Earth. Choice (4) is incorrect because although weight changes on different planets, mass does not.

Exercise 3

1. **The correct answer is (1). (Unifying concepts and processes)**
   The brighter the star, the lower the magnitude. Because every increase in absolute magnitude of 1 means that a star is 2.5 times dimmer, a star of magnitude 4 is five times dimmer than a star with a magnitude of 3. Choice (2) is the opposite of the correct answer. Choices (3) and (4) are incorrect because a star's absolute magnitude tells you nothing about its apparent magnitude. Choice (5) is unsupported by the text.

2. **The correct answer is (3). (Fundamental understandings)** As yellow main-sequence stars like the sun run out of fuel, they first become red giants and then white dwarfs. Choices (1) and (2) describe sequences of events that happen to blue giant stars. Choice (4) describes what happens to red main-sequence stars. Choice (5) is incorrect.

3. **The correct answer is (4). (Fundamental understandings)** Highest in mass are blue main-sequence stars, next most massive are yellow main-sequence stars, and least massive are red main-sequence stars.

GLOSSARY

earth and space science: the scientific disciplines that seek to understand the earth and space

geology: the study of the solid earth and the dynamic process that shapes its features

oceanography: the scientific study of the oceans

meteorology: the study of atmospheric processes, weather, and climate

hydrology: the study of water on the earth's surface and underground

astronomy: the study of the universe and earth's relationship with it

nebula: a cloud of space gas and dust

mineral: a naturally-occurring inorganic solid with a definite chemical structure

oxide: a mineral that contains oxygen

halide: a mineral salt compound

carbonate: a mineral that contains carbon

rock: material composed of aggregates of different minerals

igneous rock: rock formed as a result of the cooling and crystallization of lava or magma

magma: molten material located under the earth's surface

lava: molten material located on the earth's surface

sedimentary rock: rock formed from sediments created by weathering and erosion

metamorphic rock: rock formed from heating and pressurization of existing rock

weathering: the process whereby rock breaks down into small particles

soil: a mixture of sand, silt, or clay; decaying organic matter; living organisms; air; and water

erosion: the movement of rock or soil by forces wind, water, and gravity

plate tectonics: the theory that the surface of the earth is composed of large slabs of crust and upper mantle that are constantly shifting against one another.

lithosphere: the earth's rocky shell, composed of the crust and upper mantle

asthenosphere: a plastic region of the upper mantle on which the lithosphere glides

isostasy: balance between the thickness of crust above and below the earth's surface

folded mountains: mountains formed by sidewise compression of rock layers

fault block mountains: mountains formed by movements of the earth's crust

fault: extensive crack in rock caused by tectonic forces

normal fault: fault resulting from crustal plates moving away from each other

reverse fault: fault resulting from crustal plates moving toward one another

strike-slip fault: fault resulting from crustal plates moving past each other

absolute dating: dating method that establishes the actual age of a strata or sample

relative dating: dating method that establishes the date of a sample in relation to that of another sample

Law of Superposition: rule that states that geologic strata closer to the surface are younger than those beneath them

principle of original horizontality: rule that states that sediments are deposited in flat horizontal sheets

intrusion: an igneous rock layer that breaks through another strata

unconformity: a break in the geologic record

continental shelf: gently falling region of sea floor that extends outward from the coast to a depth of about 100 meters (325 feet)

continental slope: part of sea floor that plunges steeply toward the ocean bottom

abyssal plain: region of sea floor with a relatively constant depth of about 4 to 5 km (3 miles)

seamount: submarine volcanic peak

mid-ocean ridge: area of ocean floor of intense seismic activity and sea-floor spreading

trench: long, narrow chasm in the ocean floor where two plates meet

greenhouse effect: trapping of heat in the atmosphere by carbon dioxide

global warming: warming of the atmosphere caused by rising levels of atmospheric carbon dioxide released by human activities

troposphere: bottom layer of the atmosphere in which weather occurs

stratosphere: layer of the atmosphere that contains ozone

mesosphere: layer of the atmosphere above the stratosphere

thermosphere: top layer of the atmosphere

air mass: a large body of air with similar temperature and humidity

front: the boundary between two air masses

orographic lifting: upward air movement caused by vertical barriers, such as mountain ranges

adiabatic cooling: cooling due to decreasing air pressure

humidity: a measure of the amount of water vapor in the air

relative humidity: a measure of the amount of water in the air in comparison with the amount the air can hold

dew point: the temperature at which a given volume of water vapor causes saturation

cirrus clouds: high, thin clouds usually made of ice crystals

cumulus clouds: low, fluffy, fair-weather clouds

stratus clouds: layered clouds that blanket the sky

hydrologic cycle: movement of water on and within the earth's surface

water table: level below which water in the ground is saturated

aquifer: layers of rock and sediment that contain water

aquiclude: rock through which water can flow

watershed: network of rivers and streams that drains a particular area

orbit: an object's path around another object, such as a planet's path around the sun

rotation: the earth's movement around its imaginary axis

revolution: the earth's movement around the sun

nebular hypothesis: theory that the solar system formed from a vast cloud of gas

apparent magnitude: the observed brightness of a star, as seen from earth

absolute magnitude: the true brightness of a star

neutron star: dense object resulting from the collapse of the core of a supernova

pulsar: neutron star that sends out radio signals at regular intervals

Physical Science

Physical science is simply the study of the physical world around us. It encompasses both **chemistry**, the study of matter, and **physics**, the study of energy. But more than just these individual subjects, physical science studies the interrelated nature of these two seemingly different fields. It can be argued that physical science is the foundation of all of the other sciences. After all, life science is the study of biology and health, which is an application of chemistry, since our bodies are matter; and earth and space science is an application of physics, since it is energy that creates the attraction of celestial bodies and keeps them in motion.

But what is science? **Science** is an approach to understanding the world around us. It begins with an **observation:** something we notice that strikes our interest and makes us want to understand it. This will lead us to gathering background information, to see if the answer we seek is already known. Often, we won't find the exact answer we seek, but we find enough related information that it leads us to guess at what the answer to our question is; this guess is called a **hypothesis**. Unfortunately, a hypothesis means nothing if we have no proof, so from here we want to see if our understanding is correct by designing experiments to test our hypothesis. These tests may lead us to accept, reject, or modify our original hypothesis.

Once confident that the hypothesis is backed up by our experiment, we report our results. This gives others the opportunity to test the hypothesis and utilizes the strengths of individuality, because everybody who reads our hypothesis may find a new way to test it. If the hypothesis has been tested time and time again and has not failed, it becomes accepted as a **theory**. If the theory is tried and tested over a long period of time, it finally becomes a **law**, yet we must always remember that a hypothesis, theory, or law can be shown to be false at any time.

This may seem pessimistic, but it's really not. In essence, scientific "knowledge" is just a guess that best fits all of the experimental data gathered so far. The more data we have, the more likely our views are correct, but who knows? Maybe tomorrow some clever young scientist will devise the experiment that proves that the atomic theory is all wrong, and chemistry will have to start over again from scratch. However, this would not be viewed as a failure by the scientific community but rather as an exciting and momentous breakthrough!

UNIT 1: MOTION: SPEED, VELOCITY, AND ACCELERATION

We will begin our study of physics with motion, because the universe is filled with objects in motion. Look around you, and you will find that almost everything is in motion: flying birds, running people, falling leaves, automobiles, and even the earth, sun, stars, and galaxies. If you are sitting or standing, you are at rest with respect to the earth, but the earth rotates about its axis once every 24 hours and revolves around the sun once every year (see Chapter 3). Motion is part of our everyday lives on planet Earth: walking, running, riding a bicycle, driving a car, and traveling in an airplane. Motion can be described using terms such as speed, velocity, and acceleration. Some examples of motion and their approximate speeds are given below.

Examples of Motion and Their Approximate Speeds

Motion	Approximate Speed
Automobile on a highway	55 to 65 mph
Race car	160 to 220 mph
Person walking	3 to 5 mph
Person running	8 to 15 mph
Airplane	400 to 500 mph
Earth's revolution	66,500 mph

Average speed is obtained by dividing travel distance, D, by travel time, t.

$$V = \frac{D}{t}$$

Instantaneous speed is the speed at any one instant. The speedometer of a car gives instantaneous speed. When you drive above the speed limit and are caught speeding, the police use instantaneous speed to issue a speeding ticket. You may be familiar with the unit *mph*, miles per hour, for speed. Mph can also be written as m/h. The unit for speed is obtained by simply dividing the unit for distance (m) by the unit for time (t). Other units for speed are km/h (kilometers per hour), cm/s (centimeters per sec), ft/s (feet per sec), and m/s (meters per sec).

When you assign direction to speed, it is called velocity. **Velocity** changes if either speed or direction changes. Velocity is expressed in the same units as speed. **Acceleration**, a, is the time rate at which the velocity changes. It is obtained by dividing the change in velocity by the time it took for that change:

$$a = \frac{\Delta V}{\Delta t}.$$

The units for acceleration are mph/s, cm/s^2, ft/s^2, and m/s^2.

Motion can be described graphically. Let's say that a person, Max, is standing at a distance of 5 m from the edge of a hallway. If Max starts to walk at a constant speed away from the wall, then his distance, X, will increase at a constant rate as shown in the first graph below. On the second graph, Max's velocity is shown as a function of time. This graph shows a horizontal line, because the velocity is a constant. Since the velocity is constant we can also conclude that the acceleration is zero.

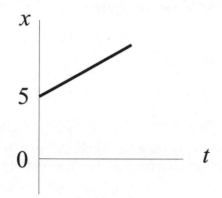

Distance (X) versus Time (t) graph for a person walking at a constant rate starting from 5 m.

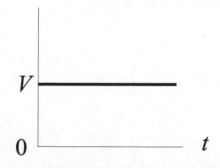

Velocity (V) versus Time (t) graph for a person walking at a constant rate.

EXERCISE 1

Directions: Choose the <u>one best answer</u> for each item.

1. What does a car speedometer measure?
   (1) Average velocity
   (2) Average speed
   (3) Instantaneous velocity
   (4) Instantaneous speed
   (5) Distance

2. During a summer vacation trip a family leaves home at 7:00 a.m. and arrives at the beach at 11:30 a.m. During the trip they took a 30-minute break for breakfast. The beach is 240 miles from their home. What is their average driving speed in mph?
   (1) 53
   (2) 60
   (3) 70
   (4) 80
   (5) 65

3. The following are the Distance (X) versus Time (t) graphs for various objects. Which graph represents an object at rest?

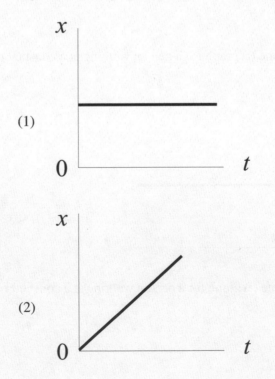

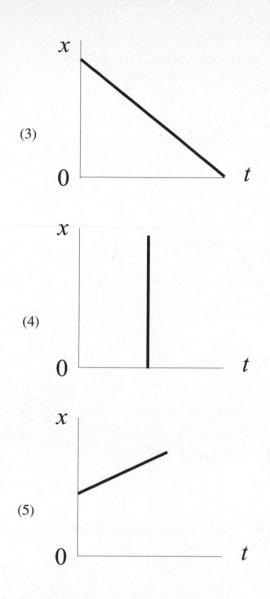

(3)

(4)

(5)

4. Acceleration is the rate of change of
   (1) time.
   (2) speed.
   (3) velocity.
   (4) distance.
   (5) displacement.

5. A sports car accelerates from 0 to 56 mph in 8 seconds. What is the acceleration?
   (1) 56 mph
   (2) 7 mph
   (3) 7 mph/s
   (4) 8 mph/s
   (5) 448 mph/s

Items 6–9 refer to the following information and graph.

A track-team member runs along a straight track. Her velocity as a function of time for the first 9 seconds is shown in the graph.

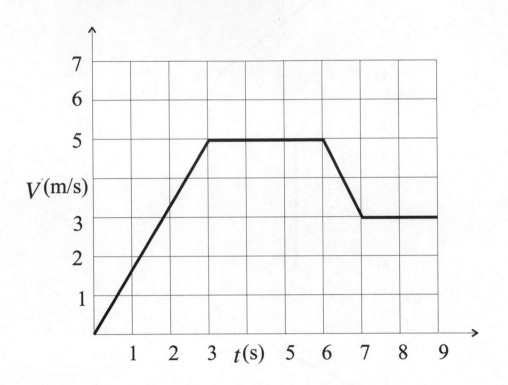

6. What is the runner's maximum velocity during the first nine seconds?
    (1)   0
    (2)   5 m/s
    (3)   3 m/s
    (4)   4 m/s
    (5)   2 m/s

7. What is the instantaneous velocity of the runner at 6.5 s?
    (1)   0
    (2)   2 m/s
    (3)   3 m/s
    (4)   4 m/s
    (5)   5 m/s

8. What is the time interval during which the runner accelerates?

    (1)   0–3 s

    (2)   3–6 s

    (3)   6–7 s

    (4)   7–9 s

    (5)   0–6 s

9. What is the instantaneous acceleration of the runner at 5 s?

    (1)   1.67 m/s

    (2)   1.67 m/s^2

    (3)   2 m/s^2

    (4)   –2 m/s^2

    (5)   0

UNIT 2: FORCE AND THE LAWS OF MOTION

We have seen how motion is described in terms of speed, velocity, and acceleration. Now we will look at how motion is created. **Force**, actually net force, is necessary for motion. For example, in a tug of war, if both teams pull with the exact same force in opposite directions, the net force is zero, the tug is in equilibrium, and no one moves. Motion will result only when there is a net force, which will be present only when one team exerts a greater force than the other.

We experience many aspects of force in our everyday lives: an object falls because of the force of gravity of the earth, we walk by pushing against the floor, and cars move because of the force exerted by the engines. We exert a force when pulling or pushing an object, throwing or kicking a ball, hitting a nail with a hammer, pushing the pedals of a bicycle, and in lifting an object.

Scientists use three basic laws of motion, named after Sir Isaac Newton, the seventeenth-century English physicist, to explain the movement of objects.

Newton's First Law of Motion states that **every body (object) will remain in a state of rest or of uniform motion in a straight line unless acted on by an outside net force.**

Inertia is the tendency of an object to remain either at rest or in motion. Newton's First Law of Motion is also known as the Law of Inertia. **Mass** is a measure of the inertia of an object.

Newton's Second Law of Motion states that **the net force acting on an object is equal to the product of the mass of the object and the acceleration of the object (F = ma)**. This law is also known as the Law of Force. It can be used to calculate the force when the mass and acceleration are known. Bold face is used for **F** and **a** because they are vectors, or quantities that have direction as well as magnitude (size). Mass, m, is a scalar quantity: it has magnitude only. Weight (**W**) is different from mass. Weight is the force of gravity acting on the mass. $\mathbf{W} = m\,\mathbf{g}$, where $\mathbf{g}$ is the acceleration due to gravity. Weight is also a vector quantity. The unit for force is the newton, N. One N = 1 kg m/s^2.

Newton's Third Law of Motion states that **when one object exerts a force on a second object, the second object exerts a force on the first that has an equal magnitude but opposite direction**. A good example of Newton's Third Law is rocket propulsion, where the force is provided by the expelling gases that push against the Earth's surface. Newton's Third Law of Motion is also known as the Law of Action and Reaction, where the action and reaction forces act on different objects. For example, when an ice skater pushes against a wall, the wall pushes the ice skater back, and this force makes the ice skater move away from the wall.

A skater moves rapidly over the ice because friction is minimized by the ice. **Friction** is the resistance to motion due to surface rubbing. Frictional forces always work in the opposite direction of motion. For example, friction produces heat in automobile engines, and oil is used to disperse this heat. We slip when we attempt to walk on ice because of the lack of friction between our feet and ice.

EXERCISE 1

Directions: Choose the <u>one best answer</u> for each item.

1. Newton's First Law is known as the law of
    (1)   inertia.
    (2)   force.
    (3)   action-reaction.
    (4)   gravitation.
    (5)   mass.

2. During the launching of a rocket, the exploding fuel leaves the rocket and exerts a force on the earth that sends the rocket skyward. Which of the following statements best explains this phenomenon?
    (1)   An object tends to remain at rest or in motion.
    (2)   Force equals mass times acceleration.
    (3)   For every action, there is an equal and opposite reaction.
    (4)   The gravity of the earth will slow down the motion of the rocket.
    (5)   You can use the position and velocity of an object to calculate its future position and velocity.

3. A net force of 3,270 N accelerates a car with a mass of 1,635 kg. What is the acceleration of the car?

    (1)   0.5 m/s^2

    (2)   0.2 m/s^2

    (3)   0.3 m/s^2

    (4)   2 m/s^2

    (5)   3 m/s^2

4. In item 3 above, if the engine exerts 4,250 N force, what are the total frictional forces acting on the car?

    (1)   0

    (2)   980 N

    (3)   3,270 N

    (4)   4,250 N

    (5)   7,520 N

5. Three students wanted to test the concept of friction. The two boys, Jeff and Ray, wear the same size shoes; Carol wears a smaller size. They tested and recorded the results of three situations: walking across an oily vinyl floor with leather-soled shoes, walking across a cement walkway with tennis shoes, and walking across a damp lawn with tennis shoes. The effort necessary to cross each surface is related to the force of friction present during each trial. The graph compares the effort of the three students using an effort scale of 0 through 10.

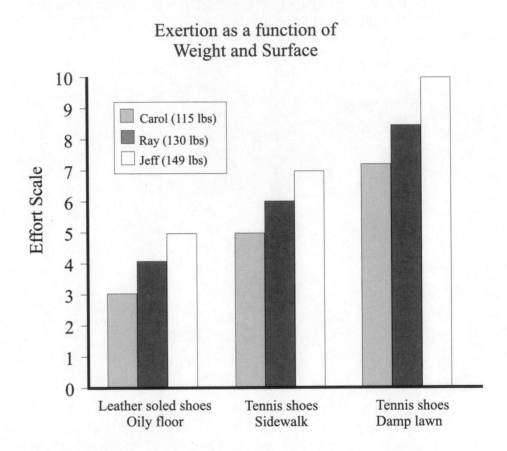

Exertion as a function of Weight and Surface

Jeff, Ray, and Carol concluded that friction depends on which of the following factors?

(1) The length of the student's stride and his or her shoe size

(2) The air temperature and relative humidity

(3) The smoothness and length of the walkway

(4) The kind of surface and the amount of force applied

(5) The length of time the object is on the surface

WORK AND ENERGY

So far we have analyzed motion using Newton's laws of motion. In this section we will study motion using work and energy. A roller coaster is a good model of how energy, work, and motion interact. A roller coaster can never go as high or travel as fast later in the ride as it does on that first hill. At the start of a roller-coaster ride, you are sitting still in a car. We have seen that inertia will keep you there all day unless an outside force intervenes. The motor that drags the cars up the hill provides the work you need to get started. **Work** is the use of force to move something over a distance. Work is defined as the product of the magnitude of the force and distance. Work is a scalar quantity.

$$Work = Force \times Distance$$

In order for a force to qualify as having done work on an object, the object must move and the force must cause that movement. Some examples of work that can be observed in everyday life are a mother pushing a baby in a stroller, a girl pushing a lawn mower across a lawn, a man pushing a grocery cart down the aisle of a grocery store, a student lifting a backpack full of books onto her shoulder, a weightlifter lifting a barbell above her head, and a person walking up the steps. There are cases where you may exert a force but no work is done on the object. For example, if you push on a stationary wall, no work is done because the wall does not move.

The unit scientists use for work is the joule, J. One joule is defined as equal to 1 nm, nanometer. The rate at which work is done is called **power**. Power is a scalar quantity. The unit for power is the watt, W. One watt = 1 J/s.

$$Power = \frac{Work}{Time}$$

ENERGY

Energy is the ability to do work. Energy comes in various forms and can be transformed from one form to another. However, the total energy will always stay the same, because energy cannot be either created or destroyed. This principle is known as the Law of Conservation of Energy. For example, the electric motor in a roller coaster uses electrical energy to drag the coaster up the hill. At the top of the hill, the electrical energy is converted into gravitational potential energy. This **potential energy**, PE, is the energy stored in an object as the result of the height it has been raised from the ground. It can be calculated using weight, which is mass times gravity, and height. Energy is a scalar quantity.

$$PE = mgh$$

As the roller coaster careens downhill, the potential energy changes into kinetic energy. **Kinetic energy**, KE, is the energy of motion. It can be calculated using mass and velocity.

$$KE = \frac{1}{2}mV^2$$

The exchange between potential energy and kinetic energy keeps the roller coaster moving up and down over the tracks.

EXERCISE 2

Directions: Choose the <u>one best answer</u> for each item.

1. According to the above definition of work, which person is doing the most work?
    (1) A stranded motorist trying to push a truck that will not move
    (2) A construction worker moving a load of bricks
    (3) A doctor listening to a patient's heartbeat
    (4) An artist making an illustration
    (5) A cashier making change

2. Two men, Joe and John, push against a stationary wall. John stops after 10 minutes, while Joe is able to push for 5 minutes longer. Compare the work they each do.
    (1) Joe does 50% more work than John.
    (2) John does 50% more work than Joe.
    (3) Joe does 75% more work than John.
    (4) John does 75% more work than Joe.
    (5) Neither of them does any work.

3. Which of the following is a newton (N)?
    (1) $kg\ m^2/s^2$
    (2) $kg/(m.s^2)$
    (3) $kg\ m/s^2$
    (4) $kg\ m^2/s^3$
    (5) $kg\ m/s^3$

4. Which of the following is a joule (J)?
    (1) $kg\ m^2/s^2$
    (2) $kg/(m.s^2)$
    (3) $kg\ m/s^2$
    (4) $kg\ m^2/s^3$
    (5) $kg\ m/s^3$

5. Which of the following is a watt (W)?
   - (1) kg m^2/s^2
   - (2) kg/(m.s^2)
   - (3) kg m/s^2
   - (4) kg m^2/s^3
   - (5) kg m/s^3

6. If the roller coaster leaves point Q from rest, how fast is it traveling at point R?

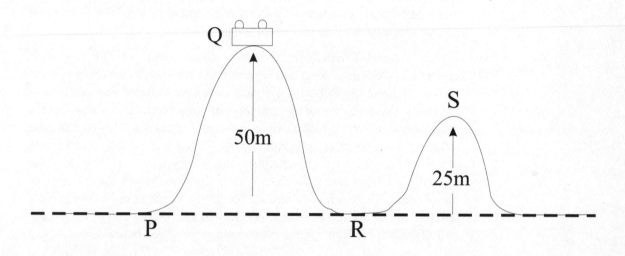

   - (1) 0 m/s
   - (2) 22.1 m/s
   - (3) 31.3 m/s
   - (4) 490 m/s
   - (5) 980 m/s

7. A 102 kg man climbs a 5 m staircase at constant speed. How much work does he do? (acceleration due to gravity = 9.8 m/s^2)
   - (1) 49 J
   - (2) 510 J
   - (3) 2,449 J
   - (4) 4,998 J
   - (5) 14,994 J

8. In the above problem, if the man takes 15 seconds to climb the staircase, how much power has he developed?
   - (1) 34 W
   - (2) 167 W
   - (3) 333 W
   - (4) 510 W
   - (5) 3,000 W

UNIT 3: TEMPERATURE AND HEAT

Temperature plays an important role in our everyday lives. In our homes we set the thermostat to a comfortable temperature. We make sure the refrigerator is set at the appropriate temperature to keep food from spoiling. We use the daily temperature forecast in planning outdoor activities. When we work outside on a hot summer day, our body perspires to maintain the body temperature. **Temperature** is a measure of how hot or cold an object is. Temperature is measured with thermometers. There are different types of thermometers: alcohol-in-glass thermometer, mercury thermometer, radiation thermometer, and resistance thermometer, to name a few. All thermometers are constructed using a measurable property of matter that changes in some way as temperature changes.

Most materials expand when their temperature increases. This expansion property is used in making liquid thermometers such as mercury clinical thermometers or alcohol-with-dye thermometers. A digital fever thermometer uses the temperature dependence of the electrical resistance of a semiconductor crystal, and a radiation thermometer uses infrared radiation to measure temperature. The Fahrenheit (°F) and Celsius (°C) temperature scales are familiar ones. The scientific community uses the Kelvin (K) scale to measure temperature. Absolute zero, 0 K, is the theoretical low limit of temperature. There is no theoretical high limit for temperature. The surface temperature of the sun is about 6,000 K, and the interior can reach as high as 15,000,000 K. Some temperature values are given below.

	Temperature in		
	°F	°C	K
Freezing temperature of water	32	0	273
Boiling temperature of water	212	100	373
Human body temperature	98.6	37	310
Absolute zero	−459.4	−273	0
Sun's temperature, surface	11,000*	6,000*	6,000*
Sun's temperature, core	27,000,000**	15,000,000**	15,000,000**

*rounded to the nearest thousand

** rounded to the nearest million

Temperatures can be converted using the following equations, where T_f stands for Fahrenheit, T_c stands for Celsius, and T_k stands for Kelvin:

$$Tf = \frac{9}{5}T_c + 32$$

$$Tc = \frac{5}{9}(T_f - 32)$$

$$Tk = T_c + 273$$

Thermal expansion has many consequences for the world around us. Engineers consider the effect of thermal expansion in designing railway tracks and road bridges. Gaps are left between two long tracks in order for them to expand and contract with changes in temperature without buckling. Expansion joints are also placed between two slabs of concrete on overhead bridges.

Heat can be used to do work. It is a type of energy that comes from the vibration or movement of molecules. More vibration creates more heat. Heat is defined as energy transfer due to a temperature difference. To raise the temperature of an object, we heat it. The unit of heat, the calorie, is defined as the amount of heat required to increase the temperature of 1 gram of water by 1° Celsius (for example, from 14.5° C to 15.5 °C). The food calorie, C, is defined as 1,000 calories. The unit for heat is the joule, or J. One calorie equals 4.186 J. Another common unit for heat is the British thermal unit, or Btu. One Btu equals 1055 J.

Heat may be transferred from one object to another by **conduction**, **convection**, or **radiation**. When the objects are connected by a solid material, the mechanism is called conduction. In convection, material moves and carries heat from a hot region to a cold region. Objects also exchange heat energy via electromagnetic waves. This mechanism is called radiation, which can take place through a vacuum. We receive the warmth of the sun via heat transfer by radiation.

Thermodynamics is the study of the movement of heat. The First Law of Thermodynamics states that **heat energy cannot be created or destroyed**. Instead, the energy changes form. For example, in a steam turbine, or jet engine, heat energy is changed to mechanical energy.

The Second Law of Thermodynamics states that **heat naturally flows from a hot place to a cold place.** The temperature difference between the hot place and the cold place represents the energy available to power an engine. Engine designers would love it if all this heat energy could be turned into work. This never happens, however, because some heat is lost through the friction of engine parts rubbing against each other, and some heat escapes to the outside.

EXERCISE 1

Directions: Choose the <u>one best answer</u> for each item.

1. If the room temperature is 22° C, what is it in °F (round to the nearest degree)
   (1) 162
   (2) 22
   (3) 72
   (4) 161.6
   (5) 0

2. The boiling point of liquid nitrogen is about 77 K. Express this temperature in °F.
   (1) −320.8
   (2) 320.8
   (3) −196
   (4) 196
   (5) 77

3. A precise steel tape measure has been calibrated at 25° C. If the tape measure is used to measure a length at 5° C, the measurement will be
   (1) high.
   (2) low.
   (3) accurate.
   (4) need the length measure to answer.
   (5) need the thermal expansion to answer.

4. A 72-kg person drinks a 140-calorie soft drink. How many stairs, height of 18 cm, must this person climb to work off the drink? (1 calorie = 4186 J, g = 9.8 m/s^2)
   (1) 45,219
   (2) 4,614
   (3) 1,102
   (4) 830
   (5) 45

5. The Thermos bottle is used to keep a liquid cold or hot. It is constructed with a double-walled container with a vacuum in between. The purpose of this construction is to minimize heat transfer by
   (1) conduction.
   (2) convection.
   (3) radiation.
   (4) conduction and convection.
   (5) conduction, convection, and radiation.

6. According to the Second Law of Thermodynamics, heat moves from a hot place to a cold place. Given this law, which of the following is most likely to occur as you make a snowball?
   (1) The snowball gets colder as it is compacted.
   (2) The warmth from your hands transfers to the snow.
   (3) The movement of your hands causes vibration of the frozen water molecules.
   (4) The temperature of the snow limits the amount of work your body can do.
   (5) Heat is lost through friction.

UNIT 4: WAVES, MAGNETISM, AND ELECTRICITY

WAVES

A wave is a disturbance in a liquid or a gas. Wave behavior is most noticeable on the surface of a liquid. Sound and light also travel in waves.

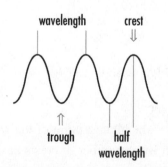

When children toss pebbles into a lake, the resulting pattern in the water is a wave. Although the wave spreads outward, the water moves only up and down when a wave passes. It does not move horizontally. The crest of a wave is the point at the top, and the *trough* of a wave is the point at the bottom. *Wavelength* is the distance between the crest of one wave and the crest of the next one. The distance between a crest and the next trough is a half wavelength.

Waves and sound. The number of crests passing a point in one second is called the *frequency* of the wave. Sound waves have high and low frequencies. A high-frequency sound has more waves per second and creates a high sound (like a dog whistle). A low-frequency sound has fewer waves per second and makes a low sound (like a bass drum). The frequency of a wave is measured in hertz. One *hertz* equals one wave per second. The human ear can hear sounds with frequencies ranging from 20 to 20,000 hertz. The range of sounds that a stereo system can reproduce is measured in hertz.

Waves and light. Light also travels in waves. The varying frequency of light waves causes varying colors. Human eyes can detect colors only within a certain frequency range. This range is called the *visible spectrum*, and it includes colors from low-frequency waves (red) to high-frequency waves (violet).

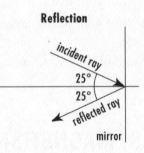

Reflection

Light normally travels in straight lines or *rays*. When a beam of light hits a flat surface such as a mirror, the light is reflected back. The light ray moving toward the mirror is called an *incident ray*. The ray of light that bounces back is called the *reflected ray*. The angle of the incident ray equals the angle of the reflected ray. The *law of reflection* states that the angle of incidence equals the angle of reflection, as shown in the diagram above.

EXERCISE 1

Directions: Choose the <u>one best answer</u> for each item.

1. Which is a true statement?
    (1)   The trough is the highest point of the wave.
    (2)   Wavelength is the number of crests passing a point in one second.
    (3)   The human ear can detect a sound with a frequency of 200 hertz.
    (4)   The distance between a crest and the next trough is a wavelength.
    (5)   A high-frequency sound has few waves per second.

Item 2 refers to the diagram below.

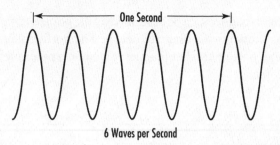

One Second

6 Waves per Second

2. Which of the following terms best describes the wave property illustrated in this diagram?
   (1) Compression
   (2) Frequency
   (3) Visible spectrum
   (4) Kinetic energy
   (5) Hertz

3. Which of the following statements best explains what happens as the frequency of a wave increases?
   (1) Wave crests and troughs cancel each other.
   (2) Wavelengths become longer.
   (3) Wavelengths become shorter.
   (4) Crest and trough are 0 wavelength apart.
   (5) Frequency cannot be measured in hertz.

4. Which statement best explains why you look taller or thinner in a fun house mirror?
   (1) The mirror reflects the light.
   (2) The curves in the mirror distort the light rays returning to you.
   (3) Light does not travel in a straight line.
   (4) Air is a different medium than glass.
   (5) Light echoes back and forth between the mirror and the walls.

MAGNETISM

Magnetism is the ability of a substance to attract iron and other iron-based metals. The earth is a giant magnet. Like all magnets, it has two *magnetic poles,* north and south, where the magnetic force is very strong.

The behavior of magnets can be described by the phrase "Opposites attract; likes repel," as shown in the diagram below. The north pole of one magnet attracts the south pole of another magnet. Two north poles move away from or repel each other.

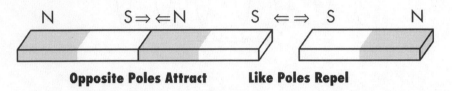

Opposite Poles Attract   **Like Poles Repel**

The poles of a magnet exert magnetic force in a *magnetic field*, the area subject to the influence of magnetism. If you sprinkle iron filings around a magnet, the filings line up in the area of the magnetic field. A common example of a magnetic field at work is in a tape recorder. In a tape recorder, a magnetic field aligns particles of metal on a cassette tape to record sound.

ELECTRICITY

Electricity is the energy produced by the movement of electrons between atoms. Most people use and experience electricity every day. Electricity takes two forms: **static electricity** and **electric current**.

Static electricity. Static electricity exists when an electric charge rests on an object. You're probably familiar with the small shock caused by static electricity when you shuffle across a carpet or pull off a wool sweater.

Electric current. When electrons flow, they produce an electric current. Electrons can move through solids (especially metals), gases, and liquids such as water. Substances (such as water) that allow an electric charge to flow easily are called *conductors*. Substances that do not conduct electricity, such as glass, porcelain, and plastic, are called *insulators*.

Electricity moves through wires much as water moves through pipes. You can measure the flow of a river by measuring how much water moves past a particular point. The strength of an electric current is measured in *amperes* (amps). An ampere measures how much electric charge moves past a point in one second.

ELECTRIC CIRCUITS

An *electric circuit* is a path for electricity. A circuit begins at a power supply, goes through wires and/or electronic devices, and then returns to the power supply. You can think of an electric circuit as a complete circle. If current doesn't pass through the entire circle, the electricity doesn't flow.

MORE RESISTANCE

Long wire

Narrow wire

LESS RESISTANCE

Short wire

Wide wire

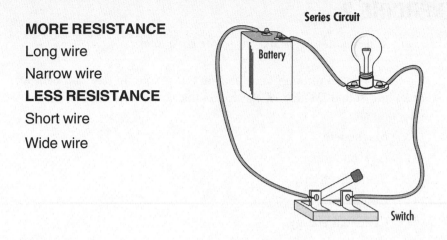

Series Circuit

As electricity moves along a wire, it meets electrical resistance, which slows down the flow. Electrical resistance is measured in *ohms*. A metal that is a good conductor has low electrical resistance. Some substances, however, have insulating qualities that offer a lot of resistance to electricity. In some cases, a particular electrical component requires a reduced flow of current, and the manufacturer intentionally puts a resistor in the circuit to control the flow. Resistance differs according to the length and width of the wire.

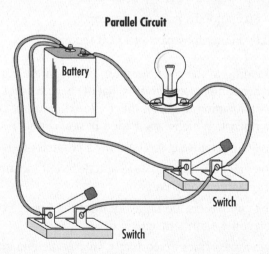

Parallel Circuit

A circuit usually consists of a power source, wires, a switch, and the item you want to power. In a *series circuit*, current must flow through every part of the electrical pathway in order to return to power.

In a *parallel circuit*, the main current is divided into two or more individual pathways, and part of the current goes through each pathway. If any part of a parallel circuit is disconnected, the design of the circuit permits the current to flow through other paths. After following independent pathways, the separate parts of the current are rejoined to complete the circuit.

EXERCISE 2

Directions: Choose the <u>one best answer</u> for each item.

1. You run a comb through your hair on a dry autumn day and hear a crackling sound. Which of the following terms best applies to this phenomenon?
   (1) Magnetism
   (2) Low humidity
   (3) Static electricity
   (4) Conductor
   (5) Chemical energy

2. The strength of a current is calculated by the following formula:

$$amps = \frac{quantity\ of\ charge\ (coulombs)}{time\ (seconds)}$$

   Which of the following situations would produce a charge of 100 amps?
   (1) 10 coulombs pass in 1,000 seconds
   (2) 100 coulombs pass in 10 seconds
   (3) 1,000 coulombs pass in 5 seconds
   (4) 1,000 coulombs pass in 10 seconds
   (5) 10,000 coulombs pass in 1,000 seconds

3. While standing at the most northern place on the earth, an explorer takes out her compass and notices that the needle points northeast. She asks her companion to check this by looking at his compass. It also points northeast. Which explanation best accounts for this?
   (1) The temperature is too cold for a compass to work.
   (2) The magnetic north pole is at a different location from the geographic North Pole.
   (3) The compass is too far away from the South Pole for it to detect the earth's magnetic field.
   (4) A compass lines up correctly only at the equator.
   (5) The earth's magnetic field cannot be detected.

4. A few nails hang in a chain from a magnet. If you pull the magnet away, the nails fall to the ground. Which of the following statements best accounts for this?
    (1) Each nail has become a permanent magnet.
    (2) The magnetic field of the earth is stronger than the field around the magnet.
    (3) Nails tend to repel each other.
    (4) As the magnet moves farther away, its magnetic field becomes stronger.
    (5) As the magnet moves farther away, its magnetic field becomes weaker.

5. Resistance is measured in ohms. You can calculate the resistance in a circuit using the following formula.

$$\text{resistance} = \frac{\text{volts}}{\text{amps}}$$

   Which of the following circuits has a resistance of 11 ohms?
    (1) a current of 10 amps on a 220-volt line
    (2) a current of 10 amps on a 110-volt line
    (3) a current of 10 amps on a 2,200-volt line
    (4) a current of 8 amps on a 12-volt line
    (5) a current of 16 amps on a 24-volt line

6. Which of the following terms is best defined as opposition to the flow of electric current?
    (1) Ampere
    (2) Volt
    (3) Resistance
    (4) Circuit
    (5) Current

7. Which of the following conditions would *decrease* the resistance of a circuit?
    (1) Lengthening the wire
    (2) Replacing a thin wire with a thicker one
    (3) Replacing a conductor with an insulator
    (4) Adding a resistor to the circuit
    (5) Breaking the circuit

Items 8 and 9 refer to the following information.

Five concepts important to electricity are defined below.

Static electricity: an electric charge resting on an object

Electric current: an electric charge in motion

Conductor: a substance through which an electric charge can flow freely

Insulator: a substance that does not conduct electricity

Earth ground: a safety device that diverts an electric current into the ground

8. Electrical wires are usually coated with plastic. This best illustrates which electrical concept?
   - (1)   Static electricity
   - (2)   Electric current
   - (3)   Conductor
   - (4)   Insulator
   - (5)   Earth ground

9. You start your car and the needle on the gauge marked amps moves to the + sign. This best illustrates which electrical concept?
   - (1)   Static electricity
   - (2)   Electric current
   - (3)   Conductor
   - (4)   Insulator
   - (5)   Earth ground

UNIT 5: CHEMISTRY

Chemistry is the study of **matter**. This definition is meaningless unless we know what matter is. By definition, matter is anything that has mass and occupies **volume**. It's easier to think of it simply as stuff. Anything you can touch, see, smell, feel, sit on, wade through, or breath, is matter.

A Few Examples of Matter and Non-Matter

Matter	Not matter
Electronic devices	Light
Food and beverages	Concepts
Air	Feelings
Furniture	Vacuum
Our bodies	Heat

The list of matter can be extended almost indefinitely, to incorporate entire celestial bodies or things smaller than a cell; the list of "not matter" is much shorter.

Mass is a measure of how much matter there is; the more matter, the more mass, and therefore, the heavier the object will be. Volume is simply a product of three-dimensional space. Length times width times height is volume. It's the amount of space an object occupies; the larger the volume, the bigger the object will be.

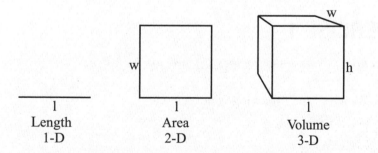

1	1	1
Length	Area	Volume
1-D	2-D	3-D

Each dimension has characteristic properties; volume is a property of the third dimension. Although the figure above represents volume as a cube, volumes are not always such simple shapes.

What about physics? Physics is the study of energy, typically thought of as the capacity to do work. It requires energy to move an object from one place to the other. This is conceptually well understood; the phrase, "I don't have the energy to lift that box," is an example of the concept. Lifting a box requires energy, and if we don't have enough energy, the box won't be lifted.

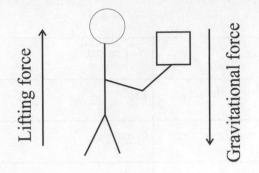

Work is force times distance; the greater the force (the heavier the box), or the further we have to move it, the more work we do. It requires energy to exert a force; therefore, it requires energy to do work.

So how do chemistry and physics relate to one another? As it turns out, they are intricately related. Of the two, physics is the more fundamental science; it's energy that holds protons, neutrons, and electrons together to make atoms, and it's energy that holds atoms together to make compounds. Without energy, matter would not exist (at least as we now understand it). On the other hand, chemistry can be viewed as applied physics. Without looking at the energy of matter, physics would really be abstract and of limited use.

In this chapter, we will explore chemistry and physics, with emphasis given to basic principles and applications. It will be difficult to see where physics ends and chemistry begins, but this simply helps delineate the relationship between the two fields.

EXERCISE 1

Directions: Choose the <u>one best answer</u> for each item.

1. Which of the following is not matter?
    (1)   Light
    (2)   Water
    (3)   Sand
    (4)   Air
    (5)   Food

2. Based on the figure below, what can we deduce about the relationship between pressure and volume of a gas?

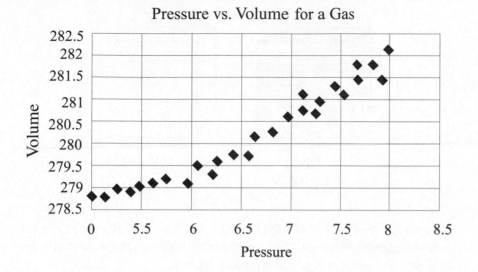

Pressure vs. Volume for a Gas

(1)   There is a relationship between pressure and volume.
(2)   Volume decreases linearly as pressure increases.
(3)   Volume increases linearly as pressure increases.
(4)   There is no relationship between pressure and volume.
(5)   The relationship between pressure and volume is not linear.

3. Right or wrong, Columbus is credited with discovering the Americas, despite evidence that the Vikings had already been here and the prior resence of Native Americans. What step in the scientific process did Christopher Columbus include that even today gives him the credit for this discovery?
(1)   Testing his findings
(2)   Doing a preliminary literature search
(3)   Seeking knowledge
(4)   Formulating a hypothesis
(5)   Reporting the findings

MATTER AND ENERGY

Matter is anything that has mass and occupies a volume. Mass is a measure of the quantity of matter; the greater the mass, the more matter there is.

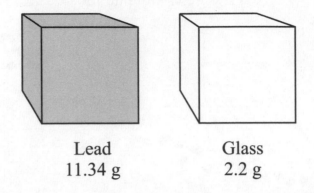

Lead
11.34 g

Glass
2.2 g

Equal volumes of glass and lead have different weight. Because the mass of lead is greater, there must be more matter in lead than in the same volume of glass. We say that lead has a greater density.

Volume is a property of the third dimension. *Length* is one-dimensional. The shortest distance, say, between you and the nearest tree (neglecting obstacles such as walls) is a straight line and could, in principle, be measured, but that straight line has only one direction; therefore, it is one-dimensional. *Area* is two-dimensional, defined as length times width. The plot of land that that tree is in, for example, is a two-dimensional area. Usually, plots such as these are rectangular in nature, with a clear width and a clear length. Notice, however, that even though the simplest two-dimensional space is a square, the concept of area can also apply to irregular plots of land. It becomes more difficult to determine the area, but the area of the plot of land is still fixed. Volume is area times height, or height times length times width. For example, there is a minimum height above Air Force bases (3,000–4,000 nautical miles) required of private aircraft. Therefore, if we take the area of our plot of land, above, and multiply it by this height, we will have defined a volume in which we should never see an aircraft.

MOMENTUM

You might be wondering why we tend to refer to "mass" rather than "weight." **Weight** is actually a force, defined as mass times the acceleration due to gravity. A force can be thought of as a motivation to move or change motion (such as changing direction). If we hold a mass, like a ball, above the ground, it will have a tendency to fall to the ground (begin to move toward the earth). You may have heard of **momentum**, usually stated as the principle that an object in motion tends to stay in motion, while an object at rest tends to remain at rest, unless acted upon by an outside force (recall the discussion of the laws of motion in Unit 2). If you yank a tablecloth out from underneath a place setting, then everything within that place setting (the plates, the silverware, the glasses, etc.) will remain where it was (if you yank quickly enough; we do not recommend that you try this), as if the tablecloth were never there. Momentum is what makes them remain in place. It requires a force to cause them to begin to move, and once they begin to move, they will continue to do so until another force causes them to stop.

Momentum can cause serious injuries in automobile accidents. When we say somebody is "thrown from the car" in an automobile accident, the person is actually not thrown at all. In fact, the car suddenly comes to a stop, but because of momentum, the passenger is still traveling at the same speed the car was moving just before the crash; thus, the passengers can go through windshields at very high velocities if they are not wearing seatbelts.

As it turns out, there is a little more to momentum than this. Momentum depends upon position, mass, and the direction the object is moving. If you are standing at a crosswalk and see a car coming, you will make several estimates before crossing the road, asking each time, *where* is the car? You are only interested in the position of the car relative to you; thus, you become the center of a frame of reference for this decision. In other words, you envision yourself as the origin, and try to estimate the distance of the car from you. Next, you estimate the direction in which the car is moving. If it is moving away from you, you won't worry about it and you'll cross. However, if it is moving toward you, you'll try to determine its velocity.

You don't do this by trying to assign actual numbers to the distance and velocity of the car; instead, you ask, knowing how quickly you move, how likely is it that the car will be at the same position as you are while you are crossing? If it is very likely that the car will strike you, you won't cross.

Finally, you worry about mass. You might be more likely to cross if it is a bicycle approaching rather than a car. The bicycle is much lighter than the car; thus if the bicycle strikes you, it is far less likely to cause serious harm than the car, even if it is moving at the same velocity as the car. Momentum is velocity times mass. Therefore, a heavier object will have more momentum at the same velocity than a lighter object; thus, a heavier object will cause more harm if you collide with it.

Consider a dump truck colliding head-on with a compact car. If they are moving at the same velocity, we all know that at the collision, the car will be pushed backward, because the truck is much heavier. Thus, the truck has greater momentum: it is more difficult to change the velocity of the truck than the car. It is possible for the car to have more momentum than the truck, but in that case, the car would have to be traveling at a much greater velocity than the truck. That is, the speed of the car would have to be far greater than the speed of the truck for the truck to be pushed backwards.

It's not always so easy to determine the nature of forces. If you roll a toy car along a flat surface, you know that eventually it will stop. Does this make sense? After all, momentum should keep it rolling indefinitely until a force acts to stop it, yet you don't see any force that can stop it. Actually, there is at least one force acting on it: friction. Friction is a form of force, because it can stop motion.

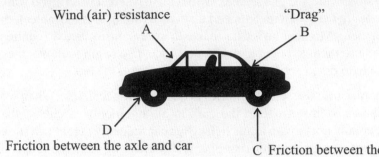

Wind (air) resistance
A

"Drag"
B

D
Friction between the axle and car

C Friction between the tire and ground

There are many forces acting to prevent a car or toy from moving continuously; were it not for these forces, then once in motion, the car would never stop. When moving downhill, there is a force (gravitational) great enough to overcome these forces that keeps the vehicle moving.

If you think about this a bit, you'll realize that this is something you already know. After all, you know that if you reduce the friction on that toy car, perhaps by applying oil to the axle, it will travel farther. If friction is increased, such as by rusting, the car will not travel as far.

MASS AND WEIGHT

Now that we have a better understanding of forces, we can examine the subtle difference between mass and weight. They are closely related to one another: as mass increases, weight increases as well. However, you can change the weight of a substance without changing its mass. For example, you can travel to another planet where the gravitational force is not so great. OK, this is a little bit unrealistic, so how about traveling to different regions of the earth?

As it turns out, the same mass (same quantity of matter) will weigh more in Anchorage, Alaska, than it will on the equator. At the equator, objects are moving faster (because of Earth's rotation) than they are anywhere else on the earth; after all, in one day, they have the farthest to travel. The centrifugal force, the force that is trying to throw us off the earth, is greatest there, so we would be lighter. This is the same force that is responsible for a weight on a string being furthest away from us as we twirl it; we know that if we tie a nut to a string, and twirl it rapidly, the string will be completely straight and the nut will feel like it is trying to pull away from us. This is centrifugal force. In Anchorage, the centrifugal force is less because it is farther from the equator, so the weight would be greater. A gold bar would not lose mass just because we've moved it from Anchorage to Hawaii, but its weight would differ.

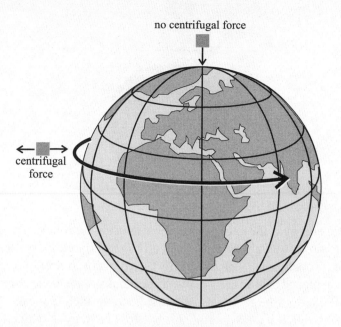

Because at the equator, centrifugal force caused by the earth's rotation creates a (very small) force acting opposite to gravitational force, objects at the equator actually have (very slightly) less weight than at the poles. However, the mass is the same because the amount of material is the same in both places.

CONSERVATION OF ENERGY

We've spoken a lot about forces, but barely mentioned energy. As we saw in Unit 2, we can classify energy into two categories: kinetic energy, or energy of motion, and potential energy, or stored energy. If you hold a mass above the ground, it has potential energy; it is not moving, because we are holding it steady, but you know that if you let it go, it will begin moving. Once you let it go, it begins accelerating, and the potential energy becomes kinetic energy, the energy of motion.

This example illustrates the Law of Conservation of Energy. The kinetic energy does not just happen; it comes from the potential energy.

Kinetic energy is the energy of motion. Because airplanes are so heavy, a rolling aircraft would be very difficult to stop (large mass means large momentum even for very small velocity). To prevent an aircraft from rolling, blocks are placed behind the wheels; these blocks prevent the conversion of potential energy (the fact that the plane is on an incline means it has the potential to roll; if it does not roll, this is "stored energy") to kinetic energy.

The Law of Conservation of Energy states that energy cannot be created or destroyed, but it can change form. That is, we can convert energy from kinetic to potential energy, or potential to kinetic energy, but the total energy cannot change. So if we were to lift a ball into the air, where does the energy come from? This is potential energy too, but it's in the form of stored chemical energy. When we eat, we obtain energy, primarily in the form of sugar; in lifting an object, your muscles utilize stored chemical energy and convert it into mechanical energy that allows you to grasp and lift the object.

The Law of Conservation of Energy has important implications for fuel use. If we cannot create energy, any fuel we use must already have energy stored within it. Thus, it is not possible to synthesize a fuel to replace natural sources (such as petroleum or natural gas), because this synthetic fuel would have to have energy incorporated into it, and the energy of the fuel cannot be greater than the energy added. In other words, if we incorporate 20 calories of energy into the production of, say, a heating mechanism for portable food, then this heating mechanism cannot release greater than 20 calories when it is used. This means that if we exhaust the natural fuel reserves of our planet (oil, coal, nuclear fuels), they cannot be replaced. Solar, wind or hydrothermal energy sources are similarly limited to what is being produced by the sun, winds, or Earth respectively. Fuels such as gasoline are useful to us because it is very easy to convert the stored (potential) energy to kinetic energy (simply by burning them); the ease of this conversion is also why these very same fuels are so dangerous to handle.

Kinetic and potential energy plays an important part in chemistry. The atoms and molecules in matter move faster if they have more energy. Energy is usually seen in chemistry as heat, which can be measured in terms of temperature. The more heat there is, the more energy in the substance, and the faster the molecules and atoms in the material are moving.

The higher the temperature, the faster (represented by the size of the arrows) the molecules move. Thus, heat energy is a form of kinetic energy. In a solid or liquid, the force that binds the atoms and molecules together is potential energy.

In a solid, strong intermolecular forces (potential energy, represented as lines) hold the atoms or molecules (represented by dots above) in place, allowing no more motion than simple vibrations. If you boil water, you must supply enough kinetic energy (heat) to overcome the potential energy holding the water molecules together, allowing them to escape the liquid and become a gas.

EXERCISE 2

Directions: Choose the <u>one best answer</u> for each item.

1. A perpetual motion machine was postulated as consisting of a pathway for water to flow over a water wheel. The water would be returned to the top of the wheel by a very long pathway in which the incline is so gradual that the water will flow through it continuously.

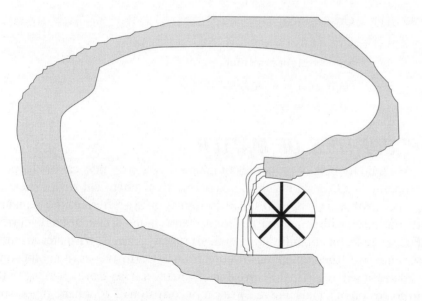

This would continually produce energy that can be tapped from the wheel. Why won't this work?

(1)   Momentum

(2)   Potential energy

(3)   The law of conservation of energy

(4)   The law of conservation of matter

(5)   Kinetic energy

2. Based on the figure below, what can we deduce about the mass and velocity of the car and truck?

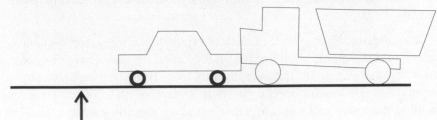

Sight of initial collision

(1)   The truck has more mass than the car.

(2)   The truck was moving faster than the car.

(3)   The car has more mass than the truck.

(4)   The truck was moving slower than the car.

(5)   The car either has more mass or was moving faster than the truck.

3. If your dance partner steps on your foot with his or her heel, it will hurt more than with his or her toe. Why?

(1)   Greater area

(2)   Greater mass

(3)   Same weight but smaller area

(4)   Same mass but smaller area

(5)   Greater weight

PROPERTIES OF MATTER

We tend to think of properties of matter in terms of physical or chemical properties. Let's start with the easy one first: **chemical properties** are properties that, if changed, result in the formation of a different kind of matter. If you end up with something different, then a chemical change has occurred. For example, flammability is a chemical property, because if a material burns, we know we'll get something different from it. Corrosiveness is another one, because it will result in the corrosion of whatever it is we are speaking of (as in corrosion of metals like rust in a car or corrosion of your hand if you spill acid on it).

Physical properties are qualities that, if changed, do not fundamentally change the type of matter. For example, density is the mass of the substance per unit volume. If we have pieces of two different materials, say Styrofoam and lead, and these pieces have exactly the same volume, we know that the lead will be heavier. The heavier a material is, for some given fixed volume, the greater its density. Viscosity, or resistance to flow, is another physical property. We know that honey flows more slowly than gasoline, so honey has a higher viscosity. But if you heat the honey so that its viscosity decreases, it's still honey. Other physical properties are size, shape, and color.

Physical properties can correspond to changes as well, provided that the material does not change chemically. For instance, ice melts at 0°C; melting point, the temperature at which solid turns to liquid, is a physical property. We change the state of ice, as it goes from solid to liquid, but it is still water. The boiling point of water is 100°C, the temperature at which liquid becomes gas. This is a physical property as well, because, after it boils, we have a new state (gas), but it's still water.

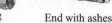

Start with a log   Process by burning   End with ashes

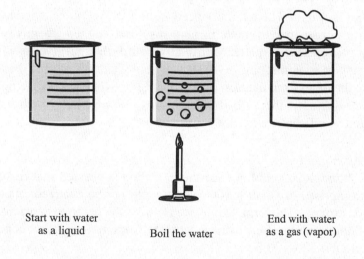

Start with water   End with water
as a liquid   as a gas (vapor)
            Boil the water

In a chemical change, we end up with something fundamentally different than what we started with. In a physical change, we can have a change in state, but we still fundamentally have not changed the material we have.

This gives rise to the concept of chemical and physical changes. In a **chemical change**, you start with one material and end up with something entirely different. You put gasoline in your car's engine; after it burns, you end up with carbon dioxide and water (as well as a variety of additional trace gases). This is a chemical change, because you started with one substance but ended up with another. In a **physical change**, you do not fundamentally change what you have. For example, if you dissolve sugar in water, you now have a solution; you've caused a change (by dissolving the sugar), but you still fundamentally have water and sugar, the same things that you started with, only now they are mixed together.

EXERCISE 3

Directions: Choose the <u>one best answer</u>.

1. Which of the following is a physical property?
   - (1) Corrosiveness
   - (2) Water reactivity (reacts with water)
   - (3) Sublimation point (the temperature at which the solid becomes a gas)
   - (4) Flash point (the temperature at which vapors above a liquid will burn in the presence of an ignition source)
   - (5) Digestibility

UNIT 6: DEVELOPMENT OF ATOMIC THEORY

Dalton's Atomic Theory

Dalton's Atomic Theory, introduced around 1805, is considered by many to be the cornerstone of modern chemistry. Before then, chemistry was a survey of properties of matter, with relatively little thought given to what was occurring at a microscopic level. It was John Dalton's atomic theory that shifted the focus from macroscopic properties to what was occurring on the atomic level. His theory had four primary components, which have not changed significantly since they were introduced:

1. *All matter is comprised of tiny, indestructible particles called "atoms."* Although he could not see them, Dalton suggested that matter was comprised of small particles that could not be changed, created, or destroyed. The term "atom" was a tip of the hat to the ancient Greek Atomist philosophical movement that had come to the same conclusion around 500–100 B.C.

When Epicurous of Samos asked, about 500 B.C., if material could be divided forever or if there would come a time when one more division would fundamentally change what you have into something else, most of the ancient Greek experimenters tried it and concluded that you can divide stone forever and it will be forever stone. A few philosophers, calling themselves the Atomists, believed you would eventually change the stone into something different and more fundamental. They were the first to propose that the world is comprised of a limited number of elements.

2. *All atoms of the same element are identical.* By identical, we mean they have exactly the same chemical and physical properties (that is, they react the same way and behave the same way when they are not reacting). The concept of the **element** also dates back to the ancient Greeks, who had proposed four elements—Earth, Wind, Fire, and

Water. In fact, there are over 100 different elements known (either through discovery or fabrication) today; they are arranged according to their chemical properties in a chart called the **periodic table**. A substance is taken to be an element if it cannot be reduced to a more fundamental set of substances through either physical or chemical means. For example, water can be further decomposed to oxygen and hydrogen by the introduction of an electrical current, but neither oxygen nor hydrogen can be further broken down.

3. *Atoms of two different elements are distinguishable* a corollary of the second component. We can tell them apart if they are different elements but not if they are atoms of the same element.

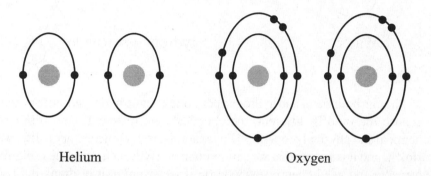

Helium   Oxygen

Dalton's Atomic Theory tells us that we should not be able to distinguish between two atoms of helium or two atoms of oxygen, but we should be able to distinguish helium atoms from oxygen atoms. Note that the atoms in the above figure are cartoon pictures of atoms and do not represent what the atoms actually look like.

For example, gold will not corrode or react except under the most severe conditions; sodium explodes on contact with water. If they were the same element, they would have the same properties; because they do not, they are clearly different elements.

4. *Atoms of two or more different elements will combine in fixed whole-number ratios to form compounds.* Probably the most important part of Dalton's Atomic Theory, this has two key components. First, we require at least two different elements to form a compound. Thus, oxygen, O_2, and ozone, O_3, are not compounds, because they contain only one type of element; oxygen. We call these *allotropes*—different forms of the same element. Second, the ratio of the elements forming a compound is fixed. If we vary this ratio, we change the compound. For example, in water, we always have two parts hydrogen to one part oxygen, written as H_2O, where the subscript "2" tells us there are two hydrogen atoms, and the assumed subscript "1" (if there is no subscript, 1 is assumed) tells us there is one atom of oxygen. The ratio of hydrogen to oxygen is 2:1. If we change this ratio, say, to 1:1 (or, as it turns out, 2:2), as in H_2O_2, we no longer have water. Indeed, we now have a nasty little chemical called hydrogen peroxide. Because the ratios of the elements

are different (the hydrogen:oxygen ratio is 2:1 for water, but 2:2, or 1:1, for hydrogen peroxide), the chemicals must be different. Thus, they have different chemical and physical properties.

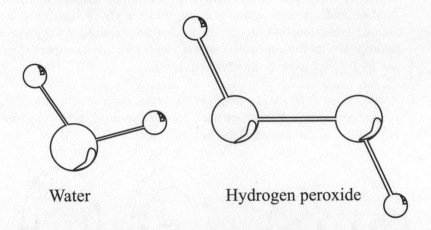

Water   Hydrogen peroxide

Although both water and hydrogen peroxide contain hydrogen and oxygen, because the ratio is different, the chemicals are different, with different chemical and physical properties. For example, water is necessary to life; we drink it, and it is so safe that we can swim in it. Hydrogen peroxide is highly corrosive and would cause severe harm if we swam in it or drank it. The solution of hydrogen peroxide that bleaches hair white is a very dilute solution; in higher concentrations, it would burn the hair off of your head, and the skin underneath as well. This is why we use hydrogen peroxide as an antiseptic: because it kills things.

Now, take a look around you and consider this: everything around you is made of elements and compounds (mostly the latter), and these elements and compounds are all comprised of the same limited set of known elements (and even a subset of those, as many are unstable).

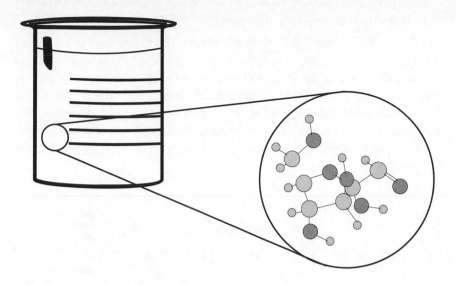

For example, if we could magnify sugar enough to be able to see it, we would discover it is comprised of only three elements: carbon, hydrogen, and oxygen.

EXERCISE 1

Directions: Choose the <u>one best answer</u> .

1. A substance can be broken down into more fundamental gases by the addition of an electrical current. One of the gases produced (always exactly three times greater than the other) is explosive in the presence of a flame, while the other extinguishes flames. What can we deduce about our original substance?

    (1)   It is a mixture.

    (2)   It is a compound.

    (3)   It is an element.

    (4)   It is a gas.

    (5)   We can deduce nothing without further information.

THE STRUCTURE OF ATOMS

Dalton's Atomic Theory was adopted rapidly and whole-heartedly by the scientific community, so you can imagine the kind of controversy it must have stirred up when one of its components—that atoms are indestructible—was challenged by the discovery of elements that not only could be destroyed but seemed to fall apart on their own. These *radioisotopes* are elements that undergo radioactive decay; the pathway of this decay causes the element to change into a different element, which elements are not supposed to do. However, as so often happens in science, what might at first glance appeared to be a calamity to our understanding of nature and the world around us turned out to be a terrific opportunity to discover more about the structure of matter.

The cathode ray tube (CRT, probably much like the one in your television and computer monitor, unless you have one of the new "flat screen" models) was actually invented to study the phenomenon of radioactive decay. A radioactive source was placed in one end of the tube, encased in lead and with a lens system that focused the radioactive beam along a tube in a vacuum. The beam would pass by plates with electrostatic charges. The electrostatic field, positive on one side and negative on the other, would cause a deflection of the radioactive particles.

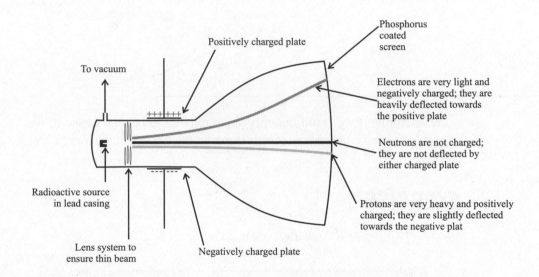

Which way radioactive particles would deflect and how much depended on their charge and mass. The negative particles would be deflected toward the positive charge and vice versa, and the heavier particles would deflect less because it would require more energy to change their momentum (in the same way that it would take more force to push a truck up a hill than it would to push a bicycle up a hill). On the opposite side of the CRT was a screen coated in phosphorous; this screen would glow wherever a radioactive particle hits.

Modern CRTs are built in much the same way, only it's a flow of electrons rather than radioactive particles, and the plates are on the sides as well as on top and bottom, and can have their charges varied as a function of time. Thus, the flow of electrons can hit any particular point, or pixel, on your screen, causing it to glow. The beam of electrons continuously sweeps back and forth and up and down, so quickly that a new electron hits the pixel before the pixel stops glowing from the previous electron strike.

Researchers were astounded to discover three particles more fundamental than the atom. One, which was exceedingly light and had a negative charge, they called the **electron**. Another, which was very heavy (relative to the electron) and had a positive charge, they called the **proton**. The mass of the electron was assigned a value of 0 (because it was so light that its mass didn't make a significant contribution to the total mass of the atom), and its charge was assigned a value of −1. The mass of the proton was assigned a value of 1 and its charge was assigned a value of +1. But, there was another particle, a very peculiar particle. Once scientists discovered the electron, the proton was not a surprise; they realized that the world was electrically neutral, so if there was a negatively charged particle, there had to be a positively charged particle as well, but *nobody* expected a third particle.

This new particle was not deflected in a magnetic field; its charge was 0. Scientists didn't know what to make of this new ray, so they dubbed it the mysterious *X-ray*. As it turns out, they had discovered **neutrons**, with a charge of 0 but a mass equal to that of a proton (mass 1).

Elementary Particles

Particle	Symbol	Charge	Mass	Location
Proton	$_1p^+$	+1	1	Nucleus
Neutron	$_1n^0$	0	1	Nucleus
Electron	$_0e^-$	−1	0	Around nucleus

Now they had discovered the three elementary particles of which all atoms are composed, but to know what particles exist is a far cry from understanding how they are put together. Their initial guess, in fact, was wrong.

It was Earnest Rutherford who, in 1910, finally discovered the true structure of the atom in an experiment that he thought was a failure. Rutherford directed a beam of radioactive particles through a thin sheet of gold foil, which was a fairly typical experiment at that time. What was different this time was that, instead of having a single small phosphorous screen target, he had wrapped the phosphorous screen around the entire apparatus.

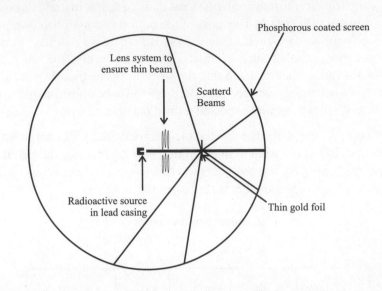

What he discovered was that there was glowing all round the screen, including almost in the exact opposite direction from the gold foil. He was so astonished by this that he wrote, "It was as if I had shot a cannonball at a piece of tissue paper and it bounced straight back toward me."

There was only one explanation for this phenomenon he could think of: somewhere, within the atom, there was a region that had matter so compact, so dense, that radiation could not penetrate it, and was actually deflected away from it. We now call that region of space the **nucleus,** the dense core of the atom that is home to the atom's protons and neutrons. The electrons are usually envisioned as being in orbit around this nucleus, although their exact behavior is, even today, not well understood. They seem to form what can best be described as clouds, but their exact path or behavior is not known.

The electrons are in shells, like the layers of an onion. We know that the outermost shell of electrons contains the only electrons that participate in the chemical and physical properties of atoms; we call these *valence shell* electrons. The remaining electrons are all between the valence shell and the nucleus; they do not really participate in the chemistry of the element, aside from giving structure on which the valence shell electrons are built. We call these the inner shell electrons.

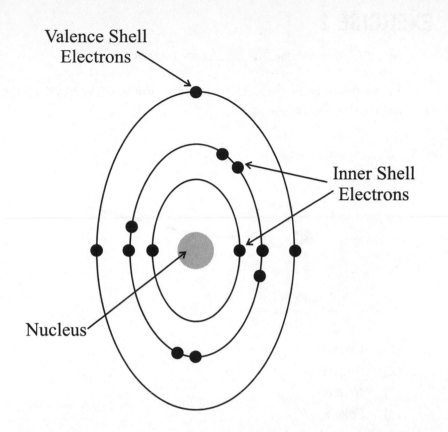

This is a cartoon diagram only; the actual structure of an aluminum atom is actually far more complicated and well beyond the scope of this book.

When atoms collide, it is only the valence shell electrons that interact; therefore, it must be these electrons that give the elements their overall chemical and physical properties. It stands to reason then, that if elements have similar electronic configurations, they must have similar chemical and physical properties. We find that this is indeed true, and it is reflected in the periodic chart.

The number of electrons can fluctuate as the element participates in bonding to form compounds. In its elemental state, the atom must be electrically neutral, so the number of electrons is exactly equal to the number of protons. This is not true of elements in a compound; it is only true in the elemental state. There is no such requirement on neutrons: an element can have as many, or as few, neutrons as it "wants"; however, if an element has too many or too few neutrons, it will be unstable.

If an atom loses electrons, which are negatively charged, it will have a net positive charge. Positively charged atoms are called **cations**. If an atom gains electrons, it will have a net negative charge. Negatively charged atoms are called **anions**. Collectively, cations or anions are referred to as simply **ions**. We'll discuss this a little later.

EXERCISE 2

Directions: Choose the <u>one best answer</u> for each item.

1. In the figure below, which elementary particle is produced by the radioactive source?

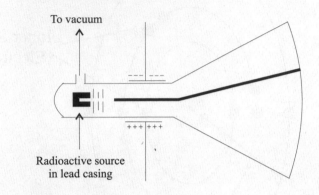

   (1)   Electron
   (2)   Nucleus
   (3)   Neutron
   (4)   Proton
   (5)   Atom

2. Before Rutherford's experiment, a model for the atom, called the "Plum Pudding" model, was hypothesized in which the electrons, protons, and neutrons were uniformly distributed in space throughout the region occupied by the atom. What feature is lacking in this model that Rutherford's experiment found?

   (1)   Neutrons
   (2)   A dense region with high mass
   (3)   Protons
   (4)   A spherical shape
   (5)   Electrons

The Periodic Chart

The periodic table shows all known elements today.

Key:

element name		
atomic number		
element symbol		
1997 atomic weight (mean relative mass)		

	1	2	3	4	5	6	7	8	9	10	11	12	13	14	15	16	17	18
	hydrogen 1 **H** 1.00794(7)																	helium 2 **He** 4.002602(2)
	lithium 3 **Li** 6.941(2)	beryllium 4 **Be** 9.012182(3)											boron 5 **B** 10.811(7)	carbon 6 **C** 12.0107(8)	nitrogen 7 **N** 14.0067(4)	oxygen 8 **O** 15.9994(3)	fluorine 9 **F** 18.9984032(5)	neon 10 **Ne** 20.1797(6)
	sodium 11 **Na** 22.989770(2)	magnesium 12 **Mg** 24.3050(6)											aluminum 13 **Al** 26.981538(2)	silicon 14 **Si** 28.0855(3)	phosphorus 15 **P** 30.973761(2)	sulfur 16 **S** 32.066(6)	chlorine 17 **Cl** 35.4527(9)	argon 18 **Ar** 39.948(1)
	potassium 19 **K** 39.0983(1)	calcium 20 **Ca** 40.078(4)	scandium 21 **Sc** 44.955910(8)	titanium 22 **Ti** 47.867(1)	vanadium 23 **V** 50.9415(1)	chromium 24 **Cr** 51.9961(6)	manganese 25 **Mn** 54.938049(9)	iron 26 **Fe** 55.845(2)	cobalt 27 **Co** 58.933200(9)	nickel 28 **Ni** 58.6934(2)	copper 29 **Cu** 63.546(3)	zinc 30 **Zn** 65.39(2)	gallium 31 **Ga** 69.723(1)	germanium 32 **Ge** 72.61(2)	arsenic 33 **As** 74.92160(2)	selenium 34 **Se** 78.96(3)	bromine 35 **Br** 79.904(1)	krypton 36 **Kr** 83.80(1)
	rubidium 37 **Rb** 85.4678(3)	strontium 38 **Sr** 87.62(1)	yttrium 39 **Y** 88.90585(2)	zirconium 40 **Zr** 91.224(2)	niobium 41 **Nb** 92.90638(2)	molybdenum 42 **Mo** 95.94(1)	technetium 43 **Tc** [98.9063]	ruthenium 44 **Ru** 101.07(2)	rhodium 45 **Rh** 102.90550(2)	palladium 46 **Pd** 106.42(1)	silver 47 **Ag** 107.8682(2)	cadmium 48 **Cd** 112.411(8)	indium 49 **In** 114.818(3)	tin 50 **Sn** 118.710(7)	antimony 51 **Sb** 121.760(1)	tellurium 52 **Te** 127.60(3)	iodine 53 **I** 126.90447(3)	xenon 54 **Xe** 131.29(2)
	caesium 55 **Cs** 132.90545(2)	barium 56 **Ba** 137.327(7)	57–70 *	lutetium 71 **Lu** 174.967(1)	hafnium 72 **Hf** 178.49(2)	tantalum 73 **Ta** 180.9479(1)	tungsten 74 **W** 183.84(1)	rhenium 75 **Re** 186.207(1)	osmium 76 **Os** 190.23(3)	iridium 77 **Ir** 192.217(3)	platinum 78 **Pt** 195.078(2)	gold 79 **Au** 196.96655(2)	mercury 80 **Hg** 200.59(2)	thallium 81 **Tl** 204.3833(2)	lead 82 **Pb** 207.2(1)	bismuth 83 **Bi** 208.98038(2)	polonium 84 **Po** [208.9824]	astatine 85 **At** [209.9871]	radon 86 **Rn** [222.0176]
	francium 87 **Fr** [223.0197]	radium 88 **Ra** [226.0254]	89–102 **	lawrencium 103 **Lr** [262.110]	rutherfordium 104 **Rf** [261.1089]	dubnium 105 **Db** [262.1144]	seaborgium 106 **Sg** [263.1186]	bohrium 107 **Bh** [264.12]	hassium 108 **Hs** [265.1306]	meitnerium 109 **Mt** [268]	ununnilium 110 **Uun** [269]	unununium 111 **Uuu** [272]	ununbium 112 **Uub** [277]	ununquadium 114 **Uuq** [289]				

*lanthanides

lanthanum 57 **La** 138.9055(2)	cerium 58 **Ce** 140.116(1)	praseodymium 59 **Pr** 140.90765(2)	neodymium 60 **Nd** 144.24(3)	promethium 61 **Pm** [144.9127]	samarium 62 **Sm** 150.36(3)	europium 63 **Eu** 151.964(1)	gadolinium 64 **Gd** 157.25(3)	terbium 65 **Tb** 158.92534(2)	dysprosium 66 **Dy** 162.50(3)	holmium 67 **Ho** 164.93032(2)	erbium 68 **Er** 167.26(3)	thulium 69 **Tm** 168.93421(2)	ytterbium 70 **Yb** 173.04(3)

**actinides

actinium 89 **Ac** [227.0277]	thorium 90 **Th** 232.0381(1)	protactinium 91 **Pa** 231.03588(2)	uranium 92 **U** 238.0289(1)	neptunium 93 **Np** [237.0482]	plutonium 94 **Pu** [244.0642]	americium 95 **Am** [243.0614]	curium 96 **Cm** [247.0703]	berkelium 97 **Bk** [247.0703]	californium 98 **Cf** [251.0796]	einsteinium 99 **Es** [252.0830]	fermium 100 **Fm** [257.0951]	mendelevium 101 **Md** [258.0984]	nobelium 102 **No** [259.1011]

Most elements were discovered, but some were artificially created. All elements in a column are *families* or *groups*, and rows are called *periods*. Metals are on the left side of the table, and nonmetals are on the right. The squiggly line toward the right-hand side of the periodic chart separates the metals from the nonmetals. Elements on this line, called *metalloids*, have properties in between those of metals and nonmetals. The elements in the square block in the middle, where the main table gets thinnest, are called the *transition metals*, while the two rows on the bottom are called the *Lanthanides* (top) and the *Actinides* (bottom).

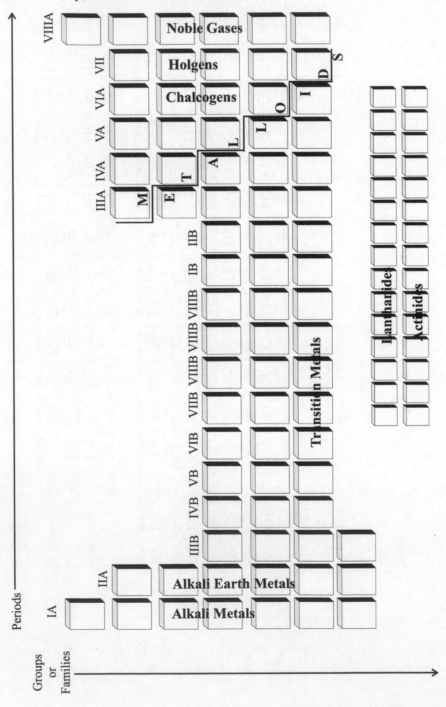

Metals tend to have all of the typical characteristics you'd expect from metals (with some exceptions): they conduct electricity and heat well, they are malleable (can be bent), they tend to be shiny, and in compounds they tend to lose electrons. **Nonmetals** are the opposite: they usually do not conduct electricity or heat, are often brittle and dull, and gain electrons in compounds.

Metalloids tend to be semiconductors (like silicon). They can be malleable or brittle, shiny or dull, and can either lose or gain electrons. They're somewhere in between metals and nonmetals.

Several columns in the periodic table have common names. For example, group IA are called the *alkali metals* (because in water they form alkaline, or basic, solutions). Group IIA, the *alkali earth metals*, include ones common in ores, like calcium and magnesium. They also form alkaline solutions when in water. Group VIIA, the *halogens,* are mostly gases that are highly corrosive and toxic; iodine, from this group, is used to clean wounds, because it kills germs. Group VIIIA are called *noble gases* because they are non-reactive, or inert.

ATOMIC SYMBOLS

You'll notice that each element has several things associated with it. First, each element has a one- or two-letter designation, or **atomic symbol**. Chemists like shortcuts as well as anybody else, so these symbols are very frequently used. Often the letters correspond with the element, like sulfur and its letter designation S. However, you'll notice that many of them do not have letters that correspond as you would expect. There are two primary reasons for this: some of them are simply historical. For example, gold has the symbol Au, which was chosen because of the Latin word for gold, *aurium*. The second reason is compromise. For example, tungsten (element number 74) was discovered in England and in Germany about the same time. There was a time when the discoverer of an element was given the privilege of naming it. In England, it was called tungsten, while in Germany, the name wolfram was assigned. Thus, the compromise was to use the English name but the German letter designation.

The now-abandoned custom of discoverers naming elements has resulted in elements that are named after the region where they were discovered, such as Californium, Americium, and Europium, or after scientists, such as "Einsteinium," and "Rutherfordium." Problems arising due to dual claims of discovery are avoided today because naming of new elements falls under the jurisdiction of the International Union of Pure and Applied Chemistry (IUPAC).

ATOMIC NUMBERS

You might also notice that each element has an **atomic number** as well, starting with hydrogen as 1, helium as 2, and so on. These numbers are not merely arbitrary. Recall that an element's chemical and physical properties are a function of its electronic configuration. It stands to reason that the electronic configuration depends on how many electrons are in an element. So we should be able to identify an element by how many electrons it has. Unfortunately, this number is subject to change when the element participates in the formation of compounds, so it is not a convenient number to use for identification of elements. However, remember that in an element the number of electrons is equal to the number of protons, and the number of protons will not change. Thus, the atomic number is best thought of as equal to the number of protons in an element.

Because the number of protons is a fixed integer (that is, we cannot have a fraction of a proton), we know that all elements have been discovered up to the last one on the periodic chart. We'll never discover an element, for example, between Calcium, Ca (element number 20) and Scandium, Sc (element number 21), because such an element would have to have an atomic number of 20½, which is impossible. Before we discuss the final number associated with each element, we must first discuss the atomic mass number.

ATOMIC MASS

As you'll recall, of the elementary particles, only protons and neutrons have mass, and their masses are very close to one another. Each had been assigned a mass of 1, while electrons were assigned a mass of 0 (not that electrons have no mass, but rather, compared to the mass of the proton and the neutron, the mass of the electron is not significant). Thus, an element's **atomic mass** number is equal to the number of protons plus the number of neutrons.

Recall that the number of protons is equal to the atomic number; thus, we are not allowed to change this number without changing the identity of the element we are discussing. However, the number of neutrons is allowed to change. Two atoms with the same atomic number (same number of protons), but a different number of neutrons will differ only in their atomic mass number, but not in their identity. We call these atoms **isotopes**.

You may notice that some elements in the periodic chart, like Neptunium (Np, element number 93) have an integral number (a whole number) associated with them (for Np, this number is 237). This is the atomic mass number of the most stable isotope. Any element with this kind of number is unstable and undergoes radioactive decay. These **radioisotopes** decay to become different elements, and they release radiation when they do.

Finally, we are ready to talk about the atomic mass. Notice that most elements have an atomic mass that is not a whole number. For example, Chlorine (Cl, element number 17) has an atomic mass of 35.543. You may wonder how it is possible to have a fractional atomic mass; this is because the atomic mass is actually the average atomic mass of a large quantity of naturally occurring atoms.

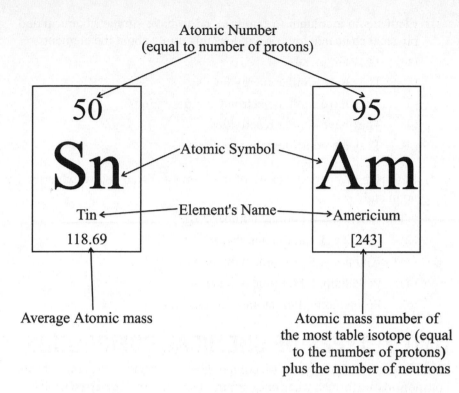

One should note that you can only deduce the number of neutrons for a specific isotope in any given element by subtracting the atomic number from the atomic mass number.

EXERCISE 3

Directions: Choose the <u>one best answer</u> for each item.

1. Referring to the periodic chart, which element has 32 protons?
   - (1) Germanium, Ge
   - (2) Gold, Au
   - (3) Sulfur, S
   - (4) Nickel, Ni
   - (5) Polonium, Po

2. Referring to the periodic chart, how many neutrons are in the most stable isotope of Americium?
   - (1) 95
   - (2) 148
   - (3) 243
   - (4) 338
   - (5) More information is needed before this question can be answered.

3. Elements in a column (a family) tend to have similar chemical and physical characteristics. What does this imply about the elements?

   (1)   They are metals.

   (2)   They have similar energy levels.

   (3)   They have similar electronic configurations.

   (4)   They have similar reactivities.

   (5)   They are coincidentally similar.

4. Referring to a periodic chart, of the elements listed below, which is a nonmetal?

   (1)   Calcium, Ca (atomic number 20)

   (2)   Fluorine, F (atomic number 9)

   (3)   Antimony, Sb (atomic number 51)

   (4)   Palladium, Pd (atomic number 46)

   (5)   Promethium, Pm (atomic number 61)

UNIT 7: TYPES OF CHEMICAL COMPOUNDS

There are two major types of compounds: ionic and covalent. **Ionic compounds** are formed when one or more electrons are transferred from one atom to another. Because electrons are negatively charged, the atom that loses electrons (loses negative charges) will be left with a net positive charge (+1, +2, +3, etc.); this is called a cation. Meanwhile, the atom that gains electrons has a net negative charge (−1, −2, −3, etc.) and is called an anion. An ionic compound is formed by the electrostatic attraction of the positively charged cations for the negatively charged anions.

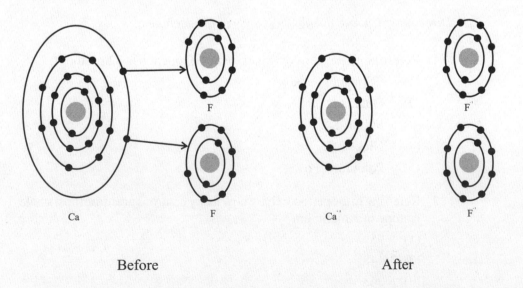

Before   After

Ionic compounds are always accompanied by a physical transference of one or more electrons. In the case above, the calcium atom loses two electrons, which are transferred to two fluorine atoms, which in turn each picks up one electron. The ionic bond is really nothing more than the attraction of these charged ions for each other.

For an ionic compound to form, one of the atoms must have a pull for electrons that is strong enough that it can literally take the electrons away; this leads to the question of what happens when one atom is not strong enough to remove electrons completely from the other. In this case, electrons must be shared. A compound in which the elements share electrons is called a **covalent compound**, and the bonds are called covalent bonds. In any covalent bond, two, and only two, electrons are shared. However, a compound can form single, double, or triple bonds (but no higher order than triple). Thus, there are two electrons shared in a single bond (one from each element involved in the bond), four electrons shared in a double bond (two in each of the two bonds), and six electrons shared in a triple bond (two in each of the three bonds).

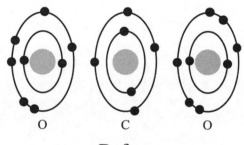

O   C   O

Before

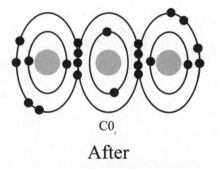

CO_2

After

For example, carbon dioxide (shown above) actually forms two double bonds (requiring that four electrons be shared on each side, two for each in the double bond).

In both ionic and covalent compounds, the atoms are trying to do the same thing: complete the octet of electrons in their valence shell. It was discovered that elements want eight electrons in their valence shells (except for hydrogen, which only wants two). This is called the **Octet Rule**. Essentially, elements will share, lose, or gain electrons to complete their octet. Since elements always have a fixed number of electrons in their valence shell, we find that they often share or exchange the same number of electrons every time they bond. For example, sodium has one electron in its valence shell; if it loses that one electron, the next inner shell becomes its valence shell, and it is already a complete octet. Thus, in compounds, sodium always forms a +1 ion (because it always wants to lose that one electron). On the other hand, chlorine has seven electrons in its valence shell; thus, it always wants to gain one electron to complete its octet, it is always −1 charge in a compound. Sodium chloride (table salt), an ionic compound, has one sodium atom and one chlorine atom, so the charges will balance out exactly.

Hydrogen wants to gain one electron, and oxygen wants to gain two electrons. Since neither oxygen nor hydrogen is strong enough to remove electrons from the other, the electrons must be shared. Since hydrogen has only one electron to share, but each oxygen wants two electrons, then two hydrogens are required for each oxygen. Thus, the resulting compound will be H_2O, which we know as water.

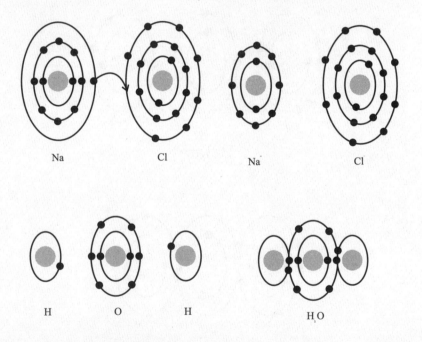

Both ionic and covalent compounds are working to fulfill the Octet Rule—the only difference is how they satisfy this rule!

Just how much an element wants an electron is called **electronegativity**. The higher an element's electronegativity, the stronger that element will pull an electron. Thus, two elements will form an ionic bond if one has a much higher electronegativity than the other. It's like two children playing with a toy: if one is much larger and stronger than the other, then that child will most likely take the toy, leaving the smaller child without it (an ionic compound). However, if the children are about the same strength, then one will not be strong enough to take the toy away from the other and the two children will share the toy (a covalent compound).

If two elements have electronegativities that are close enough that one element cannot take the electron from the other, but one is slightly higher than the other, then we have a new situation: the electron is shared, but the electron will spend more time near the more electronegative element than the less.

Large Difference in electronegativity

Small Difference in electronegativity

If the difference in electronegativity is great (as demonstrated by the relative sizes of the children in the figure above), the electron (or toy) will be taken from the less electronegative by the more electronegative. The child who lost the toy won't want to stray too far though and will always be close; this is akin to an ionic compound. If the electronegativities are closer, however, one child may not be able to actually take the toy from the other, but the toy will still spend a little more time around the slightly stronger child. This is analogous to a covalent compound.

If elements have different but similar electronegativities, what we end up with is an unequal sharing. The more electronegative element will end up with a slight, but not complete, negative charge, called a partial negative charge; and the less electronegative element will have a partial positive charge. With a partial positive charge on one side of the bond and a partial negative charge on the other, we have developed what is called a *dipole*, which can be thought of as a tiny little magnet. This is an important concept when we think of intermolecular forces (not chemical bonds, but rather the attraction of one molecule for another). These intermolecular forces are what give rise to the various states of matter.

EXERCISE 1

Directions: Choose the <u>one best answer</u> for each item.

1. Which family in the periodic chart contains elements that probably already have a complete octet?
   (1) Alkali metals
   (2) Halogens
   (3) Alkali earth metals
   (4) Chalcogens
   (5) Noble gases

2. Electrostatic forces are electronic in nature, based primarily on the attraction of oppositely partial charges on molecules. This is most similar to
   (1) metals.
   (2) metalloids.
   (3) ionic bonds.
   (4) nonmetals.
   (5) covalent bonds.

PROPERTIES OF COVALENT AND IONIC COMPOUNDS

Covalent and ionic compounds differ in behavior. For instance, covalent compounds tend to have lower melting points and be more malleable, while ionic compounds tend to have higher melting points and be more brittle.

Property	Ionic Compounds	Covalent Compounds
Melting Points	Typically very high	Ranges from low to moderately high
Malleability	Typically brittle (not malleable)	Ranges from brittle to malleable
Dissociates in water	Yes (if soluble)	No (even if soluble)

However, one of the greatest differences between these types of compounds is their behavior in water. Some compounds, called **electrolytes**, cause water to conduct electricity, while other compounds, called **nonelectrolytes**, do not.

Solid (dry) salt will not conduct electricity

Water that is VERY pure will not conduct electricity

Water with even a little bit of salt
(like from your toe!) WILL conduct electricity

Keep in mind that even a very small amount of electrolyte, like those found on floors and the ground, or in tap water, will be enough to conduct electricity; do not try this demonstration yourself!

In water, ionic compounds *dissociate*, or break down into their individual ions.

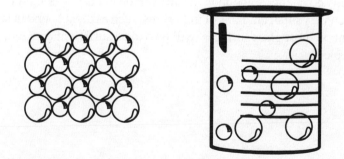

In water, an ionic compound, which is very ordered as a solid (as seen on the left in the figure above), will literally "split apart" into cations and anions in solution, as seen above by this rendition of sodium chloride as a solid in water. It is the ions that actually conduct the electricity. Because covalent compounds must have their atoms remain close enough to share electrons, covalent compounds cannot dissociate into ions.

Ionic compounds themselves do not conduct electricity, and water (if it is pure) does not conduct electricity either. However, even a minute amount of an ionic compound in water will cause the solution to conduct electricity. This is because there is nothing physically holding ionic compounds together besides the electrostatic attraction of positively charged cations for negatively charged anions. In water, these ions dissociate and become free-floating ions. Thus, an electrolyte is actually an ionic compound; in water, it's the ions that carry the charge. Without the ions, water cannot carry the charge alone any more than the compounds can carry the charge without the water.

Covalent compounds, on the other hand, remain coherent in solution.

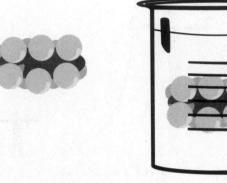

As a solid (above left) or in solution (above right), a covalent compound cannot allow its atoms to get too far apart to share electrons. Thus, a covalent compound, like this sugar molecule, cannot conduct electricity (even in water); it is a nonelectrolyte.

Because covalent bonds share electrons, the atoms are not free to move too far apart from one another as ions are in an ionic compound. Thus, because covalent compounds cannot dissociate, solutions of covalent compounds (such as sugar and water) do not conduct electricity. Thus, nonelectrolytes are actually covalent compounds. (However, do not try to verify this on your own. Even very small amounts of impurities, such as those found in tap water or present on most glass surfaces, will provide a sufficient concentration to conduct electricity.)

EXERCISE 2

Directions: Choose the <u>one best answer</u>.

1. No matter how pure the water is, and no matter how clean the floor is, if you place your foot in a puddle, the water in that puddle will be capable of conducting electricity (even if your feet are clean). What must be on your skin for this to be true?
   (1) Metals
   (2) Nonmetals
   (3) Covalent compounds
   (4) Ionic compounds
   (5) Nucleic acid

UNIT 8: INTERACTIONS OF MATTER AND ENERGY

HEAT

The interaction of matter and energy is dependent on the form of the energy. Energy can be absorbed or released by matter, but remember that the total energy is conserved; we cannot create or destroy energy. Consider, for example, heat. Heat was originally defined as that which flows from a region of high temperature to low temperature. This definition tells us little else, because, when this standard definition of heat was formulated, little was known of the effects of heat on matter.

As it turns out, heat is directly related to the kinetic energy of the molecules and atoms in matter. Thus, the higher the temperature, the faster molecules and atoms move, and the higher their kinetic energy. When a cooler body is in contact with a warmer body, heat is transferred from one body to another because of the collisions between the molecules and atoms. As it turns out, when atoms and molecules collide, they behave much as you might expect any object to. Just like their macroscopic counterparts, atoms and molecules display momentum. They move in a straight line until they collide with some object, forcing them to change direction. If that other object is another atom or molecule, then an energy transfer can be expected to occur. The atom or molecule with less kinetic energy (lower temperature) will pick up some of the kinetic energy from the atom or molecule with greater kinetic energy (higher temperature). Because the molecule with less kinetic energy now has more kinetic energy, its temperature has increased. Similarly, the faster hotter atom or molecule will lose some of its kinetic energy to the cooler slower atom or molecule it collides with; thus, its temperature will decrease.

ELECTROMAGNETIC RADIATION

Another form of energy is *electromagnetic radiation.* Light falls into the category of electromagnetic radiation, but so do many other things, such as microwave radiation, infrared and ultraviolet radiation, radio and television signals, and many other forms of energy. The major difference between all of these energies is primarily the amount of energy they have; for example, ultraviolet has higher energy than infrared.

Matter can either absorb or emit electromagnetic radiation, and both are very common occurrences. For example, if you are reading this at night, you are probably using an artificial light source to read it (a light bulb). No matter what type of light bulb you are using, the principle is the same: electricity is being used to force the electrons in the atoms in the light bulb (either the gas if it is neon or filament if it is incandescent) into a high energy state (called an *excited state*). The electrons in atoms really don't like being in a high-energy state, so they will eventually go back to the lowest possible energy state that they can, called the *ground state.* The process of going from an excited state to a ground state is called *relaxation.*

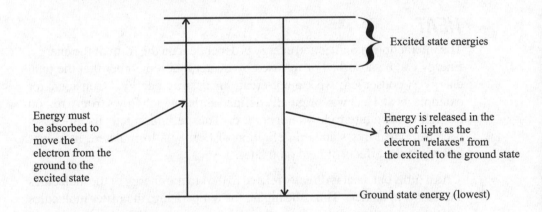

It always requires the input of energy to get the electrons into a higher energy state than their ground state, but that energy is released, often in the form of light, as the electron "relaxes" back to the ground state. Because energy cannot be destroyed, we reach that excited state when energy in the form of electrical energy is absorbed. When the atom relaxes back to the ground state, all that excess energy is again released, only this time in the form of light, but exactly equal in energy to the energy absorbed to excite the electrons in the first place.

This also occurs when we burn salts (ionic compounds) formed from various metals. Because of the high temperatures within flames, the metals in flames have their electrons excited, and they subsequently relax to release light. Each metal releases a different (characteristic) color of light; sodium burns orange, for example, while copper is green. This is seen in fireworks, as salts added to the explosives create different colors, but it is also used to detect and identify metal contamination in soil or water samples.

When matter absorbs electromagnetic radiation, something entirely different usually happens. Although absorbing light can cause the electrons to get into an excited state (which causes glowing, as in phosphorescent, or "glow-in-the-dark" toys), light usually causes a change in the behavior of the molecules present. As it turns out, bonds are anything but static; they bend, rotate, and stretch, so even in molecules that are not moving, there is still a lot of motion.

Electromagnetic radiation often excites (or increases the energy of) these motions.

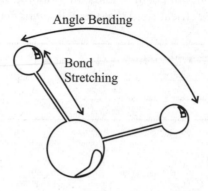

Thus, when they absorb light, these bonds might vibrate faster, or the molecules might rotate faster, or the atoms might stretch further apart. This is how a microwave oven works: the microwave radiation causes water molecules to rotate faster. As the molecules rotate faster, they collide with other molecules and transfer some of this energy to other molecules, which in turn start moving faster. Thus, the food gets hotter because the molecules are moving faster.

Energy has also provided a unique tool that can probe the nature of matter. The difference between a compound and an element, for example, is our ability to separate compounds into more fundamental (elemental) components through chemical means. This is different from solutions, which can be separated by mechanical means; for example, we can easily separate a solution of water and salt by boiling off the water. However, separating water into hydrogen and oxygen atoms is more difficult. It is because so many elements were first discovered through electrical separation that the concept of a chemical bond being electrical in nature was discovered. For example, we can separate water into its corresponding elements, hydrogen and oxygen, by applying an electrical current (in the correct conditions); however, hydrogen and oxygen cannot be further broken down. Thus, hydrogen and oxygen must be more elemental than water.

ELECTRICITY AND MAGNETISM

Electricity is the flow of electrons, the same electrons, in fact, that we find in the outer shells of atoms. Metals have an abundance of what can best be described as free-floating electrons; when we add electrons to one side, the electrons are pushed along the surface of the metal, resulting in electrical conduction. The close relationship between electricity and magnetism can be demonstrated by how electricity is produced.

Magnetism is a force that attracts metals and other magnets. We can use magnetism to create electricity. An electric generator is nothing more than a wire coil inside a permanent magnetic field; when the coil or the magnet is rotated, an electrical current is induced in the coil, just as a magnetic field can be created by running current through a wire surrounding a piece of metal. In a magnet, all of the charge imbalances in a material line up, such that the negative end and positive ends are pointing the same way. This creates an overall electrical field that we call a *magnetic field*.

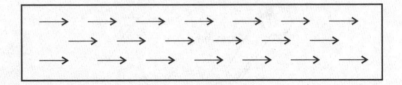

EXERCISE 1

Directions: Choose the <u>one best answer</u> for each item.

1. Argon has about 10 times the mass of helium. What can we deduce about the behavior of a mixture of these gases (assuming the temperature of the gases are the same)?
   (1)   The helium is cooling the argon.
   (2)   The argon is cooling the helium.
   (3)   The argon is moving faster than the helium.
   (4)   The helium is moving faster then the argon.
   (5)   The argon and the helium must be moving at the same average velocity.

2. A can found on a hike shows red pigments faded but blue colors still bright. Which of the following statements explains this observation?
   (1)   Red absorbs red light, and the energy associated with red light is higher energy than blue light.
   (2)   Red absorbs blue light, and the energy associated with red light is higher energy than blue light.
   (3)   Red absorbs red light, and the energy associated with blue light is higher energy than red light.
   (4)   Red must be absorbing light, while blue is emitting light.
   (5)   Red absorbs blue light, and the energy associated with blue light is higher energy than red light.

STATES OF MATTER

We all know the three major states of matter: gas, solid, and liquid. If you were shown a particular material (tricks aside), you would be able to identify its state. Gases have very low density, expand to fill the volume of their container, and assume the shape of their container. Liquids have intermediate density and a fixed volume but will assume the shape of their container. Solids have the highest density, fixed volumes, and fixed shapes.

Characteristics of the Three Major States of Matter

Property	Gas	Liquid	Solid
Viscosity (resistance to flow)	Low	Low to high	High
Volume	Container-dependent	Fixed	Fixed
Shape	Container-dependent	Container-dependent	Fixed
Relative temperature	Highest	Intermediate	Lowest
Relative density	Lowest	Intermediate (with rare exceptions)	Highest (with rare exceptions)

DENSITY

Density warrants some discussion. Not all solids have higher densities than liquids; solid iron has lower density than liquid mercury, which is easy to prove because iron will float on a pool of mercury. This is because we are comparing different elements; with very few exceptions, for any given element or compound, the solid will have a higher density than the corresponding liquid. So mercury in the solid state has a higher density than mercury in the liquid state, and iron in the solid state has a higher density than iron in the liquid state. Unfortunately, one of the extremely rare exceptions to this rule is water. This unfortunate fact led to the sinking of the *Titanic;* if solid water were more dense than liquid water, then icebergs would not float and it would not have been possible for the *Titanic* to collide with the iceberg that sank it. In fact, water is the only known compound (and there is only one known element) for which this is true. Remember that, despite the abundance of water on our planet, it is, nonetheless, an exceptionally odd compound!

This raises another issue of density: if the *Titanic* was made of steel, and if the *Titanic* floated, does this imply that steel is less dense than water? No, it does not. There are two ways to decrease density: we can remove mass from the same volume or increase volume without increasing the mass.

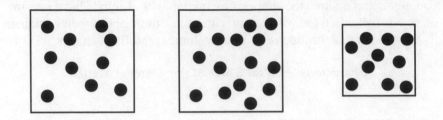

A group of iron atoms, as shown on the left in the figure above, in the form of a block are more dense than water; they will sink. However, the same number of atoms formed in the shape of a boat, as on the right in the above figure, gives a greater relative volume to the atoms, and they will float. Steel ships are designed such that the total volume of the ship is so great that the *average density* of the ship as a whole is less than that of water.

If we have a material, like Styrofoam, for example, with a lot of air pockets, then the average density of the object as a whole can be significantly less than the density of the material if it were, say, simply a cube.

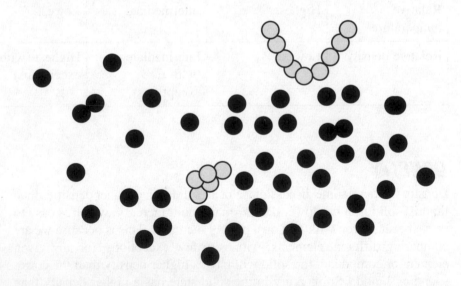

We can increase density (as demonstrated in the figure above by how close the particles are to one another) by either increasing the number of particles (middle) or decreasing the volume (right).

ELECTROSTATIC FORCES

Because of the condensed states of matter (liquid and solid), we know that there must be forces between molecules that are different from normal chemical bonds. These forces hold compounds or elements together to form condensed states; if no such forces existed, all matter would be in the gaseous state. These intermolecular forces are electrostatic in nature: an uneven distribution of electrons around an element or compound creates regions of partial charge (partial positive and partial negative, but the net charge does not change). In turn, these opposite partial charges attract one another and pull the atoms or molecules closer together.

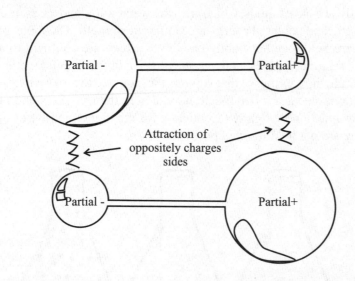

Uneven sharing of electrons will cause molecules to have partial, if not full, charge imbalances within the molecule itself. These charge imbalances must cancel each other out to have a neutral compound, but can still attract one another as any opposite charges would do. These electrostatic attractions are the foundation of intermolecular forces.

What we are discussing is a form of stored energy, or potential energy. These forces vary in strength, depending on the nature of the material, and play a critical role in the physical properties of compounds and elements. The stronger the intermolecular forces between atoms or molecules, the more strongly they will be held together. This means it will be more difficult to break them apart; in other words, it will require more energy to allow these atoms or molecules to move freely. This means that, the stronger the intermolecular forces, the higher the melting and boiling points will be, and, probably, the greater the density.

If we think about these implications, especially in light of kinetic and potential energy, we start to see a picture of what might be happening at a molecular level for various substances. In a solid, there is relatively little motion. This means that the kinetic energy, the energy of motion, must be small compared with the potential energy that is holding the elements and molecules together. Thus, we have a collection of atoms and molecules that cannot move from one place to another (although they do vibrate considerably); they are all trapped in positions that, relative to one another, will not change significantly. The atoms and molecules are held tightly and closely together.

On the other end of the spectrum, we have gases. In gases, molecules and atoms are free to move relative to one another. If this were the case, the molecules or atoms could never get far enough away from one another to allow the gas to expand to fill a container. In a gas the kinetic energy is very great, while the potential energy is almost negligible. Thus, the atoms in a gas move rapidly and at random, interacting with one another only when there is a chance collision; they are very far apart from each other.

Finally, we have liquids, which are in between solids and gases. In liquids, the kinetic and potential energy are similar in strength. The molecules and atoms are held together tightly enough that they are confined to a small volume relative to gases, and yet, they have a high enough kinetic energy that, within the confines of that volume, they are free to move wherever they like. The molecules move much more slowly than in gases and are held together much more tightly (accounting for the higher density of liquids), but they are not held in fixed positions.

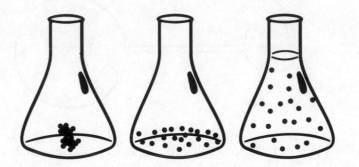

Solids are restricted by very strong potential energy that prevents them from moving (other than vibrations); they are highly dense and independent of the shape of the container. Liquids have weaker intermolecular forces when compared with their kinetic energy, and thus are free to move but only within a restricted volume; this allows them to assume the shape of the container they are in. Gases have very high kinetic energy compared with their potential energy; they are free to move anywhere within their container. As we heat up a solid, we are increasing its kinetic energy, but the potential energy remains fixed; thus, as kinetic energy becomes comparable to the potential energy, the solid will melt, and when the kinetic energy is very large compared with the potential energy, the liquid will boil and turn into a gas.

EXERCISE 2

Directions: Choose the <u>one best answer</u> for each item.

1. Vapor pressure is the pressure created in a closed container above a liquid. If a liquid has a high vapor pressure (the higher the vapor pressure, the more liquid will evaporate at a given temperature), what can we infer about the molecules in the liquid?

    (1)   The kinetic energy must be great.

    (2)   The intermolecular forces between the molecules must be weak.

    (3)   The kinetic energy must be weak.

    (4)   Nothing can be inferred from this observation.

    (5)   The intermolecular forces between the molecules must be strong.

2. The substance shown in the figure below is most likely to be a(n)

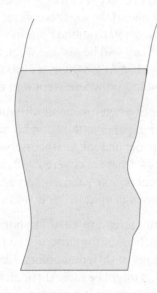

    (1)   solid.

    (2)   compound.

    (3)   element.

    (4)   liquid.

    (5)   gas.

SOLUTIONS AND MIXTURES

Much like compounds, mixtures require at least two different components. However, in mixtures, these components may themselves be compounds (and often are). In addition, unlike compounds, the ratio of these components is free to vary. You'll also notice that we are discussing mixtures at this point rather than solutions; all solutions are mixtures, but not all mixtures are solutions.

Properties of Solutions and Compounds

Property	Solutions	Compounds
Comprised of two or more things	Yes (solute and solvent)	Yes (at least two different elements)
Fixed ratios	Yes	No

A **mixture** is a combination of two or more components. We refer to mixtures as either heterogeneous or homogeneous. A *homogeneous* mixture is the same throughout; if we were to sample a homogeneous mixture at any point, it would be identical in every way to any other portion. For example, in a solution of sugar and water, if the sugar is completely dissolved (no solid particles remain), a sample taken from the bottom will be no different than a sample taken at the top. They will be just as sweet, they will look the same and have the same density. In a *heterogeneous* mixture, however, we have different properties depending on where we are in the mixture.

This book is an example of a heterogeneous mixture. We know that there are at least two components (paper and ink, and if we analyze even further we will find that both the paper and ink are themselves mixtures). However, there are portions of the paper that are covered with ink and portions that are not. Thus, we have different regions, and a heterogeneous mixture. In fact, if this were not a heterogeneous mixture, you would not be able to read it!

Often, heterogeneous mixtures are easy to spot; you'll see something floating in the solution, such as an impurity or even ice in a glass of water, or perhaps you'll see regions of different colors, like carpet with multicolored threads. Other times, it might be more difficult to spot a heterogeneous mixture, such as milk. However, as it turns out, if a solution is very cloudy or opaque, it must be a heterogeneous mixture. This is because the cloudiness or opaqueness is caused by light bouncing off very fine particles that are too small for the human eye to catch. Thus, as it turns out, so-called homogenized milk is not homogenized at all; it may look the same to us because we cannot see anything different from one point in the milk to another, but if it were truly homogenous, it would be clear (do not confuse "clear" with "colorless;" water is clear and colorless, while Kool-Aid is clear but not colorless). We call milk (and mixtures like milk) a *suspension*. It looks like a homogeneous mixture, but it is cloudy or opaque, indicating the presence of particles too small for us to see.

SOLUTES AND SOLVENTS

You might wonder what the difference is between a mixture and a solution. A **solution** is a homogenous mixture. To be a true solution, you must have a clear (but, again, not necessarily colorless) mixture of two or more components. Some common terms we use when discussing solutions are solvent and solute. The **solute** is the active ingredient; it is what is important in the solution, or the reason we create or choose to use it. The **solvent**, then, is what the solute is dissolved in; it is the delivery medium for the solute. Thus, in children's aspirin, the solute, the active ingredient or most important component, is the acetyl salicylic acid (aspirin); the flavorful syrup is the solvent.

In addition to these, there are several key terms relating to how much solute we have relative to the amount of solvent. If a solution is *unsaturated*, we have dissolved some solute but could dissolve more. If it is *saturated*, we have dissolved as much solute as possible at the given temperature. If it is *supersaturated*, we have dissolved more solute in the solution than possible. This last term seems very odd, but as it turns out, for solids to form from a solution (a process called *precipitation*), the crystals need something to form on. This so-called seed can be either a crystal of the same compound, or a scratch in the container, or some other imperfection. Without such a seed, a solution can actually be made that is supersaturated.

To make a supersaturated solution, we begin with a heterogeneous mixture consisting of a saturated solution and excess solute in the same very smooth (scratch-free) container. We heat up the solution, so that the excess solute dissolves. Once the solute has dissolved completely, we allow the solution to cool slowly back down. If we are careful to choose a container free of scratches, we can form a solution that has more solute dissolved than should be possible at the lower temperature. Supersaturated solutions are rare, because they are unstable. Typically, even slight jarring of the container or a piece of dust settling on the surface of the container will cause the excess solute to precipitate out.

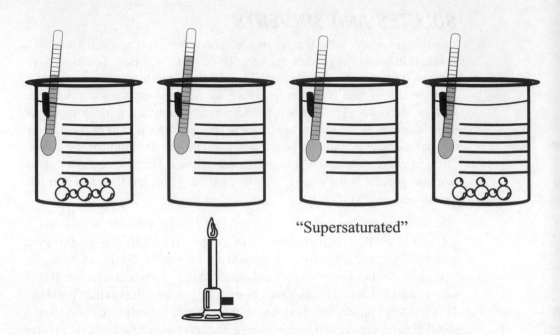

"Supersaturated"

We can also speak of a solution as concentrated or dilute. A solution is *concentrated* if it contains a lot of solute relative to the amount of solvent. It is *dilute* if it contains relatively little solute. How much solute we have relative to the amount of solvent is usually expressed in some given concentration. There are many concentration expressions, but they are basically all the same—typically, the quantity of solute per given amount of solution or solvent.

Returning to the concept of children's medicine, suppose we wish to deliver 10 mg of medicine to a child. Few of us are capable of measuring 10 mg of anything, because it is a very small amount. Thus, the pharmaceutical company has created a solution for us, in which the exact amount of medicine per quantity of solution is well known. For example, the manufacturer may have made the medicine such that it contains 10 mg of active ingredient (quantity of solute) per teaspoon of medicine (amount of solution). A teaspoon is very large relative to 10 mg, so if we measure a little bit too much or a little bit less, it will not significantly alter the amount of medicine the child is getting. This example also illustrates why we use solutions in the first place: it is more convenient to use solutions than the pure substance, either because we need too little of the pure substance to be able to measure it, or because the substance is in a state that is difficult to work with, such as a gas.

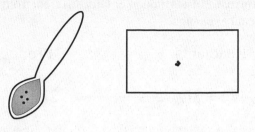

SOLUBILITY

If a substance dissolves to an appreciable extent in a solvent, we say it is *soluble*, as salt is soluble in water. However, if very little will dissolve, we say it is *insoluble*, such as pepper in water. In the special case of liquid solvent/liquid solute, we use the terms *miscible* or *immiscible* instead. Two liquids are said to be miscible if they can be mixed in any ratio without their separating out on standing. Gasoline and oil, for example, are miscible. However, if the liquids cannot be mixed without their separating on standing, they are immiscible, as in oil and vinegar.

EXERCISE 3

Directions: Choose the <u>one best answer</u> for each item.

1. A cloudy liquid is an example of a(n)
   (1) compound.
   (2) solution.
   (3) element.
   (4) solute.
   (5) heterogeneous mixture.

2. A clear liquid is known to contain a solid solute. A sample of the liquid is tested by adding an additional amount of that particular solute, which readily dissolves. Which of the following terms best describes the original liquid?
   (1) Unsaturated solution
   (2) Saturated solution
   (3) Supersaturated solution
   (4) Solvent
   (5) Solute

UNIT 9: CHEMICAL REACTIONS

When material is changed into something new, then we have caused a **chemical reaction.** The materials we started with were the *reactants*, and what we ended up with are the *products*. For example, a rust spot on a car starts out as iron and oxygen (the most reactive component of air) that combine to form rust. Rust is fundamentally different from iron and oxygen, so this is a chemical change.

Reactants   Products

$$4Fe + 3O_2 \longrightarrow 2Fe_2O_3$$

Chemical reactions are represented by formulas. Reactants, what we are starting with, are always on the left, with products always on the right. Notice that if you count the number of atoms of each element, they are the same on both sides (we have 4 iron, Fe, on the left, and $2 \times 2 = 4$ on the right). This is necessary because of the Law of Conservation of Matter (discussed below).

Chemical reactions are all around us. In fact, they are within us; *metabolism* is the term given to the collection of chemical reactions occurring within our bodies to keep us alive. For example, sugar is being converted from the foods we eat into carbon dioxide and water. This reaction releases the energy necessary to carry out other reactions that keep us alive. These reactions are typically **oxidation** or reduction/oxidation (redox) reactions. The transfer of one or more electrons accompanies all oxidation (redox) reactions. The element from which the electrons originate is said to be oxidized, while the element gaining the electron is being reduced. Oxidation cannot occur without a corresponding reduction. Burning is an example of an oxidation reaction, but there are also many other types.

CONSERVATION OF MATTER

Just as in the Law of Conservation of Energy, there is a similar law governing chemical reactions, the Law of Conservation of Matter. This law states that matter cannot be created or destroyed, but it can change form. Thus, if we burn, say, 300 tons of coal, resulting in a pile of ashes with significantly less weight, any missing mass must be present in the form of gaseous emissions. This law brings increased significance to the concept of recycling: Earth's resources are limited; if we run out of any given resource, such as aluminum, this material cannot be replaced. If we begin recycling now, we can extend the life of the resources we have, leaving more resources in reserve for future generations.

Chemical reactions are almost always accompanied by changes in energy. For example, if we burn a log, energy is released in the form of heat and light. Chemical reactions that release energy are called **exothermic**. On the other hand, if you apply a chemical cold pack to a sprained ankle, the cooling is the result of a chemical change that is occurring within the cold pack. A chemical reaction that absorbs energy (gets cold) is called **endothermic**.

The source of most of these energy changes lies within the chemical bonds. Energy is always released when a bond is formed; conversely, energy is always absorbed when a bond is broken. When we form new compounds, we are forming new bonds, but the old bonds (the bonds in the reactants) must be broken first. If we release more energy in forming the bonds in the products than is required to break the bonds of the reactants, then the reaction is exothermic. However, if it costs more energy to break the bonds in the reactants than is released in the bonds formed in the products, then the reaction will be endothermic. The heat of the reaction, called **enthalpy**, can be used to tell us the relative energies of the bonds in the products and the reactants.

$$2H_2 + O_2 \longrightarrow 2H_2O$$

In the figure above, we see two ways of writing the reaction of hydrogen with oxygen: the traditional way on top, and a more graphical way beneath. Again, notice that the Law of Conservation of Matter is conserved in both depictions. The reaction of hydrogen in oxygen is notoriously exothermic, releasing great amounts of heat; all of this energy comes from the formation of new bonds in the water (product). However, some energy first had to be absorbed to break the preexisting bonds of the hydrogen and oxygen (reactants). This reaction led to the Hindenburg disaster in which the hydrogen-filled zeppelin burst into flames and killed many passengers in what was at the time one of the most luxurious modes of transportation known. It's because of the energy required to break the hydrogen and oxygen bonds, however, that allowed the lighter-than-air craft to fly over the Atlantic before exploding over the American shores.

Keep in mind the Law of Conservation of Energy. If energy is released, it must have been stored somewhere within the reactants to begin with. Thus, the potential energy stored within reactants is being released during an exothermic reaction. Similarly, energy can only be absorbed in an endothermic reaction if that energy is being stored in the form of potential energy in the products. After a great deal of experimenting, however, it was discovered that there was another source of energy other than the bonds. In fact, if there were not, endothermic reactions would not even be possible. We call this source of energy entropy.

Entropy is typically defined as disorder: the higher the disorder, the higher the entropy. Although this is not a very good description of entropy, it is useful in predicting entropy changes. For example, we might expect a gas, whose molecules can move about freely, to have a higher entropy than a solid, whose molecules are fixed relative to one another. Since molecules cannot move in a solid (outside of vibrations), they must have low entropy..

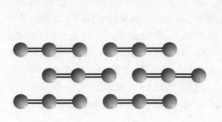 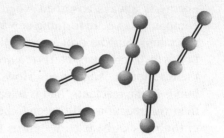

Solid; highly ordered, low entropy   Gas; randomly distributed, low order, high entropy

As it turns out, entropy has a desire to be high; to cause a reduction of entropy, we must supply energy. Because of this, we can think of entropy as a form of internal energy cost as we create change in our system.

Reversible Reactions

We have a tendency to think of reactions as being one shot only: that is, once the reaction happens, it is over. This is not always true: in fact, many reactions can proceed either forward or backward (that is, either from reactants to products or from products to reactants).

$$H_2O(l) + CO_2(g) \rightleftharpoons H_2CO_3(aq)$$

Above we have a famous reversible reaction: carbon dioxide dissolves in water to form carbonic acid, but carbonic acid can also break down to form carbon dioxide in water. Soft drink manufacturers use the forward reaction by adding a lot of carbon dioxide to form carbonated beverages (note that they are always stored under high pressure). However, the reverse reaction is very dangerous during hyperventilation; loss of carbon dioxide in hyper-ventilation causes the loss of carbonic acid, H_2CO_3, which can cause our bodies to become too basic (or alkaline, called alkalosis). The letters in parentheses provide additional information by telling us the state of each reactant and product ("l" for liquid, "g" for gas, and "aq" for aqueous, meaning "dissolved in water").

We call these reversible reactions, and they are necessary to sustain life. Consider, for example, ATP and ADP. ATP is an energy-producing molecule that, on decomposition, releases energy and creates ADP. It is found in many metabolic processes. If this were a one-way reaction, the body would have to discard the ADP, which would be a tremendous waste of material. Instead, the ADP participates in another reaction, which takes ADP as a reactant, and produces ATP, which is then available for another cellular function.

EXERCISE 1

Directions: Choose the <u>one best answer</u> for each item.

1. What can we deduce about the reaction H_2CO_3 (aq) —> H_2O (l) + CO_2 (g)?

    (1)   Nothing more can be deduced.

    (2)   It is endothermic.

    (3)   Its entropy is decreasing.

    (4)   It is exothermic.

    (5)   Its entropy is increasing.

2.   What is wrong with the reaction H_2SO_4 (aq) + NaOH (s) —> Na_2SO_4 (aq) + H_2O (l)?

    (1)   It violates the Law of Conservation of Energy.

    (2)   The compounds are written incorrectly.

    (3)   These reactants will not react.

    (4)   It violates the Law of Conservation of Matter.

    (5)   The reaction is written using the wrong notation.

3. Of the following processes, which is not a chemical reaction?

    (1)   A car catches on fire after a collision.

    (2)   A piece of bread begins to grow mold.

    (3)   Water is driven off of a solution, leaving behind salt.

    (4)   A drug combats high cholesterol.

    (5)   An athlete eats food that will later supply the energy necessary to win the competition.

KINETICS

*   **Particle Size.** Just because a reaction will occur does not mean that the reaction will occur quickly enough to be noticeable or of practical use. The study of how quickly a chemical reaction occurs is called **kinetics**. As it turns out, we have quite a bit of control over how quickly chemical reactions can occur. Among the factors that can influence reaction rate is particle size. For reactions to occur, the reactants must be in contact; the smaller the particles, the greater the surface area, and therefore the more area that is in contact and that can react. If you think about this, it means that dust is more likely to react rapidly than, say, grains. This leads to periodic (and all too often tragic) grain elevator explosions: as the grain is loaded, small particles flake off the grain in the form of dust. When these tiny dust particles begin to react, they react very rapidly, and therefore violently, leading to an explosion. Technology designed to reduce the threat of grain elevator explosions is often directed toward reducing dust accumulation in the elevator.

- **Temperature.** Another factor that can influence reaction rate is temperature. Chemical reactions occur faster at higher temperatures, because the molecules and atoms are moving faster to begin with. If you think about metabolism as a collection of chemical reactions, this leads to an understanding of a very common phenomenon in people with high fevers: rapid respiration rate. If you have a high fever, your body temperature is higher than normal; thus, all of the chemical reactions in your body increase as well. As these chemical reactions speed up, more oxygen will be required, and carbon dioxide will be produced at an abnormally high rate (the end product of the metabolic process). To get the required oxygen and dispose of the excess carbon dioxide, people with high fevers tend to breathe faster than normal.

- **Concentration.** If the reaction involves a solution, we generally find that the higher the concentration of the reactants, the faster the reaction will occur. This is because the higher the concentration, the more reactants that are present and available to react. This is seen in unusual ways; for example, one of the major metabolites (chemicals used in metabolism; food) in algae is phosphate. If we allow too many phosphates into lakes or streams, we are increasing their concentration; thus, the chemical reactions (metabolism) that result in the production of more algae increases as well. If too many algae are produced, they will use up too much oxygen in lakes, causing fish to die. This is the primary driving force behind phosphate-free detergents.

- **Catalysts.** Finally, chemical reactions can be increased by the addition of a catalyst. Catalysts are chemicals that speed up reactions but are not consumed in the reaction themselves; thus, when the reaction is complete, we will have just as much catalyst as we added in the first place. Catalysts occur both naturally and artificially. Within our bodies, enzymes are catalysts; they speed up the metabolic reactions. These reactions could occur without the enzymes, but too slowly to support life; thus, enzymes are a convenient way for the body to control our metabolism. Probably the most important artificial catalyst is the catalytic converter. These devices are placed in the exhaust manifold of automobiles and catalyze the reaction that converts carbon monoxide, a deadly gas, into carbon dioxide. Without catalytic converters, our carbon monoxide output would be at dangerous levels. Incidentally, carbon monoxide is a by-product of any burning process; thus, if you have a fireplace, gas- or oil-burning furnace, gas stove, or any other fuel-burning device in your house, it is a good idea to get a carbon monoxide detector. Carbon monoxide is colorless and odorless and can kill at very low concentrations.

Ways to Increase a Reaction Rate

Property	To speed up a chemical reaction...
Size of reactants	...make reactants smaller to increase their surface area
Temperature	...increase temperature
Concentration	...increase concentration of your reactants if they are in a solution
Catalysts	...add a catalyst

EXERCISE 2

Directions: Choose the <u>one best answer</u> .

1. Why does refrigeration make food last longer?
   (1)   Light is not a catalyst in the dark refrigerator.
   (2)   Reactions stop at a lower temperature.
   (3)   Reactions are slower at a lower temperature.
   (4)   The concentration of decay-causing microbes is smaller in the refrigerator.
   (5)   The lower temperature kills microbes.

EQUILIBRIUM

If we combine the concept of kinetics and reversible reactions, we stumble upon a concept called **equilibrium**. It is always a mistake to think of chemistry as static; there is always something going on—vibration, rotation, or, in the case of a reversible reaction, the reaction continuing to occur in both the forward and reverse direction.

If we have a mixture of reactants and products together in an enclosed container for a reversible reaction, the reaction is continuously occurring in both the forward and the reverse direction. However, if the mixture is at equilibrium, then the reaction is occurring in both directions at exactly the same rate. Thus, the forward reaction is creating products just as quickly as the reverse direction is consuming these products. The end result of this is that there is no way to detect any kind of change in the system over time.

$$2NO_2(g) \rightleftharpoons N_2O_4(g)$$

It is important to note that equilibrium does not mean we have equal numbers of reactants and products; only that, as a function of time, the relative number of reactants and products does not change. The reaction continues in both directions at equilibrium, but at exactly the same rate; thus, N_2O_4 is broken down as quickly as it is formed; thus, the total number of N_2O_4 won't change. The temperature, the pressure, and most important, the concentration of the reactants will not change from one moment to the next.

There are several ways to disturb equilibrium. If a gas is present, either as a product or a reactant, then a change in pressure will influence equilibrium; increasing pressure always favors the side with less gas. For example, consider a carbonated beverage. Carbonation means that carbon dioxide has been dissolved in the liquid. This is how the liquid remains carbonated: under high pressure, more carbon dioxide will dissolve than at low pressures, because the more carbon dioxide in the liquid, the less in the gaseous form. We see that this is true because, when we open the container, the pressure decreases. If increasing pressure favors less gas, then decreasing pressure will favor more gas; thus, the carbon dioxide in the container begins coming out of the container in the form of gas bubbles (more gas).

Increasing temperature always favors the endothermic side of equilibrium. As with any reversible reaction, one direction will absorb heat, while the other will release heat. For example, suppose we have excess solid salt in a saturated solution. Dissolution of salt into a solution is usually an endothermic process; that is, dissolving salt makes the solution colder. If we have the solid salt in contact with a saturated solution, then we have set up equilibrium, in which the rate at which the solid salt is dissolving is exactly equal to the rate at which the salt is coming out of solution. Thus, it appears as if the salt has finished dissolving. However, if we heat the solution, we will favor the side of the reaction that absorbs heat: dissolving absorbs heat, so heating the solution will favor dissolving more salt, and the solubility of the salt increases as the temperature increases. When we heat the solution up, more salt will dissolve. Consider, for example, the formation of ammonia from nitrogen and hydrogen (below). Notice that to maximize the amount of ammonia we produce, we will want to use high pressure and low temperature.

$$N_2(g) + 3H_2(g) \rightleftharpoons 2NH_3(g) + heat$$

Endothermic side
More gas (4 particles)
Favored by low pressure
Favored by high temperature

Exothermic side
Less gas (2 particles)
Favored by high pressure
Favored by low temperature

You may think that adding a catalyst will influence equilibrium. In fact, it will not. It is true that a catalyst will speed up a chemical reaction, but it always increases both directions of an equilibrium equally. Thus, adding a catalyst will not change the equilibrium at all. This may seem at odds with what you know about ozone, since scientists are concerned about the catalytic destruction of ozone through the use of CFCs (chlorofluorocarbons). If we have an equilibrium between oxygen and ozone, then a catalyst should not disturb this equilibrium at all. In fact, the CFC catalyst does NOT disturb the ozone-oxygen equilibrium, but it *does* force a mixture of ozone and oxygen to reach equilibrium concentrations more quickly.

As it turns out, the ozone-oxygen concentrations in the upper atmosphere are not at the concentrations we would expect in equilibrium. This is because the ozone is being produced too rapidly in electrical storms (most common around the equator) for true chemical equilibrium to be reached. This ozone takes time to decompose, so it diffuses from the equator toward the poles. Chemicals always move from regions of high concentration, in this case the equator, where they are produced, to regions of low concentration. We call this *diffusion*.

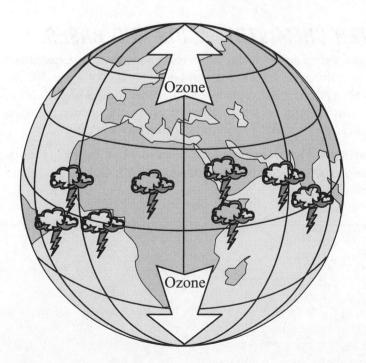

The presence of CFCs causes the ozone to decompose more rapidly than it should; thus, the CFCs are not changing the equilibrium, but they are forcing the ozone and oxygen more rapidly to reach their equilibrium concentrations, which are too low to protect us from UV light.

EXERCISE 3

Directions: Choose the <u>one best answer</u> for each item.

1. An industrial process that relies on the reversible chemical reaction (equilibrium), REACTANTS ↔ PRODUCTS, produces a better yield at high temperatures. What can we deduce about this reaction?
   (1)   The reaction increases in entropy in the forward direction.
   (2)   Nothing more can be deduced.
   (3)   The reaction is exothermic in the forward direction.
   (4)   The reaction decreases in entropy in the forward direction.
   (5)   The reaction is endothermic in the forward direction.

2. When will an equilibrium stop?
   (1)   When we have more reactant than product
   (2)   When we have more product than reactant
   (3)   Never
   (4)   When the concentrations of the reactant and product reach their equilibrium values
   (5)   When the concentrations of the product and reactant are equal

WATER CHEMISTRY: ACIDS AND BASES

Chemistry that occurs within water is of great interest to us as human beings because of the critical role water plays in both our ecology and our anatomy. On Earth, it is the great abundance of water that sustains life, while our bodies themselves are primarily comprised of water. If we are discussing water chemistry, we are usually describing acid/base reactions.

An **acid** is any ionic compound that has the hydronium ion, H^+, as its cation. A **base** is any ionic compound with a hydroxide, OH^-, as its anion.

Acids and Bases

Acid	Ions comprising the acid	Base	Ions comprising the base
Hydrochloric HCl	H^+ and Cl^-	Sodium hydroxide	Na^+ and OH^-
Hydrobromic HBr	H^+ and Br^-	Potassium hydroxide	K^+ and OH^-
Nitric HNO_3	H^+ and NO_3^-	Ammonium hydroxide	NH_4^+ and OH^-
Carbonic H_2CO_3	$2 H^+$ and CO_3^-	Calcium hydroxide $Ca(OH)_2$	Ca^{+2} and $2 OH^-$
Sulfuric H_2SO_4	$2 H^+$ and SO_4^-	Magnesium hydroxide $Mg(OH)_2$	Mg^{+2} and $2 OH^-$
Phosphoric H_3PO_4	$3 H^+$ and PO_4^{-3}	Aluminum hydroxide $Al(OH)_3$	Al^{+3} and $3 OH^-$

Thus, an acidic solution will have more hydronium ions than hydroxide ions, while a basic (or alkaline) solution will have more hydoxide ions than hydronium ions. As you might imagine, if you react an acid with a base, or H^+ with OH^-, the result is simply water, H_2O. This is referred to as a **neutralization reaction.** A neutralization reaction is a reaction between an acid and a base, and it results in the formation of water and a salt, as shown by the two examples below.

$$2HBr \text{ (aq)} + Ca(OH)_2 \text{ (aq)} \rightarrow CaBr_2 \text{ (aq)} + 2H_2O \text{ (l)}$$

$$3H_2SO_4 \text{ (aq)} + Al(OH)_3 \text{ (aq)} \rightarrow Al_2(SO_4)_3 \text{ (aq)} + 3H_2O \text{ (l)}$$

We have a very convenient and simple way of measuring and expressing the acidity of a solution, the pH scale. **pH** is an inverse measure of the concentration of hydronium ions; thus, the lower the pH, the greater the number of hydronium ions, and the more acidic the solution. On the other hand, the greater the pH, the greater the concentration of hydroxide ions, and the more basic, or alkaline, the solution will be. A pH of 7 has as many hydronium as hydroxide ions, and the solution is exactly neutral. A pH less than 7 is acidic, while a pH greater than 7 is basic.

EXERCISE 4

Directions: Choose the <u>one best answer</u> for each item.

1. A solution with pH 3.99 is
   - (1) a base.
   - (2) an acid.
   - (3) a salt.
   - (4) an ion.
   - (5) neutral.

2. Lemon juice, which contains citric acid, is added to fish to cut the fishy smell, which is attributed to an amine compound, a base. Why does lemon juice cut the fishy smell?
   - (1) Lemon is a natural cleaning solvent.
   - (2) An acid and a base form a salt.
   - (3) This is a fallacy with no foundation in science.
   - (4) An acid and a base form water.
   - (5) The smell of lemon masks the fishy smell.

ANSWERS AND EXPLANATIONS

UNIT 1: MOTION: SPEED, VELOCITY, AND ACCELERATION

Exercise 1

1. **The correct answer is (4). (Fundamental understandings)** The speedometer cannot measure direction, and hence it cannot measure velocity. It basically measures the speed at any one time, hence it cannot measure the average speed. The odometer measures the distance.

2. **The correct answer is (2). (Fundamental understandings)** Average driving speed is obtained by dividing travel distance, D, by travel time, t, expressed as $V = \dfrac{D}{t}$. In this problem, the travel distance is given as 240 miles. Total trip time is obtained by finding the time from 7 a.m. to 11:30 a.m., which is 4.5 hours. From this 4.5 hours we need to deduct the 30-minute (0.5 hour) breakfast time, to find the travel time, which is therefore 4 hours. Dividing 240 miles by 4 hours will give 60 mph.

3. **The correct answer is (1). (Fundamental understandings)** When an object is at rest, it does not move. This means that its distance does not change. In the first graph only the distance, X, is constant. It is changing in all other cases.

4. **The correct answer is (3). (Fundamental understandings)** Acceleration is the time rate at which the velocity changes. Hence the answer is choice (3).

5. **The correct answer is (3). (Fundamental understandings)** Acceleration, a, is obtained by dividing the change in velocity by the time it took for that change, $a = \dfrac{\Delta V}{\Delta t}$. The change in velocity is 56 mph – 0, or 56 mph. The time is 8 seconds. Hence, dividing 56 mph by 8 s gives 7 mph/s.

6. **The correct answer is (2). (Unifying concepts and processes)** As can be seen from the graph, the runner starts to run from rest and reaches 5 m/s in 3 s and maintains this velocity from 3 s to 6 s. After that, the runner's velocity decreases. Hence, the runner's maximum velocity is 5 m/s.

7. **The correct answer is (4). (Unifying concepts and processes)** As can be read from the graph, the velocity at 6.5 s is 4 m/s.

8. **The correct answer is (1). (Fundamental understandings)** As can be seen from the graph, the runner's velocity increases from $t = 0$ to $t = 3$ s. This means that the runner accelerates from $t = 0$ to $t = 3$ s.

9. **The correct answer is (5). (Fundamental understandings)** According to the graph, the velocity is constant at 5 m/s from 3 s to 6 s. This means that the acceleration is zero during this time interval. Since 5 s is within this time interval, the instantaneous acceleration is zero at 5 s.

UNIT 2: FORCE AND THE LAWS OF MOTION

Exercise 1

1. **The correct answer is (1). (Fundamental understandings)** Inertia is the tendency of an object to remain either at rest or in motion. Newton's First Law of Motion is also known as the Law of Inertia.

2. **The correct answer is (3). (Unifying concepts and processes)** The downward force of the exploding fuel produces an equal and opposite reaction: the skyward movement of the rocket. Although the other statements are true explanations of situations in physics, they do not apply to this example.

3. **The correct answer is (4). (Unifying concepts and processes)** Newton's Second Law of Motion can be used to calculate the acceleration when the net force and mass are given. Acceleration is obtained by dividing the net force, 3270 N, by mass, 1635 kg. The answer is 2 N/kg. Since N = kg m/s^2, N/kg is the same as m/s^2.

4. **The correct answer is (2). (Fundamental understandings)** The net force is the difference between the force exerted by the engine and the total frictional force. In other words, the total frictional force is equal to the difference between the force exerted by the engine and the net force. Hence, the total frictional force equals 4250 N – 3270 N, or 980 N.

5. **The correct answer is (4). (Science as inquiry)** The effort increases with increasing weight and is different for different surfaces. Choice (4) correctly describes these two results. The other variables are not tested in this activity.

Exercise 2

1. **The correct answer is (2). (Fundamental understandings)** The construction worker is moving the heaviest load and, according to the laws of physics, is doing the most work. None of the others is moving as heavy a load. The stranded motorist is not moving anything, and thus is doing no work.

2. **The correct answer is (5). (Fundamental understandings)** The key point here is the stationary wall. Since the wall is not moving, no work is done on the wall, although Joe and John may have had a workout.

3. **The correct answer is (3). (Unifying concepts and processes)** Newton's Second Law gives us a relationship among force, mass, and acceleration: force = mass × acceleration. Inserting the units will give $N = kg \ m/s^2$.

4. **The correct answer is (1). (Fundamental understandings)** The joule, J, is the unit for energy. Gravitational potential energy (PE) equals mass times gravity times height. Inserting the units will give, $J = kg \ m/s^2 \ m = kg \ m^2/s^2$.

5. **The correct answer is (4). (Fundamental understandings)** The watt, W, is the unit for power. Power is the rate of doing work, or work/time. Work has the same unit as energy. Inserting the units will give $W = kg \ m^2/s^2 \div s = kg \ m^2/s^3$.

6. **The correct answer is (3). (Unifying concepts and processes)** The roller coaster has gravitational potential energy at Q, $PE = mgh$. As it moves down, the potential energy is converted into kinetic energy.

   At R, it has only kinetic energy, $KE = \frac{1}{2}mV^2$. Using the conservation of energy we get $PE = KE$, or $\frac{1}{2}mV^2 = mgh$. Solving this equation will yield, $V = \sqrt{2gh}$. Substituting $g = 9.8 \ m/s^2$ and $h = 50$ m will yield $V = 31.3$ m/s.

7. **The correct answer is (4). (Unifying concepts and processes)** Work is force multiplied by distance. In climbing up the steps, work is done to lift the weight of the person. Weight is obtained by multiplying mass by gravity, $102 \ kg \times 9.8 \ m/s^2 = 999.6 \ kg.m/s^2$. Hence work = 999.6 $kg.m/s^2 \times 5$ m = 4998 $kg \ m^2/s^2$ = 4998 J.

8. **The correct answer is (3). (Unifying concepts and processes)** Power is rate of doing work, or power = work/time. We calculated the work in item (7), 4998 J. Dividing this by the given time, 15 s, we can get the power, 333 J/s = 333 W.

UNIT 3: TEMPERATURE AND HEAT

Exercise 1

1. **The correct answer is (3). (Fundamental understandings)** The temperature is given in Celsius units, and we need to convert it to the Fahrenheit scale. The temperature conversion equation to use here is

$$Tf = \frac{9}{5}T_c + 32.$$ Evaluating this will yield 71.6, and rounding that answer will yield 72.

2. **The correct answer is (1). (Fundamental understandings)** First we need to convert the temperature to the Celsius scale, then to the Fahrenheit scale. Using $Tk = T_c + 273$ will yield a temperature of

$-196°$ C. Now using $Tf = \frac{9}{5}T_c + 32$ will yield $-320.8°$ F.

3. **The correct answer is (1). (Fundamental understandings)** The steel tape measure has been calibrated at 25° C. It will shrink a little at 5° C, and it will become a little shorter. When you use this shortened steel tape measure, the measurement will be a little higher.

4. **The correct answer is (2). (Unifying concepts and processes)** The person needs to convert all the energy from the drink to gravitational potential energy, E = mgh. The total height is given by E/mg = (140 × 4186)/(72 × 9.8) = 830.5 m. The number of stairs is obtained by dividing the total height by the height of one stair, 18 cm = 0.18 m, 830.5/0.18 = 4614.

5. **The correct answer is (4). (Fundamental understandings)** Conduction and convection require a medium to transfer heat. Radiation is not affected by vacuum.

6. **The correct answer is (2). (Fundamental understandings)** Heat flows from a warm place to a cold place. None of the other choices reflects the Second Law of Thermodynamics.

UNIT 4: WAVES, MAGNETISM, AND ELECTRICITY

Exercise 1

1. **The correct answer is (3). (Comprehension)** The human ear can detect sounds with frequencies from 20 to 20,000 hertz.

2. **The correct answer is (2). (Application)** The diagram illustrates frequency. Hertz is the unit used to measure frequency. The other terms are concepts in physics but are not related to the diagram in any way.

3. **The correct answer is (3). (Analysis)** High-frequency waves have shorter wavelengths. None of the other statements is accurate.

4. **The correct answer is (2). (Evaluation)** Curves in a mirror distort the reflected light rays. None of the other answers provides an explanation of the distortion.

Exercise 2

1. **The correct answer is (3). (Application)** Static electricity causes the crackling sound you hear when you comb your hair on a dry day. Choices (1), (4), and (5) have nothing to do with this phenomenon. There is low humidity in the air on a dry day, but low humidity does not make the crackling sound as suggested in choice (2).

2. **The correct answer is (4). (Evaluation)** A charge of 1,000 coulombs divided by 10 seconds equals 100 amps. None of the other situations would produce this answer.

3. **The correct answer is (2). (Analysis)** The magnetic north pole is at a slightly different location from the geographic North Pole, so even when standing at the most northern place on the earth, you would not see the magnet pointing straight down. Neither temperature nor distance from the pole would affect this. Choices (4) and (5) are not true.

4. **The correct answer is (5). (Analysis)** The nails fall to the ground because the magnetic field of the magnet becomes weaker as it is pulled away from the nails. There is no evidence to support choice (1). The force of gravity pulls the nails to the floor—not the magnetic field of the earth, as described in choice (2). Choices (3) and (4) are not true.

5. **The correct answer is (2). (Evaluation)** A potential difference of 110 volts divided by 10 amps = 11 ohms. All of the other circuits have different resistance values.

6. **The correct answer is (3). (Comprehension)** Resistance is the term that means opposition to the flow of electric current. The other terms, although relevant to the subject of electricity, have different meanings.

7. **The correct answer is (2). (Comprehension)** Thick wire offers less resistance than thin wire. When you replace a thin wire with a thicker one, the resistance in the circuit goes down. Choices (1), (3), and (4) would increase the resistance. Choice (5) would stop the flow of electricity.

8. **The correct answer is (4). (Application)** The plastic coatings insulate the wires so that electricity is confined to the wires. In preventing the electric current from passing through alternate paths, the plastic covering acts as an insulator.

9. **The correct answer is (2). (Application)** The amp gauge measures electric current. Starting your car initiates the flow of electricity from the battery to the starter, which is a drain on electric current from the battery. Once the alternator begins working, it feeds electric current back to the battery, and you see the amp gauge move to "+".

UNIT 5: CHEMISTRY

Exercise 1

1. **The correct answer is (1). (Fundamental understandings)** Sand, water, and food all have mass and volume. Air might seem like the correct answer because, even though it has volume, it seems as though it does not have mass. In fact, air does have mass (which gives rise to air pressure); it is just difficult to measure. Light, on the other hand, does not have volume or mass. Therefore, light cannot be matter.

2. **The correct answer is (2). (Fundamental understandings)** There is some fluctuation in the graph, but the points seem to line up well. These minor fluctuations are caused by random error; we could still draw a pretty good line through all of them. Choice (1) is incorrect because it is not precise enough.

3. **The correct answer is (5). (History and nature of science)** Doubtless, Christopher Columbus did a fair amount of literature searching before the trip, but he was originally seeking a shorter trade route to China. If he suspected that the Americas existed, he would not have been looking for this alternative route. The Vikings never reported their findings because there is evidence they wanted to save the discovery for their own use, and those already living in the Americas would not have reported the discovery of their own native land.

Exercise 2

1. **The correct answer is (3). (Fundamental understandings)** A perpetual motion machine is not possible because it would represent continuous kinetic energy without potential energy.

2. **The correct answer is (5). (Unifying concepts and processes)** The car either has more mass or was moving faster than the truck. Typically, cars are lighter than trucks, but we cannot discount the possibility that, despite its size, the truck is lighter and the car is

heavier. Either way, the car must have greater momentum, which can be achieved either by having greater velocity and less mass or by having greater mass and equal or less velocity.

3. **The correct answer is (4). (Fundamental understanding)** Your dance partner does not change in mass (or weight), so it cannot be more or less mass or weight. What's more, although the mass is related, it's your partner's weight (the force pressing on your foot) that will cause the pain. If we divide the force (in this case the weight) by the area (smaller for the heel), we have pressure (weight per unit volume). The smaller the area, the greater the pressure.

Exercise 3

1. **The correct answer is (3). (Fundamental understandings)** This is a state change, such as dry ice changing from a solid to a gas, but it is still carbon dioxide. Digestibility implies that the material can be broken down into nutrients by the body; this is a chemical change.

UNIT 6: DEVELOPMENT OF ATOMIC THEORY

Exercise 1

1. **The correct answer is (2). (Fundamental understandings)** It is a compound. That it can be broken down implies that there is more than one component, and what it breaks down into has very different chemical characteristics (one is explosive, the other is not). What's more, the ratio of these gases is always the same, and it is a ratio of simple fixed whole numbers. If the products were not always the same, we would have a mixture.

Exercise 2

1. **The correct answer is (4). (Fundamental understandings)** It is attracted to the negative plate, but only slightly, implying it has a negative charge and is heavy.

2. **The correct answer is (2). (Fundamental understandings)** If the particles are spread out as in a cloud, the beam should have passed through them without hindrance. What's more, Rutherford's experiment did not address what particles were present; it merely addressed the structure of these particles.

Exercise 3

1. **The correct answer is (1). (Fundamental understandings)** Recall that the number of protons is the atomic number of the element, and the element with atomic number 32 is Germanium.

2. **The correct answer is (2). (Fundamental understandings)** For unstable elements like Americium, the integer represents the atomic mass number of the most stable isotope, in this case 243, but the atomic mass number is equal to the number of protons plus the number of neutrons. Thus, we have $243 - 95 = 148$ neutrons.

3. **The correct answer is (3). (Fundamental understandings)** Remember that when elements react, it is only their valence shell electrons that interact. If elements are behaving in similar ways, then their valence shells must have similar properties. To say that they have similar reactivities is simply repeating the question.

4. **The correct answer is (2). (Fundamental understandings)** Antimony is actually a metalloid.

UNIT 7: TYPES OF CHEMICAL COMPOUNDS

Exercise 1

1. **The correct answer is (5). (Unifying concepts and processes)** To answer this question correctly, you would have to bring together a lot of information. Recall that elements will change the number of electrons they have (in the formation of compounds) to gather a complete octet. Thus, we can assume that an element that is inert (nonreactive) does not have to change the number of electrons it has, because it probably already has a completed octet. The only family on the periodic chart that is nonreactive is the noble gases.

2. **The correct answer is (3). (Fundamental understandings)** The ionic bond is nothing more than the electrostatic attraction of cations (positively charged ions) for anions (negatively charged ions). The primary difference is that in intermolecular forces, we have only partial charges, but they still amount to attraction of opposite charges.

Exercise 2

1. **The correct answer is (4). (Fundamental understandings)** In water, only ionic compounds dissociate to make the solution capable of conducting electricity. Metals can conduct electricity, but do not dissociate, so they would not make a solution capable of carrying electricity.

UNIT 8: INTERACTIONS OF MATTER AND ENERGY

Exercise 1

1. **The correct answer is (4). (Unifying concepts and processes)** The helium is moving faster than the argon. The gases are at the same temperature, so one cannot be cooling the other. However, we know that they must have the same kinetic energy if they are at the same temperature (not the same velocity). Because kinetic energy is related to mass, the lighter gas (helium) would have to be moving much faster than the heavier gas (argon). One should note, by the way, that the helium atoms would not be moving ten times faster just because argon is ten times heavier; the relationship between velocity and kinetic energy is not linear. (In fact, the helium would have to be moving only about three times faster to have the same kinetic energy.)

2. **The correct answer is (5). (Unifying concepts and processes)** Red absorbs blue light, and blue is higher energy than red. We know the paint is not emitting light, because we require light to be able to see it. Thus, the light is being absorbed. The only color we see is that which is reflected; therefore, the color absorbed is the color we do not see, which is blue, and as stated previously, blue light has more energy than red light. Because the color red is absorbing the higher energy light, it fades before the color blue.

Exercise 2

1. **The correct answer is (2). (Fundamental understandings)** We cannot speak of the kinetic energy; this is a function of temperature alone, and temperature is not given. However, the weaker the intermolecular forces, the weaker the molecules must be held in the liquid, and therefore, the more molecules that will "escape" the liquid into the gaseous state.

2. **The correct answer is (4). (Fundamental understandings)** We can see that the material assumes the shape of the container but does not occupy its entire volume. We cannot infer if this is a compound or an element since there are examples for both in all three states.

Exercise 3

1. **The correct answer is (5). (Fundamental understandings)** Because it is cloudy, more than one component must be present. This is not a solution, though, because the cloudiness is created by undissolved solute particles.

2. **The correct answer is (1). (Fundamental understandings)** If we know there is already solute present, and if it is clear, then it must be a solution. Because additional solute will dissolve, it cannot be saturated; it must be unsaturated.

UNIT 9: CHEMICAL REACTIONS

Exercise 1

1. **The correct answer is (5). (Unifying concepts and processes)** We cannot say whether or not it is giving off heat, but notice that we start with an aqueous substance (remember that aqueous means "dissolved in water"; it is a condensed state) and end up with a liquid and a gas. Conversion from a condensed state to a gas alone would lead us to suspect an increase in entropy (greater disorder), and the breakdown of one substance into two is an increase in entropy as well.

2. **The correct answer is (4). (Fundamental understandings)** Notice that there are two sodium atoms on the product side, but only one as a reactant. Other elements are off-balance as well, but sodium is the easiest to spot.

3. **The correct answer is (3). (Fundamental understandings)** In all other processes, a chemical reaction will occur, but in the solution, we had salt and water already, only dissolved. After the process, we still have salt and water, only as a solid and a vapor.

Exercise 2

1. **The correct answer is (3). (Fundamental understandings)** Reactions are slower at lower temperatures. Light is not a catalyst, because catalysts are chemicals, and the refrigerator is not a sterilization technique. It is important to note that chemical reactions do not stop at lower temperatures, but they do slow down, including the metabolic reactions in microbes that cause food decay.

Exercise 3

1. **The correct answer is (5). (Fundamental understandings)** The reaction is endothermic in the forward direction. If we increase temperature, the equilibrium will shift to try to absorb that excess heat; this means we will favor the endothermic direction, or the products.

2. **The correct answer is (3). (Fundamental understandings)** Remember that at equilibrium, the forward and reverse reactions do not stop; however, the rate of the forward reaction is equal to the rate of the reverse reaction. Also, one cannot assume anything about the equilib-

rium concentrations: some equilibrium reactions have a large amount of product compared to reactant, but some have a large amount of reactant compared to product, and some have similar concentrations of both. Choice (4) is incorrect because this statement does not assume anything about the concentrations. However, even in this case, when no observable change is occurring, the reaction still does not stop.

Exercise 4

1. **The correct answer is (3). (Fundamental understandings)** A pH of less than 7 is acidic, greater than 7 is basic, and about 7 is neutral.

2. **The correct answer is (2). (Unifying concepts and processes)** An acid and a base form a salt. The base that causes the fishy smell becomes part of a salt (a citrate salt, named for the citric acid). Because salts are not as volatile as bases (they do not evaporate as readily), the fishy smell is reduced.

GLOSSARY

chemistry: the scientific study of matter

physics: the scientific study of energy

science: a structured approach to understanding the world around us

observation: something we notice that strikes our interest and makes us want to understand it

hypothesis: a proposed explanation that is tested by means of an experiment

theory: a hypothesis that has been repeatedly tested

law: a theory that has been repeatedly tested

velocity: speed and direction

acceleration: the time rate at which velocity changes

force: a motivation to move or to change motion

inertia: the tendency of an object to remain either at rest or in motion

mass: the amount of matter an object contains

friction: the resistance to motion caused by the rubbing of surfaces against one another

work: the use of force to move something over a distance

power: the rate at which work is done

energy: the ability to do work

potential energy: the energy stored in an object as the result of the height it has been raised above the ground

kinetic energy: energy of motion

temperature: a measure of how hot or cold an object is

heat: energy transfer due to a temperature difference

conduction: transfer of heat between objects that are connected by a solid

convection: transfer of heat by movement of material from a hot region to a cold region

radiation: transfer of heat by means of electromagnetic waves

thermodynamics: the study of the movement of heat

matter: anything that has mass and occupies volume

volume: the amount of space something takes up

weight: a force defined as mass times the acceleration caused by gravity

momentum: the principle that an object in motion tends to stay in motion, while an object at rest tends to remain at rest, unless acted upon by an outside force

chemical properties: properties that, if changed, result in the formation of a different kind of matter

physical properties: properties that, if changed, do not fundamentally change the type of matter

chemical change: change that results in a different type of matter

physical change: change that results in a change of state or of some other physical property

element: a material that cannot be broken down into simpler materials

periodic table: a chart that arranges elements according to the chemical properties

electron: fundamental particle with a negative charge

proton: fundamental particle with a positive charge and a mass of 1

neutron: fundamental particle with a charge of 0 and a mass of 1

nucleus: dense core of an atom where neutrons and protons are found

cations: positively charged atoms

anions: negatively charged atoms

ions: all charged atoms, including cations and anions

metals: elements that conduct electricity and heat well, are malleable, tend to be shiny, and in compounds tend to lose electrons

nonmetals: elements that do not conduct electricity or heat, are brittle and dull, and gain electrons in compounds

atomic symbol: an element's one- or two-letter designation

atomic number: the number of protons in one atom of an element

atomic mass: the number of protons plus the number of neutrons in an atom of an element

isotopes: atoms with the same atomic numbers but different atomic mass

radioisotopes: atoms that decay to become different elements, releasing radiation as they do so

ionic compound: compound formed when one or more electrons are transferred from one atom to another

covalent compound: compound in which atoms share electrons

Octet Rule: tendency of atoms to lose, gain, or share electrons to maintain eight electrons in their outer shell

electronegativity: the pull an atom exerts on an electron

electrolyte: compound that causes water to conduct electricity

nonelectrolyte: compound that does not cause water to conduct electricity

magnetism: a force that attracts metals and other magnets

mixture: a combination of two or more components

solution: a homogenous mixture

solute: the active ingredient in a solution

solvent: what the solute is dissolved in; the delivery medium for the solute

chemical reaction: combining different materials to create a new material

oxidation: chemical reaction that involves the transfer of one or more electrons

exothermic: chemical reaction that releases energy

endothermic: chemical reaction that absorbs energy

enthalpy: the heat of a reaction

entropy: disorder

kinetics: the study of how quickly chemical reactions occur

equilibrium: the condition when a reaction occurs in a mixture in both forward and reverse directions at the same time, resulting in no detectable change

acid: any ionic compound that has the hydronium ion, H^+, as its cation

base: any ionic compound with a hydroxide, OH^-, as its anion

neutralization reaction: a reaction between an acid and a base, resulting in the formation of water and a salt

pH: an inverse measure of the concentration of hydronium ions; the lower the pH, the greater the number of hydronium ions and the more acidic the solution

Practice Tests

PRACTICE TEST 1

Answer Sheet

1 ① ② ③ ④ ⑤   6 ① ② ③ ④ ⑤   11 ① ② ③ ④ ⑤

2 ① ② ③ ④ ⑤   7 ① ② ③ ④ ⑤   12 ① ② ③ ④ ⑤

3 ① ② ③ ④ ⑤   8 ① ② ③ ④ ⑤   13 ① ② ③ ④ ⑤

4 ① ② ③ ④ ⑤   9 ① ② ③ ④ ⑤   14 ① ② ③ ④ ⑤

5 ① ② ③ ④ ⑤   10 ① ② ③ ④ ⑤   15 ① ② ③ ④ ⑤

16 ① ② ③ ④ ⑤   21 ① ② ③ ④ ⑤   26 ① ② ③ ④ ⑤

17 ① ② ③ ④ ⑤   22 ① ② ③ ④ ⑤   27 ① ② ③ ④ ⑤

18 ① ② ③ ④ ⑤   23 ① ② ③ ④ ⑤   28 ① ② ③ ④ ⑤

19 ① ② ③ ④ ⑤   24 ① ② ③ ④ ⑤   29 ① ② ③ ④ ⑤

20 ① ② ③ ④ ⑤   25 ① ② ③ ④ ⑤   30 ① ② ③ ④ ⑤

31 ① ② ③ ④ ⑤   36 ① ② ③ ④ ⑤   41 ① ② ③ ④ ⑤

32 ① ② ③ ④ ⑤   37 ① ② ③ ④ ⑤   42 ① ② ③ ④ ⑤

33 ① ② ③ ④ ⑤   38 ① ② ③ ④ ⑤   43 ① ② ③ ④ ⑤

34 ① ② ③ ④ ⑤   39 ① ② ③ ④ ⑤   44 ① ② ③ ④ ⑤

35 ① ② ③ ④ ⑤   40 ① ② ③ ④ ⑤   45 ① ② ③ ④ ⑤

46 ① ② ③ ④ ⑤

47 ① ② ③ ④ ⑤

48 ① ② ③ ④ ⑤

49 ① ② ③ ④ ⑤

50 ① ② ③ ④ ⑤

Practice Test 1

Directions: Choose the <u>one best answer</u> for each item.

Items 1–3 refer to the following illustration and information.

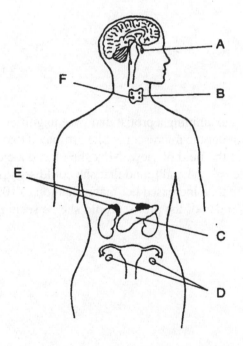

The endocrine glands pictured above secrete hormones into the bloodstream that act on certain tissues, known as target tissues, that have hormone receptors. These tissues respond to the hormones while others do not.

1. Which of the glands produce hormones that act on other glands?

    (1)   A

    (2)   A and B

    (3)   C

    (4)   D

    (5)   A and D

2. Which gland produces hormones that can increase your blood pressure and make your heart rate go up?

    (1)   A

    (2)   B

    (3)   C

    (4)   D

    (5)   E

3. Insulin and glucagon are produced by which gland?

    (1)   A

    (2)   B

    (3)   C

    (4)   D

    (5)   E

4. A student was examining a protist that was magnified 40 times larger than normal under the microscope. She estimated that the protist took up one-half of the field of view. Next she placed a clear plastic ruler under the microscope and found that she could see 4 mm in the field of view. If she then increased her magnification to 100 total magnifications, how much of the protist would she be seeing?

    (1)   0.1

    (2)   0.2

    (3)   0.4

    (4)   0.6

    (5)   0.8

5. The light reactions in photosynthesis produce more than one product. Two of these products are

    (1)   water and oxygen.

    (2)   oxygen and ATP.

    (3)   ATP and water.

    (4)   NADH and ATP.

    (5)   NADH and PGAL.

6. A student wanted to measure the rate of photosynthesis in a closed container. The implement he would most likely use is a
    (1)   thermometer.
    (2)   pH meter.
    (3)   microscope.
    (4)   barometer.
    (5)   turbidity device.

7. In the alternation of generations in mosses, the archegonium is
    (1)   the male structure and is diploid.
    (2)   the male structure and is haploid.
    (3)   the female structure and is diploid.
    (4)   the female structure and is haploid.
    (5)   part of the sporophyte.

8. A student put a rock in a graduated cylinder filled half with water. She was attempting to measure the rock's
    (1)   mass.
    (2)   volume.
    (3)   density.
    (4)   solubility.
    (5)   malleability.

9. A man drove 627.2 miles and used 14.1 gallons of gas. By dividing the former by the latter on his calculator, he obtained an answer of 44.48227. How many miles per gallon should he report?
    (1)   44.48227
    (2)   44.4823
    (3)   44.482
    (4)   44.48
    (5)   44.5

10. A volatile liquid has a density of 0.68 g/ml. What is the mass of 500 ml of this substance?
    (1)   340 g
    (2)   34 g
    (3)   735 g
    (4)   73.5 g
    (5)   34 kg

Items 11–13 refer to the following information.

Seawater is a complex solution of salts with an average salinity of about 3.5%. Salinity is a complex process that can be affected by temperature, depth, and density. Therefore, salinity varies by geography and is affected by local factors. Enclosed bays and harbors tend to have higher salinity, while polar waters tend to be slightly less salty due to the melting of ice from continental glaciers into the sea. The most common salt in seawater is sodium chloride (NaCl), or table salt. On average, over 23 grams of sodium chloride are found in 1 liter of ocean water.

11. If seawater has an average salinity of 3.5%, the amount of dissolved salts in 1 liter of seawater is about

    (1)   .35 g.

    (2)   3.5 g.

    (3)   35 g.

    (4)   350 g.

    (5)   3,500 g.

12. Over 2.5 billion tons of sediments are deposited in oceans annually, contributing the mineral base that is the source of seawater salinity. The most likely means of conveyance of the sediments to the ocean is

    (1)   beach erosion.

    (2)   rivers and streams.

    (3)   volcanism.

    (4)   offshore dumping.

    (5)   rain.

13. The passage states that it is common for bays and other restricted bodies of water to have salinity levels above 3.5%. Which of the following is likely to contribute to this situation?

    (1)   Decreased currents in the bay

    (2)   The emptying of river water into the bay

    (3)   Pollutants dumped into the bay

    (4)   Evaporation of the water in the bay

    (5)   Organic matter from plants and animals

Items 14–16 refer to the following information and illustration.

Opaque objects appear to be a certain color because they reflect light of that color. For instance, a banana is yellow because it primarily reflects yellow light and absorbs other colors, as shown in the figure. Since white light is made up of all colors, there is some light available for reflection for objects of any color.

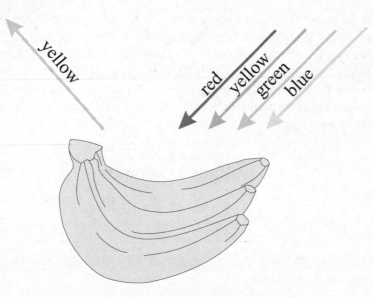

14. According to the passage above, the color of an opaque object depends on
    (1)   the color of the light falling on it.
    (2)   the color of the light transmitted through it.
    (3)   the intensity of the light falling on it.
    (4)   both (1) and (2).
    (5)   both (2) and (3).

15. A material that is red under white-light illumination appears
    (1)   green when illuminated by blue light.
    (2)   orange when illuminated by yellow light.
    (3)   dark green or black when illuminated by green light.
    (4)   red when illuminated by blue light.
    (5)   red when illuminated by green light.

16. If an object appears blue, you can conclude that it is being illuminated

    (1) only by blue light.

    (2) by a mixture of colors that includes blue.

    (3) by yellow light.

    (4) by some color of light other than blue.

    (5) by all colors except blue.

17. A permanent magnet consists of magnetic domains, which are groups of atoms aligned to make tiny magnets, as shown in the first figure below. When these domains are randomly aligned, their magnetic fields cancel and the magnet is demagnetized, as shown in the second figure below. Adding energy to the magnet tends to randomize the alignment of the domains. Which of these should be avoided to prevent demagnetization?

aligned domains

randomized domains

    (1) Heating the magnet

    (2) Striking the magnet with a hammer

    (3) Rotating the magnet through 360 degrees

    (4) Both (1) and (2)

    (5) All of the above

Items 18 and 19 refer to the following illustration.

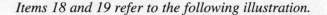

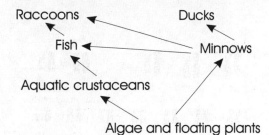

18. The diagram above shows that
    (1) algae and floating plants are the primary consumers.
    (2) aquatic crustaceans and minnows are the primary consumers.
    (3) fish and ducks are the primary consumers.
    (4) raccoons are the quaternary consumers.
    (5) fish eat raccoons.

19. If water contained 0.001 ppm of a nonbiodegradable substance, such as DDT, which of the following statements is the least likely to be correct?
    (1) The amount of DDT is more in 1 gram of duck than in 1 gram of minnow.
    (2) The amount of DDT could be as high as 10 ppm in raccoons.
    (3) The amount of DDT is higher in fish than in raccoons.
    (4) The amount of DDT is higher in crustaceans than in plants.
    (5) The amount of DDT could be as high as 1 ppm in fish.

Item 20 refers to the following illustration.

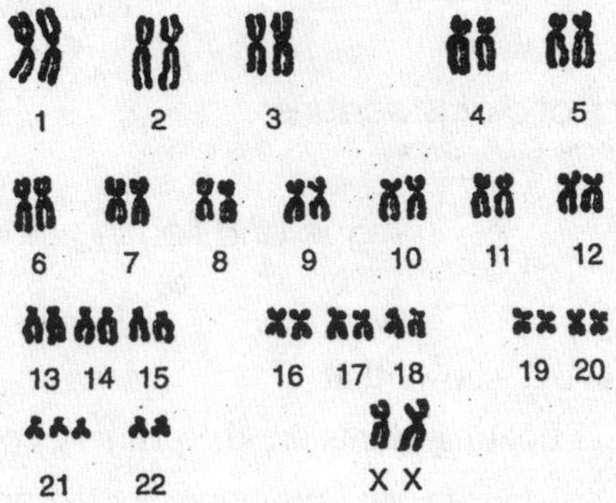

20. The above illustration is a karyotype, a picture of homologous chromosomes. Which of the following statements is most likely to be correct?

    (1) The chromosomes have to be human because there are 23 pairs, and only humans have 23 pairs.

    (2) The individual these chromosomes belong to is probably mentally affected.

    (3) The individual these chromosomes belong to is a boy with brown hair.

    (4) The individual these chromosomes belong to is a girl with black hair.

    (5) There isn't enough information in the karyotype to draw any conclusions.

21. The reason there is more biodiversity in land areas around the equator than around the 35° north or south latitude is that

    (1) plant life evolved at the equator.

    (2) there is more radiant energy at the equator.

    (3) there are fewer mountains at the equator.

    (4) the rain shadow effect is more pronounced at the equator.

    (5) animal life evolved at the equator.

22. After Watson and Crick discovered the structure of DNA in 1954, it was years before anyone could do anything like genetic engineering. The most important scientific discovery that led to the manipulation of DNA strands from one organism to another was the discovery of

    (1) restriction enzymes.
    (2) gel electrophoresis.
    (3) ethidium bromide.
    (4) triple helical DNA.
    (5) reverse transcriptase.

23. In order to elucidate the structure of DNA, Watson and Crick used information previously gained by

    (1) Stanley and Cohen.
    (2) Alfred Hershey and Martha Chase.
    (3) Messelson and Stahl.
    (4) Rosalind Franklin and Maurice Wilkins.
    (5) all of the above.

24. Atoms consist of a small, heavy nucleus surrounded by a cloud of electrons. The nucleus contains most of the mass of the atom. Which force holds the electrons in place around the nucleus?

    (1) Gravity
    (2) Electric
    (3) Magnetic
    (4) Nuclear
    (5) Caloric

25. Shorter-wavelength light scatters more efficiently from particles than longer-wavelength light, if these particles are much smaller than the wavelength. Air molecules are much smaller than any visible wavelengths, so more light on the blue end of the spectrum is scattered from the sun. This makes the sky blue. The Blue Ridge Mountains of North Carolina and Virginia are outlined in blue for much the same reason. From this, what conclusion can be drawn?

    (1) The mountains are made of blue rocks.
    (2) There is more air near the mountains than in most places, making them more blue.
    (3) The mountains are so high that they pick up some color from the sky.
    (4) The blue color is an illusion.
    (5) Small particles must be causing additional scattering near the mountain ridges.

26. A block slides down an inclined plane with little friction, as shown in the figure below.

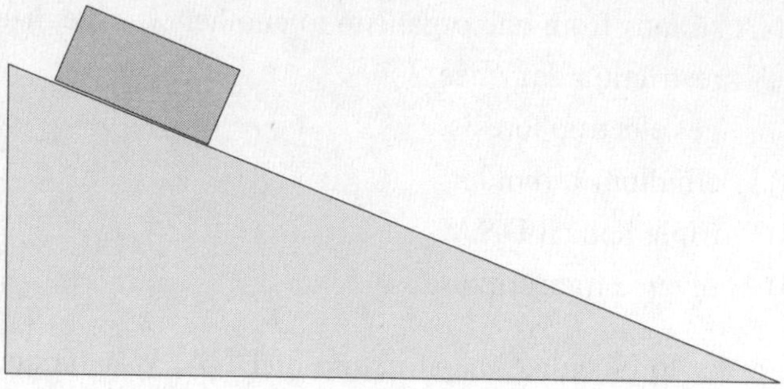

What would happen if the incline were made steeper?

(1) The block would slide more slowly because the incline pushes on the block more.

(2) The block would slide more slowly because there is more friction.

(3) The block would slide more quickly because the incline is not pushing the block up as much.

(4) The block would slide more quickly because the force of gravity is greater.

(5) The block would slide in the same amount of time because gravitational acceleration is a constant.

Items 27 and 28 refer to the following table.

Element	Molar mass
Hydrogen	1
Carbon	12
Nitrogen	14
Oxygen	16

27. Ammonia is made by the Haber process, which combines hydrogen and nitrogen according to the following formula:

$$3H_2 + N_2 = 2NH_3$$

How many grams of nitrogen would be needed to make 51 grams of ammonia?

(1) 46

(2) 42

(3) 31

(4) 28

(5) 21

28. A compound was analyzed and found to be composed of 40% carbon, 6.667% hydrogen, and 53.33% oxygen. What is the empirical formula for this compound?

    (1) CHO

    (2) C_2HO

    (3) CH_2O

    (4) C_2H_2O

    (5) CH_2O_2

Item 29 refers to the following diagram of ionization energies.

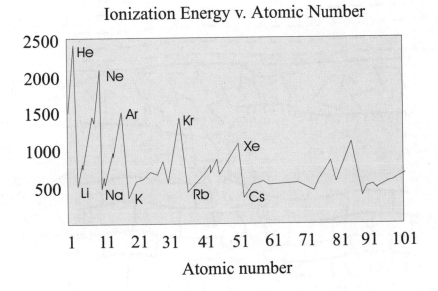

Ionization Energy v. Atomic Number

29. Within a row, the ionization energies generally increase from left to right. The above illustration and statement can be explained best by which of the following statements?

    (1) The buildup of electrons between the nucleus and the outer-most electrons shields those outermost electrons, which will be removed.

    (2) The increase of electrons in the lower energy levels is more important than the distance of the outermost electrons from the nucleus.

    (3) The increase in the number of electrons in the outermost shells will cause the ionization energies to increase.

    (4) The increase in ionization energy is the result of an increase in nuclear charge without an increase in shielding.

    (5) The increase in nuclear charge affects those electrons closest to the nucleus.

30. Which of the following is the correct formula for iron (III) oxide?
    (1) Fe_2O_3
    (2) FeO_2
    (3) Fe_2O_2
    (4) FeO_3
    (5) Fe_3O_2

Items 31–33 refer to the following illustration.

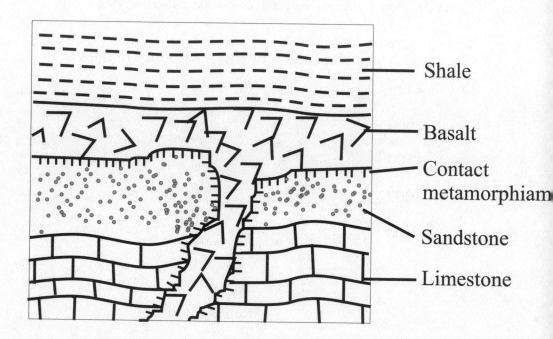

31. According to the law of superposition, which of the illustrated layers is the youngest?
    (1) Shale
    (2) Basalt
    (3) Sandstone
    (4) Limestone
    (5) Not enough information is given

32. Which of the layers in the diagram illustrates an igneous intrusion into sedimentary rock?
    (1) Shale
    (2) Basalt
    (3) Sandstone
    (4) Limestone
    (5) Not enough information is given

33. Which of the rock types listed below could be substituted for the basalt layer without changing the accuracy of the diagram?

    (1) Conglomerate
    (2) Marble
    (3) Schist
    (4) Granite
    (5) Chalk

Items 34 and 35 refer to the following illustration and information.

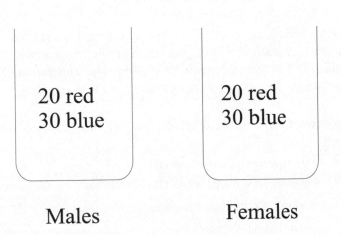

Males   Females

Each beaker represents the frequency of certain alleles of a gene pair in a sexually reproducing population. Assume that the beaker on the left represents males and the one on the right represents females.

34. If the act of sexual reproduction is the union of one allele from each container, what is the probability that the first union will be one red and one blue?

    (1) 0.24
    (2) 0.36
    (3) 0.48
    (4) 0.50
    (5) 0.60

35. If these ratios represented the allele frequency of a genetic disease that would affect a person with two blue alleles, what percentage of the population is affected?

    (1) 24%
    (2) 36%
    (3) 48%
    (4) 50%
    (5) 60%

Items 36 and 37 refer to the following illustration and information.

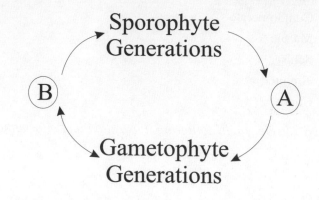

Green plants and their ancestors go through a unique life cycle known as the alternation of generations. In one generation or life stage the plant structures are haploid, and in the other they are diploid. The illustration shows that these two stages are called sporophyte and gametophyte.

36. To correctly fill in the diagram, the (A) and (B) spaces would be labeled
    (1) fertilization (A), meiosis (B).
    (2) meiosis (A), fertilization (B).
    (3) spores (A), meiosis (B).
    (4) meiosis (A), gametes (B).
    (5) spores (A), gametes (B).

37. Which process must occur before the gametophyte generation?
    (1) Fertilization
    (2) Mitosis
    (3) Germination
    (4) Meiosis
    (5) Evolution

38. Which of the following will result in a lower chance of developing arteriosclerosis?
    (1) Eating a high-fiber diet
    (2) Exercising regularly
    (3) Smoking cigarettes
    (4) Eating large quantities of polyunsaturated fats
    (5) Having several alcoholic drinks each day

39. The part of the digestive tract that is mainly responsible for the digestion of proteins is the
    (1)   esophagus.
    (2)   stomach.
    (3)   small intestine.
    (4)   large intestine.
    (5)   liver.

40. Which of the following has the greatest effect on stream erosion?
    (1)   Climate
    (2)   Clevation
    (3)   Temperature
    (4)   Water depth
    (5)   Slope

41. In which layer of the atmosphere does all life reside and weather occur?
    (1)   Mesosphere
    (2)   Troposphere
    (3)   Stratosphere
    (4)   Ionosphere
    (5)   Lithosphere

Items 42 and 43 refer to the following information.

The height and wavelength of a water wave depends on several factors. The depth of the water, the wind speed, the length of time the wind has blown, and the size of the area over which the wind blows all contribute to a wave's height and length. The largest water waves are produced by strong winds that blow for many hours over large areas.

42. In which of the following locations would waves likely be highest?
    (1)   Pacific Ocean
    (2)   Lake Superior
    (3)   Mediterranean Sea
    (4)   Red Sea
    (5)   Gulf of Mexico

43. When a wave reaches shallow water, its wavelength decreases. The ocean bottom slows the wave down, but the crest continues to move forward. What is the result of this situation?
    (1)   A current pulls the wave away from the shore.
    (2)   The crest tumbles over and the wave breaks on shore.
    (3)   The wave comes onto the beach at a steep angle.
    (4)   The crest grows higher.
    (5)   The trough moves faster.

Items 44 and 45 refer to the following illustration, which shows two different gases at the same temperature, pressure, and volume.

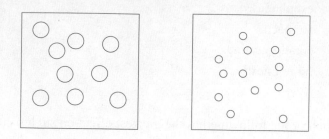

44. The diagram depicts equal numbers of molecules in each container, although they are different elements. The person who developed the idea that equal volumes of gases at the same temperature and pressure contain the same number of molecules was

    (1) Leonardo daVinci.

    (2) Plato.

    (3) Avogadro.

    (4) Boltzman.

    (5) Boyle.

45. Assume that the container on the left has 0.1 mole of oxygen in it and the one on the right has nitrogen in it. Which statement is correct?

    (1) The masses of the gases are the same.

    (2) The number of moles of gases are identical.

    (3) The number of particles in the two containers are different.

    (4) If a tube were placed between the containers, more oxygen molecules than nitrogen molecules would diffuse.

    (5) The pressure in the container on the left will rise faster because of the larger molecules.

46. Momentum is always conserved in a collision between two objects. If the collision also conserves kinetic energy, it is called elastic; if not, it is inelastic. Consider two objects, A and B, that collide and stick together. They encounter a third object, C, in a collision. The kinetic energy of all three objects before the first collision is greater than the sum of their kinetic energies after the second collision. What conclusion can be drawn?

    (1)   Both collisions were elastic because momentum is conserved.

    (2)   Both collisions were inelastic because kinetic energy is conserved.

    (3)   Both collisions were inelastic because kinetic energy is not conserved.

    (4)   At least one of the collisions was inelastic because kinetic energy is not conserved.

    (5)   At least one of the collisions was elastic because kinetic energy is not conserved.

Items 47 and 48 refer to the following illustration.

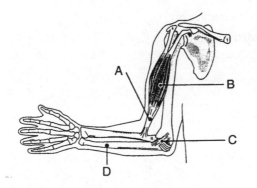

47. Based on the diagram, which answer is correct?

    (1)   A is a ligament, and B is the femur.

    (2)   A is a tendon , and C is a ligament.

    (3)   A is a ligament , and B is the triceps.

    (4)   C is a tendon, and B is the triceps.

    (5)   None of the above statements is true.

48. The bone labeled D is the

    (1)   phalanges.

    (2)   carpel.

    (3)   radius.

    (4)   ulna.

    (5)   humerus.

49. Which of the following factors does not favor a change in gene frequency, and therefore does not favor evolution?

(1)   Large populations

(2)   Mutations

(3)   Emigrations

(4)   Genetic drift

(5)   Sexual selection

Item 50 refers to the following illustration.

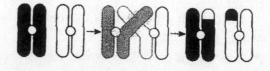

The drawing above is an illustration of

(1)   independent assortment.

(2)   sex determination.

(3)   nondisjunction.

(4)   karyotyping.

(5)   crossing over.

ANSWERS AND EXPLANATIONS

1. **The correct answer is (5). (Fundamental understandings)** The pituitary gland is the master gland that can control other glands, although it is under the guidance of the hypothalamus. The ovaries also produce hormones that provide feedback to the pituitary and to the hypothalamus.

2. **The correct answer is (5). (Fundamental understandings)** Epinephrine is produced in the adrenal glands, which are anterior to (on top of) the kidneys.

3. **The correct answer is (3). (Fundamental understandings)** The pancreas produces these important hormones, which regulate blood glucose levels.

4. **The correct answer is (5). (Unifying concepts and processes)** The field of view at 40 magnifications was 4 mm in diameter; therefore the protist was 2 mm. If she increased her magnification to 400, she would only be seeing 0.4 mm, but she can see four times that amount at 100 magnifications, or 1.6 mm. Therefore, $1.6 \div 2$ is 0.8 or 80% of the protist.

5. **The correct answer is (2). (Unifying concepts and processes)** In the light reactions, water is split into oxygen and hydrogen. The former is given off, and the latter is associated with NADP to become NADPH. ATP is formed in the light reaction and is used to power the production of PGAL in the Calvin cycle, or the light-independent reactions.

6. **The correct answer is (2). (Science as inquiry)** A pH meter allows you to detect the assimilation of carbon dioxide, which results in an increase in the pH.

7. **The correct answer is (4). (Fundamental understandings)** When the sperm, produced in the antheridia, meets the egg in the archegonium, the resulting embryo will be diploid.

8. **The correct answer is (2). (Unifying concepts and processes)** She might measure the density eventually, but she can't find that out without knowing both the volume and the mass of the rock.

9. **The correct answer is (5). (Unifying concepts and processes)** This question deals with significant digits, which are limited to the smallest number of digits in the calculation.

10. **The correct answer is (1). (Unifying concepts and processes)** To calculate the mass, use the formula for density and rearrange it:

$$D = \frac{m}{v}, \text{ therefore } m = D \times v$$

11. **The correct answer is (3). (Science as inquiry)** One liter of water is 1,000 ml. 3.5 % of 1,000 is 35.

12. **The correct answer is (2). (Fundamental understandings)** Flowing water is a significant mover of sediments. Rain deposits little in the way of sediments and overall would dilute the concentration of minerals, choice (5). Volcanism, choice (3); human action, choice (4); and beach erosion, choice (2), would contribute to some degree, but not nearly as systematically as water erosion and runoff.

13. **The correct answer is (2). (Fundamental understandings)** Fresh water dumped into a bay would actually decrease salinity. Estuaries are ecosystems based on brackish waters with reduced salinity.

14. **The correct answer is (1). (Fundamental understandings)** The color reflected to the eye determines the object's perceived color, which depends on the color of the light falling on it. The intensity does not determine the color, and light is not transmitted through opaque objects.

15. **The correct answer is (3). (Fundamental understandings)** The red object primarily reflects red light. Since it may reflect a little green light, it may appear slightly green under green light. Under illumination by other colors, it cannot appear red, so choices (4) and (5) are incorrect. Choices (1) and (2) are wrong because the material cannot change the color of incident light.

16. **The correct answer is (2). (Fundamental understandings)** Blue light must be reflected to the observer for the object to appear blue. White light contains blue light, but the other colors are not required. Choice (1) is wrong because other colors may be present in the illuminating light.

17. **The correct answer is (4). (Unifying concepts and processes)** Heating the magnet adds thermal energy and striking it adds mechanical energy. Both tend to randomize the orientation of domains. Rotating the magnet does not add energy to the magnet.

18. **The correct answer is (2). (Fundamental understandings)** Primary consumers are herbivores, which eat the green plants, or producers.

19. **The correct answer is (3). (Fundamental understandings)** As one moves up the food chain, each level will accumulate nonbiodegradable poisons in the tissues. This buildup is termed biological magnification.

20. **The correct answer is (2). (Science and technology)** The karyotype reveals three chromosomes in the twenty-first pair, a product of nondisjunction, a symptom of which is mental retardation.

21. **The correct answer is (2). (Fundamental understandings)** Plants use radiant energy to make sugars, which other organisms depend on for food. If there is sufficient water, the equator will have the most plants and, therefore, the greatest biodiversity.

22. **The correct answer is (1). (Science in social and personal perspective)** Restriction enzymes cut specific sequences in DNA and are used as chemical scissors.

23. **The correct answer is (4). (History and nature of science)** Franklin and Wilkins supplied the x-ray image of the cross section of the molecule. Hershey and Chase demonstrated that DNA is the genetic material. Meselson and Stahl found that DNA replication is semi-conservative. Cohen helped to develop a cloning technique. Stanley helped to discover viruses.

24. **The correct answer is (2). (Fundamental understandings)** The electrons are attracted to the protons in the nucleus by the electric force.

25. **The correct answer is (5). (Unifying concepts and processes)** Small particles are causing additional scattering, thereby enhancing the blue color. Since the air is no different in North Carolina and Virginia than it is elsewhere, some other small particles must be the cause.

26. **The correct answer is (3). (Fundamental understandings)** The force of gravity on the block does not depend on the angle of the incline. The block slides down more quickly at steeper angles because the incline's force on the block is smaller. This force balances part of the downward gravitational force.

27. **The correct answer is (2). (Fundamental understandings)** Fifty-one grams of ammonia is 3 moles of ammonia. (The number of moles is 14 + 1(3) = 17 g/mole). The molecules combine in a 2:1 ratio, so 3 moles of ammonia require 1.5 moles of nitrogen. Since nitrogen is diatomic here, the number of grams in 1.5 moles is 14 × 1.5, or 42 g.

28. **The correct answer is (3). (Unifying concepts and processes)** Since the amount is given as a percentage, assume that the total number of grams is 100, which means one has 40 grams of carbon or 3.33 moles. One also has 6.67 moles of hydrogen and 3.33 moles of oxygen. The ratio becomes $C_{3.33}H_{6.67}O_{3.33}$, which reduces to CH_2O.

29. **The correct answer is (4). (Fundamental understandings)** No increase in shielding occurs, because electrons are added to the same outer energy levels and therefore do not shield one another.

30. **The correct answer is (1). (Fundamental understandings)** The (III) refers to the oxidation number assigned to iron. Since there are 2 atoms, the positive charge is 6. Oxygen usually carries an oxidation number of −2, so it would take 3 atoms to neutralize the positive charge.

31. **The correct answer is (1). (Fundamental understandings)** According to the law of superposition, the bottom layer was formed first, and the other layers, which were deposited later, are progressively younger.

32. **The correct answer is (2). (Fundamental understandings)** Basalt, an igneous rock, crosses several layers diagonally, forcing its way through existing rock layers. Intrusions are younger than all layers they pass through.

33. **The correct answer is (4). (Unifying concepts and processes)** Granite is an intrusive igneous rock. Marble and schist are metamorphic, while chalk and conglomerate are sedimentary in origin. Only igneous rocks can form intrusions.

34. **The correct answer is (3). (Fundamental understandings)** The proportion of red is 20/50 or 0.4, and that of blue is 30/50 or 0.6. The chances of drawing a red from the male is 0.4, and the chance of drawing a blue from the female is 0.6. The probability of two simultaneous events is the product of their individual probabilities, or 0.24. However, one could also draw a blue from the male and a red from the female (another 0.24 probability), so that there are 2×0.24 or a 0.48 chance.

35. **The correct answer is (2). (Fundamental understandings)** The frequency of the blue allele is 0.6. Those that have two copies of the allele would be 0.6×0.6, or 36% of each population.

36. **The correct answer is (5). (Fundamental understandings)** Sporophytes produce spores and gametophytes produce gametes.

37. **The correct answer is (4). (Fundamental understandings)** Meiosis produces haploid spores, which germinate into haploid gametophytes, which produce haploid reproductive structures that become diploid with fertilization.

38. **The correct answer is (1). (Science in social and personal perspective)** Eating a high fiber diet reduces the amount of cholesterol in one's system, a major cause of arteriosclerosis.

39. **The correct answer is (2). (Fundamental understandings)** Protein digestion is completed in the small intestine, but begins in the stomach.

40. **The correct answer is (5). (Fundamental understandings)** Of the choices, the one with the greatest effect on stream erosion is slope, or incline, because water moves more rapidly on a steep slope. Elevation may sound correct, but change in elevation—slope—is the key. Water in a high elevation on flat terrain collects in a lake.

41. **The correct answer is (2). (Fundamental understandings)** Weather and life are found in the layer of the atmosphere closest to the earth's surface. The greatest temperature instability (promoting weather) and over 75% of the air mass (including oxygen) is found in the troposphere. The lithosphere, choice (5), the surface of the earth, contains life but not weather.

42. **The correct answer is (1). (Unifying concepts and processes)** The Pacific Ocean is the world's largest body of water, with strong winds that blow constantly. Waves have the opportunity to build across the entire span, reaching dozens of feet high.

43. **The correct answer is (2). (Fundamental understandings)** As the bottom of the wave is slowed, the crest continues to move forward at the original speed. Momentum carries the crest over, and the wave begins to break. Choice (1) is incorrect because a current may or may not be acting on a wave. Choice (3) is true but is not the result of slowing of the wave. Choices (4) and (5) are incorrect.

44. **The correct answer is (3). (History and nature of science)** It was significant that Avogadro came up with this idea before the ideal gas law was formulated.

45. **The correct answer is (2). (Fundamental understandings)** Since there are 6.02×10^{23} particles in a mole, and the number of particles are equal, the number of moles has to be the same.

46. **The correct answer is (4). (Fundamental understandings)** Since kinetic energy was not conserved from beginning to end, at least one of the collisions must have been inelastic, perhaps both. There is not enough information to conclude that both were inelastic. Momentum is always conserved and does not affect the answer.

47. **The correct answer is (2). (Fundamental understandings)** Ligaments connect bone to bone and tendons connect bone to muscle. B is the biceps muscle, and the femur is the thigh bone.

48. **The correct answer is (4). (Fundamental understandings)** The radius sits above the ulna and can rotate around it.

49. **The correct answer is (1). (Unifying concepts and processes)** Small populations can cause a change in gene frequency because they are more susceptible to changes.

50. **The correct answer is (5). (Fundamental understandings)** Homologous chromosomes cross over and exchange segments of DNA during the first stages of meiosis.

SCIENCE PRACTICE TEST 1 ANALYSIS CHART

Use this table to determine your areas of strength and areas in which more work is needed before you go on to Practice Test 2. The numbers in the boxes refer to multiple-choice questions in the practice test.

Content Area	Fundamental understandings	Unifying concepts and processes	Science as inquiry	Science as technology	Science in personal and social perspective	History and nature of science
Chapter 2 **Life Science**	1, 2, 3, 7, 18, 19, 21, 34, 35, 36, 37, 39, 47, 48, 50	4, 5, 49		20	22, 38	23
Chapter 3 **Earth and** **Space Science**	12, 13, 31, 32, 40, 41, 43	25, 33, 42				
Chapter 4 **Physical Science**	14, 15, 16, 17, 24, 26, 27, 29, 30, 45, 46	8, 9, 10, 28	6, 11			44

Answer Sheet

1 ① ② ③ ④ ⑤   6 ① ② ③ ④ ⑤   11 ① ② ③ ④ ⑤
2 ① ② ③ ④ ⑤   7 ① ② ③ ④ ⑤   12 ① ② ③ ④ ⑤
3 ① ② ③ ④ ⑤   8 ① ② ③ ④ ⑤   13 ① ② ③ ④ ⑤
4 ① ② ③ ④ ⑤   9 ① ② ③ ④ ⑤   14 ① ② ③ ④ ⑤
5 ① ② ③ ④ ⑤   10 ① ② ③ ④ ⑤   15 ① ② ③ ④ ⑤

16 ① ② ③ ④ ⑤   21 ① ② ③ ④ ⑤   26 ① ② ③ ④ ⑤
17 ① ② ③ ④ ⑤   22 ① ② ③ ④ ⑤   27 ① ② ③ ④ ⑤
18 ① ② ③ ④ ⑤   23 ① ② ③ ④ ⑤   28 ① ② ③ ④ ⑤
19 ① ② ③ ④ ⑤   24 ① ② ③ ④ ⑤   29 ① ② ③ ④ ⑤
20 ① ② ③ ④ ⑤   25 ① ② ③ ④ ⑤   30 ① ② ③ ④ ⑤

31 ① ② ③ ④ ⑤   36 ① ② ③ ④ ⑤   41 ① ② ③ ④ ⑤
32 ① ② ③ ④ ⑤   37 ① ② ③ ④ ⑤   42 ① ② ③ ④ ⑤
33 ① ② ③ ④ ⑤   38 ① ② ③ ④ ⑤   43 ① ② ③ ④ ⑤
34 ① ② ③ ④ ⑤   39 ① ② ③ ④ ⑤   44 ① ② ③ ④ ⑤
35 ① ② ③ ④ ⑤   40 ① ② ③ ④ ⑤   45 ① ② ③ ④ ⑤

46 ① ② ③ ④ ⑤
47 ① ② ③ ④ ⑤
48 ① ② ③ ④ ⑤
49 ① ② ③ ④ ⑤
50 ① ② ③ ④ ⑤

Practice Test 2

Directions: Choose the <u>one best answer</u> for each item.

Items 1–6 refer to the following information and illustration.

The central dogma of modern biology states that DNA is transcribed into RNA, which is translated into protein. The diagram above is a model that explains, in part, how that process works.

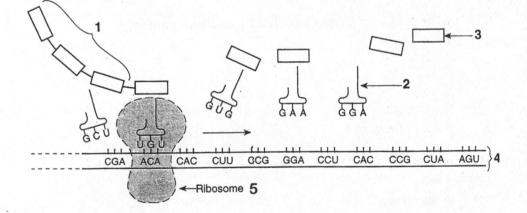

1. Which of the following numbers represents tRNA (transfer RNA)?

   (1)   1
   (2)   2
   (3)   3
   (4)   4
   (5)   None of the above

2. Which of the following numbers represents mRNA (messenger RNA)?

(1)   1

(2)   2

(3)   3

(4)   4

(5)   None of the above

3. Which of the following structures represents an amino acid?

(1)   1

(2)   2

(3)   3

(4)   4

(5)   None of the above

4. Which of the following represents DNA?

(1)   1

(2)   2

(3)   3

(4)   4

(5)   None of the above

5. The anticodon is most closely associated with which number?

(1)   1

(2)   2

(3)   3

(4)   4

(5)   None of the above

6. If the protein being made was for secretion, the event is most likely taking place

(1)   in the nucleus.

(2)   on the rough endoplasmic reticulum.

(3)   in the cytoplasm.

(4)   either in the nucleus or the cytoplasm.

(5)   either on the rough endoplasmic reticulum or in the cytoplasm.

Items 7–9 refer to the following equation.

$$H_2O + CO_2 = H_2CO_3$$

7. In the above equation, how many molecules of water react to form carbonic acid?

    (1)   1
    (2)   2
    (3)   3
    (4)   6
    (5)   12

8. How many atoms of oxygen are participating in the reaction?

    (1)   1
    (2)   2
    (3)   3
    (4)   6
    (5)   12

9. How many grams of water would be required to combine with 44 grams of carbon dioxide?

    (1)   6
    (2)   12
    (3)   18
    (4)   44
    (5)   62

Items 10–12 refer to the following passage.

Desertification is a process by which formerly fertile land is transformed by drought, climatic change, and human development. One classic example of desertification occurred in the U.S. Midwest during the Great Depression. At that time, a severe drought hit the Midwest. Farmers lacked resources to plant and irrigate their properties, and massive crop failures resulted. Land that was formerly cultivated went without crops, and the prairie winds blew away much of the rich topsoil. Many years passed before the affected farms were productive again.

10. According to the passage, which agent of erosion is primarily responsible for desertification?

    (1)   Flooding
    (2)   Gravity
    (3)   Wind
    (4)   Glaciers
    (5)   Drought

11. Which of the following factors was least relevant to the formation of the Midwest dust bowls during the Great Depression?

    (1) A coincidental drought

    (2) No money for crop planting

    (3) Lack of irrigation water

    (4) High winds over the plains

    (5) Especially dense subsoil composition

12. Which of the following actions would be least likely to assist in the recovery of the land mentioned in the passage?

    (1) Replace topsoil

    (2) Add nutrients to soil

    (3) Plant vegetation to hold soil

    (4) Harvest planted crops

    (5) Irrigate land to minimize drought effects

Items 13–15 refer to the following information and illustration.

The graph below shows the absorption of optical fiber used to carry data and voice in telecommunications networks. Fibers with less absorption are desired because they can carry signals farther before they need to be amplified. The distance between amplifiers is inversely proportional to the absorption coefficient, which means that if the absorption is doubled, the distance is halved. While lower-absorption fiber is generally more expensive, the higher cost of the fiber is more than compensated for by the lower total cost of amplifiers.

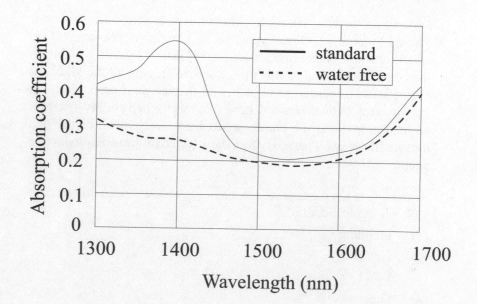

13. Why is the absorption important in optical communication?

   (1)   Data is lost when light is absorbed in the fiber.

   (2)   More data can be sent down a fiber with less absorption.

   (3)   Data can be sent over longer distances with less absorption.

   (4)   Absorption determines the spacing of optical amplifiers.

   (5)   Low-absorption fiber is more expensive.

14. For a communications system operating at 1,400 nm with 20 amplifiers using standard fiber, how many amplifiers can be saved by converting to water-free fiber?

   (1)   None

   (2)   5

   (3)   10

   (4)   15

   (5)   20

15. The owner of an optical link that uses standard fiber at 1,310 nm is considering upgrading the link. Which change would result in the greatest savings in the number of amplifiers?

   (1)   Change the wavelength to 1,550 nm.

   (2)   Install water-free fiber.

   (3)   Install water-free fiber and change the wavelength to 1,400 nm.

   (4)   Install water-free fiber and change the wavelength to 1,550 nm.

   (5)   None of the above changes would save amplifiers.

16. Newton's Third Law of Motion states that every action has an equal and opposite reaction. This means that if one object exerts a force in one direction on a second object, the second exerts an equal force on the first, but in the opposite direction. Airplanes in level flight do not fall to Earth. How can Newton's Third Law of Motion be used to explain this?

   (1)   The engine pushes the airplane up, while the air pushes the airplane down.

   (2)   The airplane pushes air down, while air pushes the airplane up.

   (3)   The engine pushes the airplane forward to generate lift.

   (4)   The shape of the wing generates lift.

   (5)   The airplane is moving so fast that it cannot fall.

17. In Newtonian physics, energy can neither be created nor destroyed, only transformed. This is the principle of conservation of energy. When a match is struck, a flame is produced and heat is released. Energy appears to have been created. How is this reconciled with conservation of energy?

    (1)   Heat is not a form of energy.

    (2)   Heat is produced from friction as the match is struck.

    (3)   Heat stored in the match is released by friction.

    (4)   Nuclear energy stored in the match is released by friction as the match is struck.

    (5)   Chemical energy stored in the match is released by friction as the match is struck.

Items 18–20 refer to the following information and illustration.

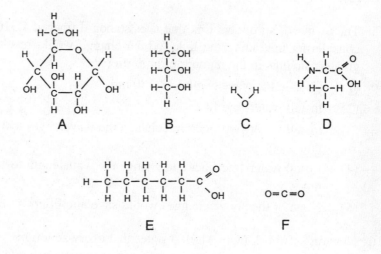

Scientists use formulas and models to help them visualize molecules.

18. Which of the drawings represents glucose?

    (1)   A

    (2)   B

    (3)   C

    (4)   D

    (5)   E

19. Which of the drawings represents an amino acid?

    (1)   A
    (2)   B
    (3)   C
    (4)   D
    (5)   E

20. Which of the following represents a saturated fatty acid?

    (1)   A
    (2)   B
    (3)   F
    (4)   D
    (5)   E

Items 21–23 refer to the following information.

Stuart wanted to know what types of music would help his plants grow best. He obtained 10 bean seeds, planted each in a quart container of commercial potting mix, and placed them around his living room. For 10 hours each day he would play one of four different types of music: classical, jazz, rap, or pop. At the end of each day he would weigh the plants and see how much mass they had gained that day.

21. What was Stuart's biggest mistake in his experimental design?

    (1)   He didn't use enough beans.
    (2)   He placed the beans in different areas of his living room.
    (3)   He switched music too often.
    (4)   His balance scale wasn't tested when he began.
    (5)   He can't tell how much a plant grows by weighing it.

22. What is the dependent variable in this experiment?

    (1)   The amount of sunlight
    (2)   The types of music
    (3)   The types of beans
    (4)   The mass of the plants
    (5)   The number of bean seeds

23. What is the independent variable in this experiment?

    (1)   The amount of sunlight
    (2)   The types of music
    (3)   The types of beans
    (4)   The mass of the plants
    (5)   The number of bean seeds

24. Advances in science often depend on advances in technology. Which of the following technological advancements helped the advancement of science?

    (1)   Biological stains

    (2)   The microscope

    (3)   The computer

    (4)   Gel electrophoresis

    (5)   All of the above

25. A block is pushed by a constant force, at constant velocity, on a horizontal surface with friction. In this process

    (1)   mechanical energy is converted to electrical energy.

    (2)   mechanical energy is converted to heat.

    (3)   mechanical energy is conserved.

    (4)   heat is transferred from the block to the surface.

    (5)   no work is done on the block.

26. The graph below shows the orbital period, as a function of radius, for a satellite orbiting the earth.

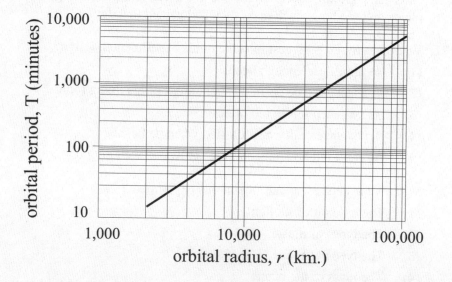

    If the satellite is to orbit the earth once every 2 hours, what should the radius of the orbit be?

    (1)   2,000 m

    (2)   8,000 m

    (3)   2,000 km

    (4)   8,000 km

    (5)   20,000 km

27. The Principle of Archimedes states that buoyant force is equal to the weight of water displaced. This means that a floating object pushes up an amount of water weighing the same as the object. The drawing below shows a glass filled to the brim with ice and water. Since ice is about 9% less dense than water, it floats. Under what conditions will the water overflow the glass after all the ice melts?

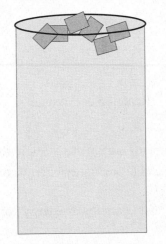

    (1)   The water will never overflow the glass.

    (2)   The water will overflow as soon as any ice melts.

    (3)   The water will overflow if there is more than 9% ice.

    (4)   The water will overflow if there is more than 18% ice.

    (5)   The water will overflow if there is more than 91% ice.

28. Objects in free fall experience constant acceleration. This means that their velocity is

    (1)   highest at the beginning of the fall.

    (2)   highest in the middle of the fall.

    (3)   highest at the end of the fall.

    (4)   constant throughout the fall.

    (5)   constant until they hit the ground.

29. Water boils at 212° F and freezes at 32° F. Water boils at 100° C and freezes at 0° C. If someone raised the temperature of water 20° F, how many degrees C would that person be raising it?

    (1)   About 4

    (2)   About 11

    (3)   About 21

    (4)   About 36

    (5)   About 43

Item 30 refers to the following graph.

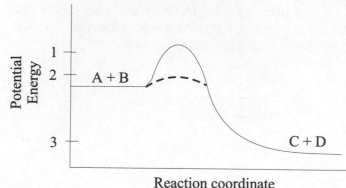

30. Which of the following statements is supported by the graph?
    (1) Products C and D are higher-energy compounds than reactants A and B.
    (2) Products C and D are lower-energy compounds than reactants A and B.
    (3) One can form twice as much C and D by doubling the temperature.
    (4) It takes about 5 minutes for A and B to be converted to C and D at 50° F.
    (5) A and B are gases, but C and D are liquids.

Items 31–33 refer to the following diagram.

Aquifers are an important source of water in the United States. The following figure shows the structure of a section of an aquifer.

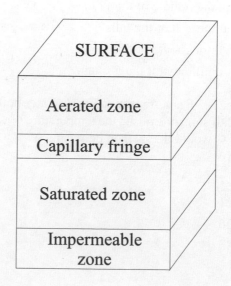

31. What is the zone of maximum penetration of the water?
    (1) Aerated zone
    (2) Capillary zone
    (3) Saturated zone
    (4) Impermeable zone
    (5) Water would only sit on the surface.

32. Which of the following rock types is most likely to be found in the saturation zone?
    (1) Granite
    (2) Gneiss
    (3) Sandstone
    (4) Basalt
    (5) Shale

33. If one were to drill a well into the ground at the section illustrated above, to what level would you have to drill to guarantee a productive well?
    (1) Into the impermeable zone
    (2) Into the capillary zone
    (3) To the top of the saturation zone
    (4) To the bottom of the saturation zone
    (5) Any well deeper than 30 feet would be productive

Items 34–36 refer to the following information.

In the human population in America there is a genetic condition known as sickle-cell anemia. This genetic disease is the result of an individual inheriting two recessive alleles, causing his or her red blood cells to become sickle-shaped under some conditions. Individuals who have one normal allele and one sickle allele are said to have the sickle-cell trait, which does not cause them pain or discomfort. The number of people in the United States with sickle-cell anemia is 4 in 10,000.

34. What is the gene frequency for the sickle-cell allele in the U.S. population?
    (1) 0.0004
    (2) 0.004
    (3) 0.04
    (4) 0.0002
    (5) 0.02

35. What percentage of the people in the population cannot pass on the sickle-cell allele?

    (1)   96%
    (2)   48%
    (3)   4%
    (4)   52%
    (5)   None of the above

36. What percentage of the population has the sickle-cell trait?

    (1)   7.68%
    (2)   3.92%
    (3)   15.36%
    (4)   0.768%
    (5)   0.392%

Item 37 refers to the following illustration.

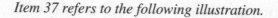

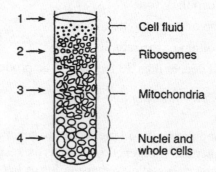

37. In the drawing above, the organelles were separated by

    (1)   gel electrophoresis.
    (2)   protein electrophoresis.
    (3)   ultracentrifugation.
    (4)   their polarity.
    (5)   their charge.

38. Charles Darwin is credited most justifiably with which of the following ideas?

    (1)   The theory of evolution
    (2)   The theory of natural selection
    (3)   The theory of kin selection
    (4)   The theory of punctuated equilibrium
    (5)   Gradualism

Items 39 and 40 refer to the following illustration.

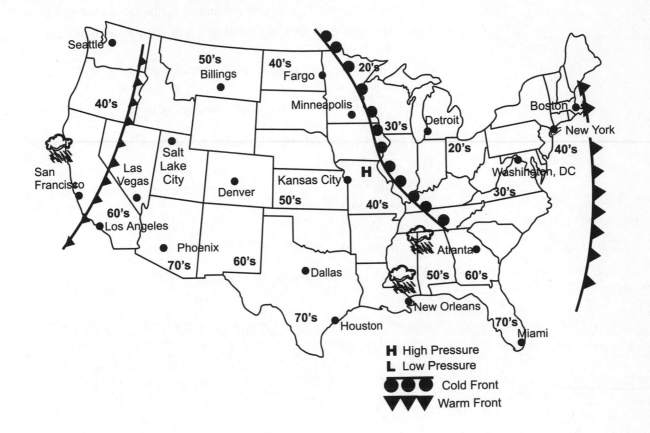

39. According to the illustrated weather map, in which city is it raining?

    (1) Miami

    (2) Dallas

    (3) Minneapolis

    (4) Las Vegas

    (5) San Francisco

40. The movement of fronts across the United States is generally from west to east. The local forecast in one city on the map is for clearing skies and colder temperatures in the 20s. Which of the following cities is this forecast for?

    (1) Washington

    (2) Atlanta

    (3) Denver

    (4) Los Angeles

    (5) Houston

41. Which of the following is evidence that the earth's crust has undergone great changes during its history?
    (1) The constant pounding of ocean waves on the coastlines
    (2) The occurrence of a large number of earthquakes each year
    (3) The continued flow of vast amounts of river water into the sea
    (4) The presence of marine fossils in rock making up high mountains
    (5) The presence of glaciers in mountain valleys

42. The gas that scientists believe is most responsible for global warming is
    (1) carbon dioxide.
    (2) ozone.
    (3) nitrous oxide.
    (4) methane.
    (5) argon.

Items 43–45 refer to the following illustration.

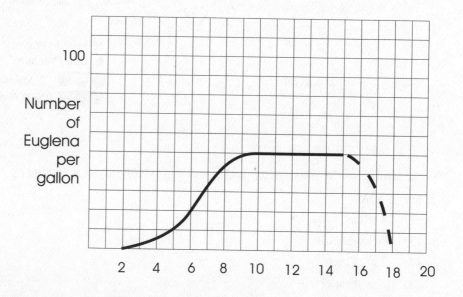

43. According to the graph, the carrying capacity for Euglena in that environment was
    (1) 50 Euglena per gallon.
    (2) 12.5 days.
    (3) 16 days.
    (4) 100 Euglena per gallon.
    (5) none of the above.

44. The period through which the population grew the fastest was days
    (1)   2 to 4.
    (2)   4 to 6.
    (3)   6 to 8.
    (4)   8 to 10.
    (5)   16 to18.

45. A possible reason for the decline in the number of Euglena is a(n)
    (1)   increase in the natality rate.
    (2)   decrease in the predation rate.
    (3)   increase in the nutrient level.
    (4)   decrease in the mortality rate.
    (5)   increase of waste products.

46. The one hormone listed below that is not associated with the pituitary gland is
    (1)   calcitonin.
    (2)   follicle-stimulating hormone.
    (3)   thyroid-stimulating hormone.
    (4)   growth hormone.
    (5)   ADH.

47. Which of the following are incorrectly paired?
    (1)   Xylem and water
    (2)   Phloem and sap
    (3)   Stomata and guard cells
    (4)   Sieve cells and xylem
    (5)   Xylem and wood

Items 48–50 refer to the following information.

The pH scale measures the concentration of an acid or base. Acids have pH values of less than 7. Bases, which can neutralize acids, have pH values greater than 7. Neutralization reactions create salts. The pH scale, like the Richter scale, is logarithmic. Water is considered neutral and has a pH of 7. The chart below lists the pH levels of several substances.

<u>Substance</u>	<u>pH</u>
Lime	1.9
Grapefruit juice	3.5
Human blood	7.5
Seawater	8.2
Magnesium hydroxide	10.5
Lye	13

48. According to the information given, which substance should be used to neutralize grapefruit juice?
    (1) Lime
    (2) Blood
    (3) Seawater
    (4) Magnesium hydroxide
    (5) Lye

49. Which substance has the highest concentration of acid?
    (1) Lime
    (2) Grapefruit juice
    (3) Seawater
    (4) Magnesium hydroxide
    (5) Lye

50. Lime is how much more acidic than seawater?
    (1) About 6 times
    (2) About 8 times
    (3) About 100 times
    (4) About 1,000 times
    (5) About 1,000,000 times

ANSWERS AND EXPLANATIONS

1. **The correct answer is (2). (Fundamental understandings)** The tRNA ferries amino acids to the ribosome, site of protein synthesis.

2. **The correct answer is (4). (Fundamental understandings)** mRNA is a complementary copy of DNA.

3. **The correct answer is (3). (Fundamental understandings)** The amino acids are assembled into polypeptide chains as the ribosome moves down the mRNA.

4. **The correct answer is (5). (Fundamental understandings)** The DNA has already been transcribed into mRNA. From left to right, the DNA sequence would read GCT TGT GTG GAA, etc.

5. **The correct answer is (2). (Fundamental understandings)** The anticodon is the three bases at the end of the tRNA that are complementary to the mRNA.

6. **The correct answer is (2). (Fundamental understandings)** The best answer is choice (2) because, while protein synthesis takes place on both free and attached ribosomes, proteins destined for secretion are most often synthesized on ribosomes attached to the ER (rough endoplasmic reticulum).

7. **The correct answer is (1). (Fundamental understandings)** The number of molecules is the coefficient in front of the molecule. In this case it is understood to be 1.

8. **The correct answer is (3). (Fundamental understandings)** There are 3 on the reactant side and 3 on the product side.

9. **The correct answer is (3). (Unifying concepts and principles)** Even without a periodic chart, a student should know some of the basic formula masses such as oxygen, carbon, and hydrogen. Forty-four grams of carbon dioxide is the mass of 1 mole of carbon dioxide ($12 + [16 \times 2]$). Since water and carbon dioxide react in a 1:1 ratio, 1 mole of water will react, which is the same as 18 grams ($[1 \times 2] + 16$).

10. **The correct answer is (3). (Fundamental understandings)** The primary agent for the movement of soil in this case would be wind. Water, choice (1), would also have some effect, but due to the essentially flat topography, water would move little soil. Similarly, the drought, choice (5), was a factor but the passage states that wind blew the soil away.

11. **The correct answer is (5). (Fundamental understandings)** Desertification is primarily a problem of topsoil erosion. High winds, barren

fields, and lack of water would all be factors. Compaction of subsoil would be least relevant.

12. **The correct answer is (4). (Fundamental understandings)** Any efforts to replace the soils, increase nutrients, and increase ground cover would speed recovery. Harvesting crops would actually increase erosion if alternative vegetation was not planted.

13. **The correct answer is (4). (Science as technology)** As the passage explains, lower absorption allows the amplifiers to be more sparsely spaced. The absorption does not affect the data capacity of the fiber, choices (1) and (2), nor the total range of fiber transmission, choice (3). While low-absorption fiber is more expensive, it is not the reason that absorption is important.

14. **The correct answer is (3). (Unifying concepts and processes)** The absorption is reduced from about 0.55 dB/km to 0.27 dB/km: a factor of two. Since the amplifier span is inversely proportional to the absorption, the distance between amplifiers can be doubled, reducing the number of amplifiers by half, from 20 to 10.

15. **The correct answer is (4). (Unifying concepts and processes)** The lowest absorption is for water-free fiber at 1,550 nm, so the greatest savings of amplifiers is achieved by changing to that fiber type and wavelength.

16. **The correct answer is (2). (Fundamental understandings)** Newton's Third Law of Motion requires that something be pushed down for the airplane to be pushed up against gravity. That "something" is the air. The engine does not push the airplane up. While choices (3), (4), and (5) may be true, they do not explain the source of the upward force.

17. **The correct answer is (5). (Fundamental understandings)** A chemical reaction transforms stored chemical energy in the match head into heat and light. While there is some friction in striking the match, it is a negligible part of the energy released, so choice (2) is incorrect. Nuclear energy is not involved, so choice (4) is wrong.

18. **The correct answer is (1). (Fundamental understandings)** This configuration represents glucose, the ring structure most associated with biological activity. It is written as $C_6H_{12}O_6$.

19. **The correct answer is (4). (Fundamental understandings)** Amino acids have an amine group (NH_2), a central carbon with a variable group attached (in this case CH_3), and a carboxyl group (COOH).

20. **The correct answer is (5). (Fundamental understandings)** Saturated fatty acids lack double bonds and are composed of hydrocarbon chains with a carboxyl group.

21. **The correct answer is (2). (Science as inquiry)** All variables, including light, need to be controlled as tightly as possible so that one can best determine the effect of the experimental variable (sound).

22. **The correct answer is (4). (Science as inquiry)** The dependent variable is what is measured as a result of the independent variable. Stuart was using the mass as a measure of plant growth.

23. **The correct answer is (2). (Science as inquiry)** Stuart was changing the types of music to see if they had an effect on plant growth (mass).

24. **The correct answer is (5). (Science and technology)** This question was designed to illustrate the stated principle and to show that computers are used in scientific research in many fields, such as phylogenetic analysis, protein structure and function, CAT scans, and many other applications.

25. **The correct answer is (2). (Fundamental understandings)** Friction results in the conversion of mechanical energy to heat. No electrical energy is produced. Work is done on the block because a force acts on it over a distance.

26. **The correct answer is (4). (Science as inquiry)** Since 2 hours is 120 minutes, the graph indicates that the orbital radius should be about 8,000 km.

27. **The correct answer is (1). (Fundamental understandings)** The ice has more volume than the water it displaces, but its volume will be reduced when it melts, since it is less dense than water. The Principle of Archimedes guarantees that the volume of water added from melting ice is equal to the volume of water displaced since their weights are the same.

28. **The correct answer is (3). (Fundamental understandings)** Constant acceleration means that the speed is increasing at a constant rate, so the velocity continues to increase until the end of the fall.

29. **The correct answer is (2). (Unifying concepts and principles)** It takes 180 units of °F to go from freezing to boiling. It only takes 100 units of °C. Therefore, each 18 units of °F is the same as 10 units of °C.

30. **The correct answer is (2). (Unifying concepts and principles)** There is no indication of physical states or exact times. However, compounds higher on the y-axis have more energy. Thus, C and D are lower in energy than A and B.

31. **The correct answer is (3). (Fundamental understandings)** Gravity would pull water down until it reached a layer that is impermeable. Choices (1), (2), and (3) are all above the impermeable rock layer.

32. **The correct answer is (3). (Fundamental understandings)** Many samples of sandstone would allow water to pass through. All other choices are much denser and nonporous.

33. **The correct answer is (4). (Fundamental understandings)** A well drilled to the bottom of the saturation zone would be productive as long as some water existed within the ground. The impermeable zone contains no water, and wells drilled to the layers outlined in choices (1), (2), and (3) could dry up. The diagram is schematic only, so there is no way of knowing if a 30-foot-deep well, choice (5), would be deep enough.

34. **The correct answer is (5). (Fundamental understandings)** If there are only two alleles in the population, their sum is 1, or $p + q = 1$. Squaring both side gives $p^2 + 2pq + q^2 = 1$. People with sickle-cell anemia are the q^2 group, and are equal to 0.0004. By taking the square root of q^2, we get $q = 0.02$.

35. **The correct answer is (1). (Fundamental understandings)** The only people who can't pass along the gene are the p^2 group, which is 0.982 or about 96%.

36. **The correct answer is (2). (Fundamental understandings)** The people with the sickle-cell trait are the $2pq$ group, or 3.92%.

37. **The correct answer is (3). (History and nature of science)** Ultracentrifuges separate things according to their density.

38. **The correct answer is (2). (History and nature of science)** Darwin was not, as many people suppose, an original thinker about evolution. His claim to fame is stated in the title to his book, *On the Means of Evolution by Natural Selection.*

39. **The correct answer is (5). (Science as inquiry)** The map key indicates that bands of diagonal stripes indicate rain. Of the listed choices, only San Francisco shows rain.

40. **The correct answer is (1). (Science as inquiry)** The weather immediately west of Washington shows the profile mentioned in the question. Given that weather fronts move eastward on the prevailing winds, Washington is likely to experience the stated weather soon.

41. **The correct answer is (4). (Fundamental understandings)** The presence of marine fossils in mountainous regions implies either that those regions were once at lower elevations or there once was an ocean covering the region in question. Either way, the crust must have undergone great changes. Choices (1), (2), (3), and (5) represent agents of erosion, but the fact that they change the surface of the earth today is not proof that they did so in the past.

42. **The correct answer is (1). (Science in personal and social perspective)** Carbon dioxide traps heat within the atmosphere. Methane also has heat-trapping properties, but carbon dioxide is many times more abundant.

43. **The correct answer is (1). (Science as inquiry)** The graph shows that the line parallel to the *x*-axis is about halfway to 100.

44. **The correct answer is (3). (Science as inquiry)** The fastest rate is the steepest slope, since slope is proportional to rate.

45. **The correct answer is (5). (Fundamental understandings)** All other factors would serve to increase the number, and organisms can and do suffocate in their own wastes.

46. **The correct answer is (1). (Fundamental understandings)** Calcitonin is produced in the thyroid gland.

47. **The correct answer is (4). (Unifying concepts and processes)** Sieve cells are associated with phloem, the tissue that transports sugars or sap.

48. **The correct answer is (4). (Science in personal and social perspective)** Magnesium is as far to one side of neutral as grapefruit juice is to the other.

49. **The correct answer is (1). (Fundamental understandings)** The lower the pH value, the more concentrated the acid.

50. **The correct answer is (5). (Unifying concepts and principles)** Since this is a logarithmic scale, each increase in a whole number is a tenfold increase.

NOTES